ENTREPRENEURSHIP & TECHNOLOGY: WORLD EXPERIENCES AND POLICIES

Editors: Wayne S. Brown & Roy Rothwell

Longman

ENTREPRENEURSHIP AND TECHNOLOGY

Longman Group UK Limited, Professional Reference and Information Publishing
Division, Longman House, Burnt Mill, Harlow, Essex CM20 2JE, UK
Telephone: Harlow (0279) 442601

First published 1986

British Library Cataloguing in Publication Data

Entrepreneurship and technology : world
    experiences and policies.
    1. Technological innovations——Economic
    aspects
    I. Brown, Wayne S. II. Rothwell, Roy
    338'.06   HC79.T4

ISBN 0–582–90122–7

Typeset by The Word Factory, Rossendale, Lancashire.

Printed and bound in Great Britain by Biddles Ltd, Guildford and King's Lynn

49.00

Entrepreneurship and Technology: world experiences and policies

Longman Guide to World Science and Technology

1   Science and Technology in the Middle East
        by Ziauddin Sardar
2   Science and Technology in Latin America
        by Latin American Newsletters Limited
3   Science and Technology in China
        by Tong B. Tang
4   Science and Technology in Japan
        by Alun M. Anderson
5   Science and Technology in the USA
        by Albert H. Teich and Jill B. Pace

Forthcoming books in the series to cover

United Kingdom
South-east Asia
Australasia, Antartica and the Pacific
Africa
USSR

Other books published by Longman Group UK Limited

Rothwell, R. & W. Zegveld: Reindustrialization and Technology
Kaplinsky, R. : Automation: the technology and society
Herman, R. : The European Scientific Community

Longman Reference on Research: directories of organizations and programmes

Pacific Research Centres
European Research Centres
Industrial Research in the United Kingdom

Contents

Foreword

Two of the most universally admired attributes of American society are the inventive spirit and the entrepreneurial drive of our people. Innovation and the attendant process of technological change are the cornerstones of the new industrial revolution now taking place throughout the world. Fueled by the limitless intellectual capacities of the human mind, the applications of high technology will afford opportunities for growth and expansion unheralded in the history of mankind.

The power of the American economy has been the result of the independent entrepreneur. Driven by a fierce need for achievement, reward and freedom of action, the new entrepreneur of the 1980s and 90s will lead the people of the world into the 21st century with a vision of boundless horizons. The creation of new products and new businesses are essential to the economic stability of a rapidly changing world.

Economic policy-makers throughout the world are increasingly turning to technology-related business activities to encourage economic growth. Most of the developed nations spend large sums of money on research and development to create essential new technology. However, translating this technology into commercial products, services, and jobs is invariably a frustrating and difficult task. The First International Technical Innovation and Entrepreneurship Symposium brought together leading authorities from industry, government and universities to discuss programmes and techniques for solving this problem.

This first symposium was an international effort to establish an enduring forum to explore policy initiatives affecting technology transfer, commercial product development, accelerated innovation, entrepreneurship, economic development, new business creation and international economic interdependence relevant to high technology. The goal of this book is to summarize, highlight and focus the presentations on those issues.

Peter O. Crisp
Managing Partner
Venrock Associates
Rockefeller Family & Associates   May 1986

Introduction

For many years, outside the United States, there existed the belief that technological entrepreneurship was largely a US phenomenon and, certainly, there have been many more high-technology entrepreneurs in the US than anywhere else during the past forty years or so. There are many reasons for this. For example, in contrast to Europe, the US is a young, lively and socially and culturally dynamic society, which is forward looking. It is rich, and its people demand innovations of many kinds. The US is essentially the bulwark of the democratic nations' defences, and the pursuance of its role as a major world power has resulted in many innovations – associated with defence and space r&d and procurement activities – that have had immense civilian commercial significance; and this seems likely to continue to be the case during the coming decades.

For the past few centuries there has been a continuous flow to the US of dynamic individuals from Europe and elsewhere. These were often the risk- takers, people who wanted to 'buck the system' but who were constrained economically and socially, or who were oppressed, and they journeyed to the US to realize their ambitions and release their creativity. Today, Europe is moving towards a more entrepreneurial mode. In all the countries of Europe venture capital is increasingly available and governments, universities and some large companies are taking steps to stimulate and foster new technology entrepreneurship.

The Japanese have proved themselves singularly capable of adopting, adapting and extending foreign (mainly US) technology. Coupled to their unique capacity for quality control, this has given Japanese companies a large and growing share of the world market across a wide variety of product types. Moreover, Japan has recently decided to attempt a significant leap ahead through its Fifth Generation Computer Technology Programme. At the same time, steps have been taken in Japan to increase the flow of venture capital, and recent reports note a significant increase in the number of new technology entrepreneurs. It would appear that those who believe Japan is good only at imitation and adaptation may be in for a rude awakening!

In terms of technological innovation and entrepreneurship, we are currently in an exciting period, with significant developments taking place in many nations. Associated with the emerging cluster of 'new' technologies (eg information technology, biotechnology, advanced materials technology) there is a burgeoning of entrepreneurship, and many and diverse attempts are being made in all the advanced market economies – and in several of the newly developing countries – to stimulate and foster entrepreneurial endeavours. It is for this reason that the First International Technical Innovation and Entrepreneurship Symposium was timely.

The First International Technical Innovation and Entrepreneurship Symposium was organized by the Utah Innovation Foundation and held in Salt Lake City during 11–13 September 1985. The authors of this introduction were co-chairmen of the symposium. It brought together three hundred assorted researchers, policymakers, academics, entrepreneurs and venture capitalists from fifteen countries to hear and discuss more than thirty presentations from speakers from over eleven countries. The size and the diverse professional and national affiliations of both the audience and the speakers reflect the intense and widespread current interest in the subject of technological entrepreneurship.

Given the considerable heterogeneity in the background and interests of the speakers, the style of the papers varied enormously. Some were traditionally academic in style; some reflect the practical bias of the authors; others were more personal in presentation. In bringing together an edited collection of the majority of the papers presented at the symposium, we have deliberately attempted to preserve those stylistic variations in order to convey both the flavour and the excitement of the symposium to the reader.

In this book we have divided the papers into three broad – and overlapping – parts: taking an overview; public policies; science parks, innovation centres and the role of higher education establishments. The latter category, which represents the 'cutting edge' of the technological entrepreneurship field, is the largest of the three. Given that there are more than twenty chapters in the book, we will not attempt here to review them all. Rather we will mention several representative chapters from each of the three sections in order to highlight the main themes.

Part 1 begins with a discussion by Dr Bruce Merrifield, of the US Department of Commerce, on the forces of change affecting high technology industries. Among these are the impact of inflation and technical and economic change within the framework of the Kondratieff long wave scenario. He points to the influence, in Japan, of the targeted industry strategy and describes the recent growth of collaborative r&d in the United States. The US government, according to Merrifield, has a catalytic role to play in mobilizing US technological capabilities and in removing barriers to, and enhancing incentives for, further inter-firm collaboration.

Yoriko Kishimoto discusses innovation in Japan. She suggests that while the Japanese have succeeded in the 'catching-up' mode, they are experiencing some difficulty in shifting towards a new 'innovation' mode. She points to a number of crucial differences between the financial systems in Japan and the United States, the former being considerably less well adapted than the latter to funding entrepreneurship. A number of cultural and institutional barriers to entrepreneurship in Japan are also discussed. Despite the various problems, Kishimoto concludes that 'Japan is slowly but surely changing'.

Jiro Tokuyama, apparently often referred to as 'Mr Pacific', makes a strong case for furthering the concept of the Pacific Economic Community. This would involve the encouragement of human resources development, the establishment of communications networks and the development of improved transportation systems. The goal of establishing a viable Pacific Community relies on the advanced countries of the region playing a leadership role in all three areas.

In the final 'overview' paper, Roy Rothwell discusses the role of small firms in technological innovation. On the basis of the data presented, he concludes that generalizations regarding the role of small firms in innovation can be misleading, and that any analysis should proceed on a sector-by-sector basis. Dynamic analysis is also necessary, since the innovatory role of small firms can alter significantly across the industrial spectrum. Rothwell also stresses the interrelationships and interdependencies that frequently exist between small and large firms; they often play different but complementary roles in furthering industrial technological change. Hence, both are desirable and both are necessary.

Part 2 begins with a paper by Walter Zegveld on government incentives to encourage technical innovation. According to Zegveld, a 'balanced and integrated reindustrialization and technology policy' contains three interrelated elements determining the innovative potential of the industrial sector: technological opportunity; the structure of the industrial sector (including finance); and the size and structure of market demand. Public policies can influence all three elements. To be fully effective, they should do so in a balanced and coherent manner.

Gerhardt Bräunling describes Federal German government activities to promote the commercialization of research, with particular emphasis on an experimental programme to support new technology-based firms. This programme focuses on creating an effective 'innovation infrastructure'. In doing this, the traditional role of promotion through financial assistance has become less relevant and greater emphasis has been placed on the role of government as a catalyst to change. This requires more acceptance of risk and more imagination on the part of government, and less use of money and authority by the governmental institutions involved in the process.

Walter Plosila describes a state programme aimed at stimulating and facilitating local economic development, namely the Ben Franklin Partnership. This represents a decentralized approach which relies on local initiatives to identify critical technologies, develop entrepreneurial effects and redirect existing education and training programmes towards the manpower requirements of the future. There are four university-based centres involved in the programme, each of which provides assistance with joint university–private sector research and development, education and training, and entrepreneurial development. Essentially, the programme represents an innovative partnership between private business, higher education and local government.

In the final paper in Part 2, Nimmervoll and Balzer describe policy initiatives in Australia to promote innovation and new technology-based businesses. These involve providing access to adequate funding, mechanisms for fostering new ideas and the establishment of an appropriate support infrastructure. An interesting Australian initiative is the Centre for Innovation Development, founded in 1982, which grew out of a university engineering faculty. The same institution has also founded a Nascent Technology Ventures Programme, which offers a variety of services in support of new technology-based start-up companies.

Part 3 of the book opens with a paper by Edward McMullan on the economics of entrepreneurship education. According to the author, available evidence suggests that entrepreneurship education, as part of an economic development strategy, complements public actions to increase venture capital availability and to encourage business incubator formation. Notable development activity may be generated, both short-term and long-term, through providing educational assistance to existing and potential future entrepreneurs, and new venture programmes can facilitate technology transfer from universities to industry.

The contribution by Nick Segal and the subsequent paper by William

Bolton both describe various aspects of the so-called 'Cambridge phenomenon' in the UK. Segal's paper describes the complex set of factors that resulted in a substantial growth in numbers of new technology-based firms in the Cambridge area, placing the role of Cambridge University and its science park in their proper context. Bolton describes public-sector funded university–industry collaborative schemes in the UK, notably the Post-graduate Teaching Company Scheme with which he was involved. An innovative undergraduate engineering course is also described in which students are required to prepare a new business proposal, thus integrating engineering subjects with those of a financial and management nature.

Everett Rogers, in his paper on university spin-off high-technology companies, begins with a discussion on the information society and the role of the research university as a key institution in the information society. He describes the trend to closer university–industry relationships in the United States during the 1980s, the manner in which government initiatives promote high-technology industry and the benefits and costs of university–industry relationships.

Staying with the same general theme, Robert Colton describes the role of several US National Science Foundation (NSF) initiatives in stimulating increased university–industry interactions. These are the Engineering Research Center, Cooperative Research Project, and Cooperative Research Center programmes. Colton provides data to substantiate his claim that NSF-sponsored programmes have successfully accelerated technology transfers from universities to industry, thus effectively stimulating industrial innovation in the US.

The remaining ten papers deal variously with innovation centres, science parks and technology parks and are based on experiences in six countries. The initiatives described include the recently established Aston Science Park in the UK, the long-established Stanford Research Park in the United States, the Shannon Innovation Centre in Ireland, the Dutch Inventors Centre, the Berlin Centre for Innovation and New Enterprises, science parks in Canada, and the Utah Innovation Foundation. Also included is an analysis of new business incubators in the United States. The descriptions and analyses included in these papers represent a rich vein of information and guidance for those who would wish to establish such initiatives elsewhere.

Wayne S. Brown, Utah Innovation Foundation
Roy Rothwell, Science Policy Research Unit   April 1986

Acknowledgements

The authors gratefully acknowledge the assistance of the Utah Innovation Foundation and its staff in preparing this book with special thanks to DoAnn Lauthers, J. Gregg Goodwin, and Bradley B. Bertoch.
Dr Rothwell would like gratefully to acknowledge the financial support of the Leverhulme Trust during his time spent editing this book.

Part 1 Taking an overview

Forces of change affecting high technology industries

Bruce Merrifield
US Department of Commerce

This paper addresses some of the major forces in the world that are restructuring not only the US economy but the world economy as well. These forces are so powerful that management in the next decades will be the management of continuous change.

One of the great forces will be the targeted industry strategy that the Japanese have modelled so effectively. It is now being copied worldwide by Europe and other countries. Another force is the emergence of the lesser developed and the underdeveloped countries that have natural resources such as natural gas that are currently just wasted. These countries have realized that they can build turn-key plants and add value to their raw material products. Ultimately, these investments will have an impact on much of the $250 billion worldwide business in commodity petrochemicals. A third major force for change is the technology explosion which has generated something like 90 per cent of all of our knowledge in the sciences in the last thirty years. It will double our knowledge again in the next ten or fifteen years, and will tend to make major investments obsolete long before their useful life can be realized.

Impact of inflation

In the United States there are also special problems relating to an adverse synergism between past tax laws and chronic inflation. Figure 1 illustrates the simple arithmetic that describes what has happened to 'smokestack America' over the last decade. Return on equity (ROE) is an after tax number that averages about 15 per cent for all companies in the United States, but it is not a realistic number. It first needs to be corrected for dividend pay-out which averages about 47 per cent in the US. So if one takes away 7 per cent of that 15, it leaves 8 per cent. Then it is necessary to subtract inflation which operates as a direct hidden tax on equity, and over the last several years has averaged 10 per cent. The net result is that even starting with a 15 per cent return on equity there is a negative 'real' return on earnings.

Figure 1 Inflation: a direct tax on equity

$$\left[\begin{array}{c}\text{return on}\\\text{equity}\end{array}\right] - \left[\begin{array}{c}\text{dividends}\\\text{paid out}\end{array}\right] - \left[\begin{array}{c}\text{inflation}\\\text{rate}\end{array}\right] = \left[\begin{array}{c}\text{real retained}\\\text{earnings}\end{array}\right]$$

$$15\% \quad - \quad 7\% \quad - \quad 10\% \quad = \quad -2\%$$

The Kidder Peabody Financial Quality Profiles that adjust earnings for inflation and identify discretionary cash flows, have shown that a majority of the companies that make up the Dow Jones, for example, have been liquidating themselves in seven or eight out of the last ten years. Moreover, many companies have much less than a 15 per cent return on equity, and they are eroding their assets at a very significant rate. Figure 2 is another way to illustrate this effect. If a million dollars is invested in a piece of equipment or a facility that has a useful life of twenty years, that investment could be recovered under previous tax laws over that period of time. But at 10 per cent inflation, it would cost $8 million to replace it. The other $7 million would not have been reserved and would have been falsely reported as profits on which 46 per cent taxes would have been paid and of which perhaps 40–50 per cent would have been paid out as dividends.

Figure 2   Effects of inflation

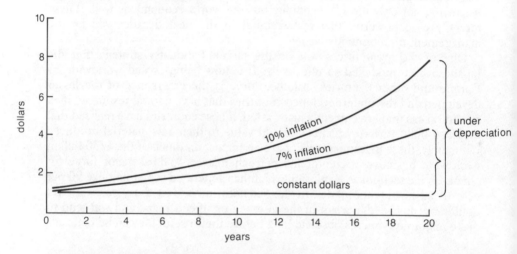

It is important to understand that increased innovation and productivity are required if inflation is to be brought down permanently. General guidelines that emerge include: the necessity of managing capital intensive operations for cash flow; harvesting or divesting cash traps, and re-investing in high-growth, low-equity intensive, proprietary systems that have a high asset turnover ratio; or in assets or operations that are indexed to inflation, such as oil and gas, timber, land, financial services, and marketing distribution systems.

Kondratieff long wave

It is interesting to speculate about why 'smokestack America' is in such trouble. One oversimplified but useful concept involves the 'Kondratieff long wave'. Kondratieff was a perceptive Russian who, back in the 1920s, disagreed with Marx and Lenin that the capitalist countries would self-destruct. He pointed out that they seem to do that every fifty-four years, but then they come back again. Of course, that wasn't very popular at the time, and they exiled him to Siberia. The concept has been very controversial, but recently Dr Jay Forrester at the Massachusetts Institute of Technology (MIT) has rationalized the long wave in terms of four phases. The last long wave started in 1929.

The first phase is a fifteen-year collapse in which many obsolescent facilities in overcapacity are written down, taken over, or go into Chapter 11. Then at the end of that period (in 1945) an excess demand over supply developed in the capital sector, which fuelled the second stage, a massive twenty-year capital re-investment. Forrester points out that the best technology existing at that time tends to fuel the entire cycle. In the steel industry this was the open hearth furnace. Hundreds of millions of dollars were being invested in new steel facilities, with significant economies of scale. Prices were going up faster than costs, so cash flows were great, and profit margins large. Forrester further points out that this process rejects new technology on the basis that it is risky to try something new when everything is going so well with the present systems. So, when the basic oxygen furnace came on the scene it was rejected in the US, but under Marshall Plan money it was put into Japan and Germany. By about 1965, a world balance in demand and supply for steel had developed, but the steel business did not see itself in the materials business, and consequently continued to invest in steel. The third phase, then, is a period in which there is excess steel capacity perhaps by 25 per cent worldwide. Competition holds down prices as costs continue to rise and the business begins to erode its assets in real terms. In addition, engineering plastics are beginning to take away markets from steel; also at the present time graphite fibre reinforced epoxies that are stronger than steel and lighter than aluminum, that do not stress fatigue or corrode, will begin to replace steel in many applications as the price of graphite fibres continues to decrease. Steel will never disappear, but with enormous worldwide overcapaicty much of the older US plants will inevitably be shut down. This introduces the fourth phase of the Kondratieff/Forrester cycle, a period of economic turbulence in which the recession cycles deepen and the next collapse occurs. 1982 is the fifty-third year of the fifty-four-year cycle. But actually, the decline of the capital intensive commodity businesses started about ten years ago, and many obsolescent overcapacity facilities have already been written down. If it weren't for the emergence of new technologies, the economy would be in far worse trouble than it is. But fortunately, as Forrester points out, the fifty-four-year cycle that rejects new technology has also seen a spectacular explosion of new products and systems.

Technology explosion

As mentioned above, this last thirty-year period has generated something like 90 per cent of all scientific knowledge. This pool will double again in the next ten or fifteen years. Moreover, 90 per cent of all the scientists who have ever lived are now living and working, and they will double again in that period. As a result, a tremendous build-up of under-utilized technology is already fueling the next cycle – in electronics, communications, engineering, plastics, biogenetics, specialty chemicals, pharmaceuticals, and so forth.

The new systems will take on increased significance in the next few years, and we are looking into one of the most interesting periods the world has ever seen. Basically we have two economies: one is in trouble and the other is exploding. Thousands of new companies have formed in the last several years and are now offsetting the decline of the capital intensive commodities so that the net GNP is even inching up a little bit.

The US a decade ago, with only 5 per cent of the world's population, was generating something like 75 per cent of the world's technology. Now the US share is about 50 per cent. In another decade, it may be 30 per cent, not because it is generating less – it will be generating a great deal more – but because the other 95 per cent of the world will also be contributing. All countries in the world now see technology as essential to quality of life and are getting into this business. There are a billion people in China, for example, one out of four in the world, and they intend to be at the leading edge of every technology by the end of the century. Perhaps half the new scientists and engineers will be emerging in underdeveloped countries.

This explosion of technology, therefore, is much more significant than is easily realized and it will change our lives continuously. Some of the areas in which major new developments will occur will be in materials science, agriculture and in hundreds of derivative areas. For example, in the materials area ceramic engines (now being tested in Japan) may make current internal combustion engines obsolete. Graphite fibre reinforced plastics will progressively erode markets in construction, aircraft, automobiles, and appliances, as will engineering plastics, alloys, and laminates. The biochemical area is a fascinating one with major developments occurring in understanding the learning process, and in realizing the total conquest of viral diseases including cancer. The ability to correct genetic defects will develop, as will the ability to produce plants that grow in cold and arid climates. The cloning of superior livestock and of genetically assembled hybrid organisms are reasonable possibilities.

Electronic systems will pervasively restructure our lives, with electronic mail providing access to the Library of Congress, from home to most of the important university courses, and to continuous news updates. The frontier of education will be adult education as the pace of change requires a continual learning process. This period will, at the least, be an interesting one.

Targeted industry strategy

Another great force that is restructuring the US economy is the 'targeted industry strategy'. It is based on the 'learning curve' first articulated as a strategic planning concept by the Boston Consulting Group in the late 1960s. Japan adopted this concept as a basic strategy at that time and targeted steel, automobiles, consumer electronics, and microchips as priority areas.

The concept is simple. If, in Figure 3 the log of the cost of a product over its lifetime is plotted against the log of its cumulative volume, a straight line results. Every time the volume doubles the cost goes down about 20 per cent. The traditional price history is illustrated by the top line where a new product is marketed in small volume, but as volume increases economies of scale result and costs decrease. Typically, a general manager will leave the price where it is allowing competitors to come in under that price umbrella and trading market share for short-term profits. Traditionally, after half the market is given up, the price collapses and a commodity situation results. However, if the price had been decreased as shown by the dotted line to a point below anyone's entry point, the resulting profits might be ten times as much. Moreover, even a late entry can forward price below anyone else's cost and take all the new market growth. All that is required is to carry the negative cash flow in the interim.

Figure 3 Japanese national strategy: the 'learning curve'

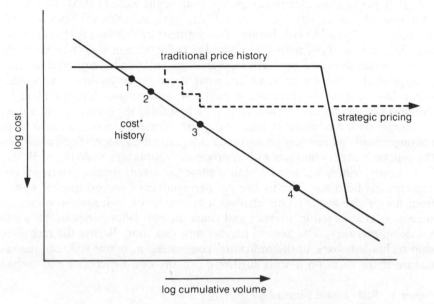

*costs decrease about 20% for every doubling of total industry volume

That is quite feasible for most American companies. However, a nation such as Japan can do this as well. The procedure is first to target the industry, then bring together all of the players in that industry such as in steel; next, the small companies are eliminated to concentrate the business and imports are closed off to further base-load economies of scale in the home market. Then r&d objectives based on manufacturing engineering improvements are parcelled out to avoid redundant effort and the new systems are leveraged 80–90 per cent with low cost capital. Incremental pricing then puts all the costs into the first eight-hour shift for the home market, and the next two shifts are for export at substantially less, and finally the product is forward priced below the existing costs of American companies. Market share is gained very rapidly until economies of scale catch up with the prices.

This is a very astute strategy and has been very successful. However, it must be understood that it is limited to those areas where there are large volume markets, and where there is a long enough time period to recapture the negative cash flow and pay out the major investments. Economies of scale then become the dominant factor, even over the best technology.

Collaborative r&d in the US

This strategy is so effective that it is now being adopted by other countries as well. Therefore, it is important that we begin to collaborate in the US on an equivalent scale of effort. US antitrust laws, however, have prevented such collaboration. Modifications to these laws must be considered, but in the meantime there is a need to find ways within the antitrust laws to collaborate on a scale equivalent to those that are now used by the Japanese and other consortia around the world. One such way involves the use of an r&d limited partnership concept. This concept allows large companies to collaborate without antitrust implications.

In Figure 4 let us assume that the consortium shown in the upper left-hand corner is perhaps an electronics group, that might include IBM, Bell Labs, Motorola, Digital Equipment, Control Data, Intel, and others. They would not normally be allowed to collaborate. The antitrust guidelines say that no more than 25 per cent of any market is allowed to collaborate in a given consortium. This concept, therefore, sets up a separate legal entity called a general partner. The general partner then identifies what the user group (the consortium) would like to have. In this case, it might be a megabyte chip, a million bit dynamic random access memory chip. The first thing the general partner does is contract with the 'users' to take or pay for a certain number of these chips contingent only on meeting pre-agreed cost–performance specifications. Then the general partner contracts with appropriate laboratories to do the work that is necessary. These are arms-length contractual arrangements that avoid any antitrust implications. Thirdly the partner syndicates venture capital money from the private sector. This involves a relatively low risk since commercial success is guaranteed in advance and since the best laboratories in the world are doing the work. The general partner now can either license the megabyte chip technology back to the individual companies or, better still, can manufacture it for them on a scale further down the cost experience curve than

Figure 4 R&D limited partnership

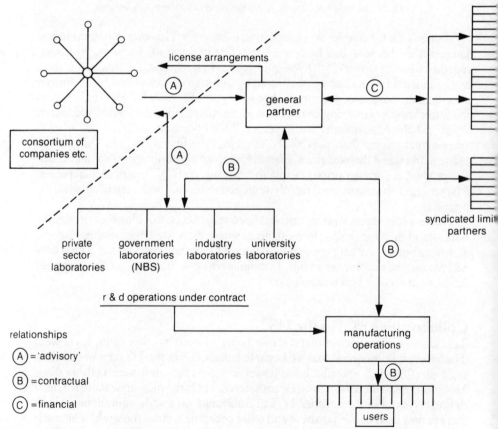

anything the Japanese or anyone else could achieve. Alternatively, the general partner can license it to an individual company for manufacture on a large scale. The consortium gains proprietary rights to the megabyte chip without putting money into it (because of their original take-or-pay orders) and their laboratories doing work that they would like to do, but are being paid to do it.

This basic structure is now being developed for all sorts of consortia in flexible manufacturing, biogenetics, and so forth. The general partner can be a university, an industry association, or a group of individuals. One of the key factors is that once the limited partners are paid off, then the cash flow continues to come back to the general partner. If the general partnership is set up as a nonprofit operation, then the continuing cash flow is available to fund second and third generation projects. It then becomes a cash machine for continuing developments, funded out of the private sector which is the important thing. The role of the government here is strictly limited to a catalytic one, that develops guidelines and advises groups when desirable. This is a major aim of the Department of Commerce.

Conclusion
It is important to remember that the US has by far the world's most advanced technology in almost every area of interest; it has an incomparable industrial infrastructure with which to translate new developments into products and processes; it has the world's most effective capital formation capability. All that is needed are the initiatives required to mobilize these capabilities, remove the barriers that impede collaboration and further enhance the incentives for doing so. The US, with all its remarkable resources and capabilities, can then be the major beneficiary of this period of change.

Innovation in Japan

Yoriko Kishimoto
Palo Alto, California

The pressure on Japan today to adjust its system to a more innovative mode is tremendous. It sees itself as being backed into a no-growth corner: fewer and more expensive technologies are available on the world marketplace; competition is closing in from the lesser developed countries; world markets are becoming increasingly closed to substitutable products; and Japan has largely caught up with the major industrial technologies which exist today.

In casting around for models, many in Japan have been intensely interested in the 'Silicon Valley model'. This model is a complex process difficult to characterize, but its chief players are the venture capitalists and the entrepreneurs. How complex this system is and how difficult it is to transfer is being appreciated by the Japanese today. Of course, this model is not the only one to support innovation, which raises the interesting question of what new models for an innovation system will be developed by Japan itself.

Japan is currently in its second 'venture capital' boom. The first one, which took off in the early 1970s, had largely collapsed by 1975. Approximately eight so-called venture capital companies were established in this first rush of interest, mainly by Japan's major securities companies, insurance companies, and banks. In the euphoria of the high growth period which had characterized the 1960s, a number of aspiring businessmen left their secure positions in large companies to try their hand independently. Most of these companies barely got off the ground, and by the late 1970s, many of the so-called venture capital companies had degenerated to no more than factoring or commercial finance companies.

The second round of activity began around 1982. A number of new enterprises (which the Japanese call venture businesses) became significant successes. These include Sord Computers and Cosmo Eighty. The older venture capital companies revived their investment activity, and a number of new ones have been established. The economic and business newspapers are filled with stories on newly discovered venture businesses. Will this second boom last?

Financing systems

The bottleneck in Japan today does not lie in an absolute lack of financial resources. The problem, rather, lies in the lack of the infrastructure necessary to re-allocate the existing financial resources to new sectors, and the lack of experience to manage investment in these fields.

Two of the obvious differences between the United States and Japan have been in their treatment of capital gains and in their over-the-counter (OTC) markets.

Japan's zero capital gains tax is well known and envied in the United States. This tax, with certain qualifications, was eliminated in the 1950s for *individual* investors. *Corporations*, however, are not exempt: their capital gains are taxed at the regular rate, which averages close to 50 per cent. This obviously makes venture capital investment less attractive for institutional investors. Even for individuals, there are important exceptions. The investor must limit his transactions to less than fifty times per year and less than 200 000 stocks per year. More importantly for the venture capitalist, a major holder of a certain company's stock cannot sell more than 5 per cent of that company's total outstanding stock or more than 15 per cent over a three-year period. Otherwise, the gains are subject to general tax rates.

Japan's over-the-counter market has not deserved its label. It has not been a functioning stepping stone for young companies which are aspiring to the major stock markets. By 1982, it had only 134 companies listed. These companies' stocks, furthermore, are not always actively traded. The OTC market seems to have been used mainly as a vehicle for closely held family- managed businesses to liquify some of their assets on a one-shot basis. Since the companies have not been allowed to issue at a higher market value, they have not had the incentive to issue more stock which, in turn, has limited their growth prospects.

The treatment of capital gains and the nature of the OTC markets are, of course, symptoms of the two national systems. Below, we will discuss the various components which define the two systems, then their implications for the various stages of financing.

Major players

The ultimate sources of the funding for the early stages of a new company must be willing to accept some risk and to evaluate investment opportunities with no historical track record. In both countries, relatives and friends are still the source of what is called 'seed money'. Japan's high savings rate means that most relatives will have relatively large bank accounts, but this money is not necessarily used for risk capital. It is most likely earmarked for specific future needs such as college tuition or retirement. The United States has more risk capital, ie, more people with the ability to absorb the total loss of a substantial investment. Japan lacks a number of the ultimate capital sources which the United States seems to enjoy.

Pension fund managers and other institutional investors are willing to invest in higher risk, high return funds. In the United States, these investors provided 34 per cent of the total venture capital funds in 1982. In Japan, the Ministry of Finance has been the source of some of the constraints. Another brake has been the extreme conservativeness structured into the investment process, in which mediocrity is definitely favoured over a possibility of failure. The concept of spreading the risks over a large portfolio is not accepted in Japan's investment community.

The financial markets in Japan have been so regulated and protected that the fund managers have not been striving to maximize returns, but to merely stay within the given parameters. These regulations, and hence the structural incentives, have significantly changed and there is much more of an incentive to maximize profits today.

The 'virtuous cycle' of venture investment has not yet produced a community of successful entrepreneurs in Japan which has the inclination and financial ability to invest in the next generation of new companies. In the United States, entrepreneurs are able to make millions of dollars if their companies successfully go public. In Japan, there are some examples of this (such as Takeda Riken's founder investing in the company A&R started by one of his former employees) but not enough.

Venture capital in the United States was started with the funds of extremely wealthy private families, such as the Rockefellers. Until 1981, wealthy individuals were still the single largest source of venture capital in the US (*Venture Capital Journal*). The single largest venture capital fund today is that of Mr Henry Hillman (the Hillman Company). In Japan, the famous Mitsubishi and Mitsui conglomerates were once controlled by powerful families, but these were dissolved with the reforms which were enforced at the end of World War II.

The institution of venture capital (vc) companies is integral to the operation of risk capital management and the creation of new companies, new technologies, and new industries in the United States. These are professionals specializing in screening companies in their start-up stages for investment. Depending on the venture capitalists' capabilities and inclinations, they may also provide management assistance, provide introductions to other types of financial sources such as banks and investment bankers, or even send in a new president.

As noted above, a number of so-called vc companies have been established in Japan over this past decade. A number of historical, institutional, legal and regulatory constraints prevent them from fulfilling the roles that vc companies of the United States play. Most of them are subsidiaries of either securities companies or banks. The parent companies in most cases have sent managers who have been trained in normal credit analysis to the newly created subsidiaries, so that the background and training of the vcs are considerably different from those in the United States. Also, most of the Japanese vcs are under pressure to produce revenues and profits in a relatively short time frame. Thus, the vcs created by the major securities companies are attempting to find medium-sized companies which are preparing to go public, and making their profits from the underwriting fees as well as from capital gains.

There is a further obstacle in the rulings from the Fair Trade Commission which forbid venture capital companies from holding a majority share of any company and from sending a representative to hold a director's seat. This obviously deters large investments in risky companies.

Facilitators

In Japan, the venture capital companies have marketing staffs which search for and attempt to interest small businesses which are likely to go public in the near future. In the United States, most venture capital companies are flooded every week with cold calls from aspiring entrepreneurs and young companies. A more important channel for spotting good investments, however, is the informal network of lawyers, consultants, professors, former investees, and other business colleagues who 'pre-screen' the prospects.

The concept of having a community, or network, is essential to a smoothly operating system. Part of the problem in Japan is simply the short history of venture capital – it may take several decades to develop fully, as it has in the United States.

Government and legal framework

Often the most simple yet most powerful measures to change the behaviour of a system is to change one or more of its ground rules. In the United States, for example, it is recognized that the reduction of capital gains tax to 28 per cent, then to 20 per cent, has been the major cause of the flood of venture capital over the past several years. There is no concept in the Japanese fiscal system which corresponds exactly with that of capital gains in the United States. We have noted above that individuals, but not corporations, are eligible for tax exemptions on some profits from trading securities.

The United States also has some corporate forms and financial instruments which Japan does not have. For example, many high technology companies have been forming r&d partnerships to raise funds, including both start-ups and major, established corporations. The r&d partnerships reduce the risks for the investors as well as offering the companies a method of raising funds 'off the balance sheet', ie, without immediately diluting the earnings per share figure.

Another example is the variety of financial instruments which are available to the venture capitalist in structuring the arrangements with the young company. Since the objective is to combine capital with management and technology, and provide each party with a proper share of the profits and control and the appropriate incentives, a variety of financial instruments is desirable. Venture capitalists in the United States frequently use warrants, convertible bonds, and build up clauses to allow the managers to 'earn' back control over their company by making the company financially successful.

Japan has begun to allow more and more of these financial instruments. For example, warrants have been authorized since 1982. A more significant constraint may be the vagueness of contractual relationships. Contrary to popular belief, laws are very important in conducting business in Japan. However, most legal constraints are structured vaguely, which is used to the advantage of the stronger party. Concretely, this means that although a large investor may not have the legal right to appoint a representative director or to determine major management policies, a small company owner will still attempt to prevent any investor from gaining a significant share of his firm's equity.

Financial system characteristics

Although Japan's financial system is being discussed in another paper, I would like to note some of its characteristics which have implications for the allocation and regulation of capital in the Japanese economy.

Rationing is one of the principles which have governed its operations. Since the economy had to be rebuilt with almost all of its capital stock destroyed by World War II, capital has been a most precious commodity which had to be carefully allocated to maximize its effect. This has meant that major corporations with high economies of scale were favoured. Also, the Ministry of Finance controlled the interest rates, which prevented the market mechanism from working. Some organizations, namely the Ministry of Finance, Bank of Japan, and the major banks retained the right to allocate capital to a large degree.

Indirect financing is one of the results of rationing. Indirect financing means the channelling of capital from the savers to the users via banks, rather than direct ownership of stocks via the various stock exchanges. Whether it is a result or cause, this has meant that the stock markets have not cultivated the full infrastructure of support which is necessary for its full functions. For example, the investors need full disclosure and a diverse set of evaluations and The Ministry of Finance has full regulations on disclosure, but consolidated statements are still not required for most companies. Also, there are few independent security analysts or investment advisors – most are affiliated or directly employed by the securities companies. The usefulness of such independent advisors may be limited in any case since the buying and selling power of the major securities companies often dominate any evaluation of a stock's value.

Protection of investors is a principle which governs the regulations over Japan's stock markets. This has been necessary because of the immature state of the stock market operations, as just outlined. Until October 1983, a company had to have more than two years operating record and the ability to pay dividends in order to be listed on the over-the-counter markets. A Genentech would never have made it on Japan's OTC market.

A few changes were made in October 1983. Regulations for the OTC market were slightly loosened and a third market was created in Osaka in autumn 1983.

Bank lending

Above, we discussed inadequacies in the equity markets in providing risk capital. Needless to say, the banks have not been more receptive to supporting the growth of new enterprises.

In the high growth era, Japan channelled most of its funds to its major corporations. Small companies saw little, and the little they did see came via the larger manufacturing or trading companies, which acted as financial intermediaries for their subcontractors. Today, the banks are eager to make more loans, but rarely will they lend without concrete collateral.

Many small companies have based their financial strategies on real estate. Graphica, a small colour graphics company, chose to locate its building in an area just outside Tokyo which was expected to rise in value most sharply, which would allow a larger loan to be taken out.

Summary

Allocation of capital is perhaps the most obvious and most political determinant of the shape of a country's economy. Capital alone, of course, is not sufficient to induce innovation, but it is necessary. Let us examine the financial support for each stage of growth in summary.

Seed money.   Japan's economy is wealthy enough to provide the initial funds necessary to test out an idea, and its family and social structure will support with mutual assistance. However, the actual probability that an entrepreneur will be able to succeed in launching a new company is so low that the prospect is rarely raised.

Early stage financing.   This is the stage where the United States' venture capital companies play their full role. They have the experience and infrastructure necessary to help new companies to become established, and the right financial incentives exist to justify the higher risk and talent required up front. In Japan, the original investors face little prospect of being able to liquidate their investments in the medium term, and will find their earnings are heavily taxed. The new companies have little prospect of being able to grow rapidly given the corporate environment, as will be discussed later.

'Cash-out' stage.   Investors must liquidate, or 'cash-out' their positions at some stage, of course, to claim their return on investment. In the United

States, this can be done by taking their companies public, or by selling to a large corporation. This stage is hampered in Japan due to differences in the OTC markets, and also the lack of an active market for mergers and acquisitions. Some partial solutions being used today include establishing a subsidiary or related company in the United States (or Hong Kong) and taking that company public. However, we have seen that the OTC market has been changing and may well come to play a more active role than it has in the past in Japan.

Going public.   Taking the company public is the ultimate goal of all venture capital investments. This marks the public acknowledgement of the company as a long-term, established organization and the stocks can enjoy wide distribution. In Japan, the step of taking a company public has great implications when recruiting new employees, and in other ways. The process is time-consuming, however. The securities companies interested in becoming its underwriters begin preparing the company six to seven years before the event. The standards for going public (to either the first or second tier) are very strict, by US standards.

The financial systems involve several key components, as we have seen. There must be the original fund suppliers, the middlemen, and there must be a large enough return in the medium and long-term to justify the risk and investment. In Japan, the first condition is satisfied, but not the second or third, for venture capital.

Innovation investment in large corporations
Before we move on to the next topic, it is worth examining the investment and resource allocation pattern within large corporations.

There is no axiom that innovation must take place in small entrepreneurial companies. Even in the United States, there has been much interest in corporate venturing, which can take one of several forms. The large company, such as 3M or Texas Instruments, can encourage individuals and/or small teams to be responsible for initiating, championing, and implementing new business lines. In another form, the larger company may spin off subsidiaries which will be partially owned and be independently managed by one of its key employees – this is the form adapted by Cetus/Cetus Madison/Cetus Palo Alto, for example. In yet another approach, the large company may choose to make an investment in a smaller company. Inco, for example, was one of the original investors in Genentech. IBM has bought significant shares in Intel and Rolm, although only after they became industry leaders on their own. Many large companies have simply acquired small, high-technology companies as well.

In Japan, there is also a great deal of interest in developing new approaches to encouraging innovation within the large corporations. Large electronics companies such as Fujitsu have begun to cultivate a group of subsidiaries or affiliated companies to develop software, for example.

The incentive system within established corporate channels encourages hard work, but punishes mistakes: this means there are active incentives *against* risk taking. Since the employment system assures a reasonably stable rise up the corporate ladder, there is little reason to take that extra risk. In addition as we shall see later, there are few rewards for those who do make an unexpectedly large contribution to the company.

The decision-making process is another barrier to risk taking. It is difficult to gain the consensus on a new venture, one whose outcome is unknown. The idea must have an extremely strong champion. This is why the first customer for a new product is usually an unbureaucratic company whose president or other executive is willing to accept the responsibility for potential failure.

Human resource systems

The financial system is one aspect of the infrastructure to support innovation. Human resources are even more important, and are proving to be as much, or perhaps even more, of a bottleneck in Japan.

Major players

The path to creating a new technology or a new industry, simplified, includes basic research, development, early commercialization, and mass marketing and production.

Scientists.   Basic research requires a good environment for scientists. Although there are a few fields, such as physics, which have produced Nobel Prize level research in Japan, the United States generally has provided a much more conducive atmosphere. Government support of universities, major research institutes, and major corporate research projects has been generous in direct and indirect ways. Generous grants from the National Institute of Health, for example, have made it possible to pursue research topics which have no foreseeable applications in the medical or industrial worlds. Genetic engineering and new anti-cancer drugs have resulted, however, from such initiatives.

Japan as yet lacks this critical mass of scientific researchers. The structure of university research and teaching positions also hampers the emergence of promising young researchers. Many excellent researchers are not able to pursue their projects freely until they have been named full professor and are free of the political pressures of their department.

Another aspect is the technology transfer between basic research and corporations. The transfer of ideas can only be done by a person who has a good understanding of both worlds. In the United States, this is done by venture capitalists themselves in some cases, but more often engineers and manager/engineers who are already working on current systems and conceive of new methodologies, new products, or new markets.

Entrepreneurs.   The central person who not only has the idea, but has the will and ability to create a company around it, is the entrepreneur. The requirements called for in this person are tremendous. He/she must be a great motivator to be able to assemble the team of initial managers, engineers, venture capitalists, and other workers. He must have the experience of being able to guide a company from its conception through its early, high-growth stages. When the company becomes more mature, he must either be able to shift gears to adjust to the entirely new set of needs, or be able gracefully to step aside for more suitable managers.

There has been much debate about how an entrepreneur is created. One requirement may be a social mythology. The entrepreneur, by definition, does not depend on the opinions of others for support, but at some level of development he must win the acceptance of the larger society – at least from the people he wishes to hire and the companies he wishes to sell to. The entrepreneur in Japan has faced obstacles on almost all levels. First, young people are not raised with the dream of creating one's own company. Even successful entrepreneurs cannot win the same respect in society at large as a high-level executive in a major corporation.

If the individual leaves a secure position in Japan to begin or join a new enterprise, the risk is large indeed – much larger than would be the case in the United States. The option of rejoining the society of large, established corporations is essentially shut off. Since most work given to smaller companies is sporadic, of low-level sophistication, and carries a small margin of profit, generally only a low level of worker can be attracted. It is very difficult to break this vicious circle, and the decision to leave the world of established companies is an irrevocable one. The lack of entrepreneurs certainly finds one root cause here.

It is also difficult for an aspiring entrepreneur to gain the experience he needs. In Silicon Valley, would-be entrepreneurs can design themselves a progression of positions which will give them experience in a number of fields, and can 'practice' by taking the responsibility of managing an independent profit centre. This experience can be partially gained by the age of thirty or so, at which stage a more experienced manager may be hired or brought in as a partner.

There are young presidents in Japan – such as the trio which presides over Ascii, a successful publishing and software company – but they are rare. Furthermore, in Japan's hierarchically structured society, it is rare to see a capable older person reporting to a significantly young person.

Japanese society's strengths come from using the concept of 'superior averageness'. The energies and talents of the average worker are fully mobilized. The trade-off made is that extremely talented people cannot be excessively rewarded for fear of demoralizing the average man. Top executives in major corporations draw salaries of no more than $100 000 to $150 000. Top-flight researchers and engineers may be promoted a little faster than their peers, but not much faster.

Thus, Japanese are always impressed with the United States' 'creme de la creme': how extremely motivated, hardworking, and fulfilled they are. Unlike top Japanese researchers who may have to waste their time making do with inadequate research facilities, and sometimes even washing their own lab equipment, top talent in the United States can find venture capital backers, recruit good managers and researchers if they wish to see their research commercialized, and receive plentiful government grants if they wish to pursue basic research.

Middle managers and engineers.   The other side of the coin becomes evident when we examine what follows after the first couple of years of creating a new company. The United States continues to hold its edge when it comes to attracting the necessary number of middle managers and engineers, since the labour market is fluid in the high-technology area. It is often said that the engineer need not even change parking lots in making a switch, since many of these companies exist side by side. The Japanese system however, has the advantage when the newness of the field, or the necessity for proprietariness, calls for the company to invest in the education and training of its own employees. At least in the larger companies, it is still rare to find employees leaving their jobs, and almost inconceivable that they would leave to join a rival company.

The advantage of the Japanese system becomes even more pronounced when the product cycle matures to the stage of large-scale production and competitive factors become more incrementally determined. Japan has a large crop of engineers who bridge the gap very well between the manufacturer and the users, ensuring that the products are custom-made for user needs, that continuous improvements are made, and that the quality of the equipment stays high. Proportionally more attention is paid to the manufacturing process as well, its costs, quality, and automation.

The strengths of the US system are its flexibility which allows resources to flow where they are most needed, and the reward system which provides the incentive to the most talented to move as necessary. Almost all the incentives and the resource allocation mechanisms in Japan, on the other hand, are designed for the mass-production, mass-marketing mode. Is this changing at all?

Changes in the Japanese human resource system
Allocation among companies.   There is yet little change here. College graduates from the better universities still prefer to enter the larger electronics companies, such as Hitachi and NEC, rather than a smaller company which may give them a freer environment to work on interesting projects. Smaller companies which are able to, do pay better for engineers of comparable age and experience than larger companies, but not significantly more. Also, it is impossible to transfer from a smaller company to a larger company later. Until the entire labour market becomes more flexible to lessen the risk for the individual, and until smaller companies can offer some substantial attraction that larger ones cannot, small start-up companies will always lack top-grade engineers.

Reward system within companies.   There is no reason why there cannot be great inventiveness within large corporations. If the company is able to spot the most promising engineers, give them the financial and labour support that they need, and give them the incentive to do their best, large companies should do very well. Indeed, many of the most important discoveries made in the United States were made in Bell Laboratories and other large companies.

Japanese companies still cannot reward the most productive scientists and engineers ostentatiously. Brilliant young researchers may receive much recognition, but their salaries will not be significantly higher than their less productive peers. Moreover, they may not be able to carry out the research that they would like to do. This is changing in some companies in Japan. For example, Suntory Inc. started a biomedical research institute in 1979. It recruited many capable young researchers from universities and other companies. It still does not pay startlingly high salaries, but it is extremely generous with research budgets and it provides very generous fringe benefits, such as high-class housing. Also, it allows its researchers to maintain ties with the academic community by publishing and giving papers at conferences. Still, it remains impossible for a researcher or engineer to become wealthy.

University–industry relations.   The barriers erected in the 1960s between the universities and industry as a result of vehement objections from the students, are still largely in place. Controls at national universities are especially strict. Both formal regulations and general social sanctions make professors very careful about their interaction with private sector companies. For example, in the biotechnology field, professors who discover new types of useful vectors for genetic engineering are at a loss as to how to diffuse their know-how. Since their academic reputation may be at risk, many are reluctant to release their discoveries to the private sector; it seems easiest to keep them, unknown and unused.

Product market systems

The emergence of excellent products in itself is insufficient without markets which are able and willing to receive them. It is often overlooked that the nature of the product markets in a system is as much a variable as the nature of the companies and technologies which supply them.

In the high-technology field, it is especially important to have users which demand even higher levels of performance. The 'leading edge' country thus enjoys a virtuous cycle. Related to the above is the receptivity of the markets to new companies. In a slow-moving economy, existing buyer–seller relationships are very difficult to break into. In a quickly growing or changing business community, new relationships are much easier to establish. Venture companies make natural customers for venture companies.

Companies which are attempting to launch a new type or category of product must build up a 'critical mass' of credibility. They must convince potential customers that the new product is here to stay, and that it will be supported by a growing infrastructure of support. The users are asked to invest in a new product whose long-term value will be determined by the market. The ability to create this credibility is generally held by already dominant companies. IBM's entrance into the personal computer market is, of course, a perfect example. Many observers have pointed out that IBM's entrance has both stabilized and enlarged the overall market by providing legitimacy and leadership.

It is also obvious that IBM was not the pioneer in this field. The initial market was created by Apple Computer, a start-up company. Likewise, the biotechnology industry was initiated by Genentech, also a venture-capital funded start-up. Since Japan has so long thrived by being a fast follower, there are few companies which are educated and financed enough to pioneer a new field. This is well illustrated by the experience of a medium-sized company which developed a new type of equipment for cutting wafers for semiconductor production. The product was first well-received by American semiconductor companies before it was accepted by Japanese firms.

Finally, the simple size of the market cannot be overlooked. The United States' gross national product is twice the size of Japan's. Since the development costs for a new product are so high, they must be spread over as large a market as possible.

Conclusions

The basic premise of this chapter is that innovation is an enormously complex system which needs a fully supportive infrastructure. This framework of structural incentives can be changed significantly by changing some laws and regulations, eg, the tax rate on capital gains and the patent protection enforcement, but it also requires several generations for a complete change. The system, after all, is comprised of human beings.

Japan is slowly but surely changing. Some of the right debates are taking place, and some of the regulations are changing, such as on the stock markets. More importantly various structural incentives will make themselves felt by everyone in Japan. These incentives include those mentioned at the beginning of this paper: fewer and more expensive technologies are available on the world marketplace; competition is closing in from the lesser developed countries; world markets are becoming increasingly closed to substitutable products; and Japan has largely caught up with the major industrial technologies which exist today.

Translated into the impact on the daily life of the average man in Japan, this will mean a gradual levelling or decline in the standard of living, fewer promotion opportunities, and less interesting work. This is already happening to some of Japan's most prestigious corporations. This means that the necessary structural change will certainly follow.

The Pacific Economic Community

Jiro Tokuyama
Nomura School for Advanced Management, Tokyo

For many years past, the sheer expanse of the Pacific Ocean served as a physical barrier for the surrounding countries to form any sort of community and generated an extraordinary diversity of cultures, races and economic as well as political systems. It is precisely because of this wide range of disparities that the creation of a Pacific community calls for a broad and open approach, precluding such a close-knit institutional union as was appropriate for the countries of Western Europe.

However, many of the drawbacks created by distance have been dispelled in recent years by the advent of the jet age and advances in telecommunications and computer technology. Thus, geographical distance no longer poses any serious problem in an effort to bring together the Pacific countries into one community. But what is to be done with the problem of establishing a common identity as members of an economic community among nations possessing different ethnic, regional, cultural and technological backgrounds and degrees of economic development?

Alvin Toffler, in his book *The Third Wave*, offers an encouraging statement. He says that the second wave, which represents a certain stage of industrial development supported by backbone industries such as coal, steel, petroleum, textiles, railways and cars, was a social, cultural and political phenomenon characterized by standardization, synchoronization, centralization and massification. However, Toffler argues that the third wave, which is a socio-economic manifestation of the telecommunications era, is a force to dis-member the centralized society and instead to foster the creation of a de-centralized social system.

If we apply this to the concept of the Pacific economy, it is possible to perceive the region's cultural and socio-economic diversity as the process of the third wave in dynamic motion. What appears to be emerging as a major political, cultural and socio-economic force is neither a multinational corporation-dominated future, nor global government. We are witnessing a far more complex system similar to what can be called matrix organization. Rather than one or a few pyramidal global bureaucracies, we are, consciously or not, weaving matrices that mesh different kinds of organizations with common interests. The concept of the Pacific Economic Community itself demonstrates pioneering efforts in such matrix formation.

Let us now turn to the administrative problem of how we must proceed to establish a decentralized regional system that shares a common goal of economic growth in the Pacific region. I believe three projects can be immediately initiated.

One is to encourage human resources development throughout the region. There is an imperative need for modern management and vocational education for the industrialization and modernization of the region as a whole. In order for a more efficient decentralized, and yet coordinated economic community to be realized, it is essential that each country in the Pacific possess a large enough number of managers who have a similar level of management skills and tools. In fact, the dissemination of management and vocational skills is indispensable for technology transfer on the part of recipient countries.

In order to disseminate management as well as engineering skills, it is advisable to establish training schools in major industrial cities within the region, so that the students will not only be exposed to classroom instruction, but also will have opportunities to visit various worksites to receive on-the-job training. As a start, for instance, we might open in Tokyo or Los Angeles an institution to which able individuals from the Pacific area would be invited on a non-exclusive basis to live and study together for a certain period of time under the guidance of a faculty of an international mix. Simple arithmetic shows that by training two hundred managers each year, the school would create a band of two thousand graduates in ten years and likewise a hundred engineers each year would yield another thousand trained graduates in ten years. Out of these programmes will emerge groups of competent managers and engineers who will serve as prime contributors to their respective economies. In other words, a personal network will be established within the Pacific region.

As for vocational training, former Japanese prime ministers Suzuki and Fukuda both proposed to establish various training centres during their premierships. Several institutions have already been established on the initiative of the Japanese government. Such efforts should continue in the years ahead. Promotion of training for capable managers, engineers, and factory workers in the overall region should be carried out with equal priority, the aggregate of which, I believe, will help in the long run to fill the cultural gap and balance out the existing discrepancies in stages of economic development.

Another task which we should start tackling in earnest is the construction of a communications infrastructure within the region. The remarkable progress in the means of communications in recent years has greatly reduced the disadvantage arising from the vast expanse of the Pacific Ocean. However, for realization of the Pacific Community concept, there must be forthcoming the full-fledged cooperation of the nations of the region for further reduction of the handicaps of distance. Such improvements as replacement of obsolescent submarine cables, development of fibre-optical networks, and wider use of facsimile equipment and communications satellites, and other work for expansion and intensification of multilateral flow of information between the countries of the region, should be undertaken on a joint basis. Several international conferences have already been held with the participation of technical experts to discuss this aspect of regional collaboration. I strongly recommend that future work of these gatherings be directed towards standardizing procedures to ensure full utilization of the telecommunications facilities for efficient and economical exchange of information throughout the Pacific.

There are many ways in which Japan can contribute to make the region 'a smaller world'. As Mr Kobayashi, Chairman of NEC suggests, Japan should be willing voluntarily to launch communications satellites and make them available for free voice and data transmission to every other country of the region.

The third type of project which is of immediate importance, is to develop more economical and convenient air transportation systems within the region. The appearance of jet aircraft reshaped the characteristics of the Pacific region dramatically in the 1960s. Along with the drastic reduction in flight hours, there has been a dramatic cut in costs as well. But the region that experienced the most conspicuous decrease in air fares has been the Atlantic. Of course, one has to take into account the effect of intense price competition in flights over the Atlantic, but the oligopoly airfare rate for flying over the Pacific should be cut to a more reasonable level. In fact, the Japanese airline industry is on the verge of deregulating its operations. It is anticipated that the Japanese aviation constitution will eventually be rewritten to allow two to three Japanese air carriers to compete for international flights over the Pacific in the not-too-distant future. By reducing transportation costs, the movement of people and freight will be greatly increased. This lowering of airfare costs for both passengers and cargoes will be more stimulating to the economy than any alternative economic assistance.

Encouragement of human resources development, establishment of communications networks and advances in transportation systems are the three main pillars of developmental policy in the Pacific region. To achieve the goal of a viable Pacific Community, it is crucial that the advanced countries of the region play a leadership role in each of the three projects mentioned. However, their role should be that of unqualified support and encouragement for the process rather than as the dominating participants – as dinner preparers rather than dinner guests, as it were, with the places of honour reserved for the less-developed nations of the region, since it is for their prime benefit that the Pacific Economic Community will emerge. Whether or not the Pacific Community will take shape, and then play the leading role in revitalizing the world economy, is totally contingent upon all-out efforts of every nation involved.

So far I have pointed out what sorts of joint projects are needed in the next ten to fifteen years in the context of Pacific economic cooperation. Statistical data indicates that the economic centre of gravity of the world is shifting towards the Pacific region. US trade with the Pacific countries topped that with Europe for the first time in 1978, and the disparity continues to grow. What is more, the economic growth performance of the Pacific region is greater than any other region of the world. The 1983 figures indicate that the Pacific region has enjoyed an average growth rate of roughly 7 per cent, in sharp contrast to the ten nations of the EC which recorded only 1.2 per cent. (GNP growth rate in 1983: US 3.7 per cent, South Korea 4.4 per cent, Taiwan 6.2 per cent, Hong Kong 7.8 per cent, Singapore 8.8 per cent.)

What is noteworthy is that of all the Pacific countries, Japan, and the so-called newly industrialized countries (NICs) of the region including South Korea, Taiwan, Singapore, Hong Kong, in particular are enjoying dynamic growth in terms of both industry and the economy as a whole.

What are the reasons underlying the economic success of the Asian–Pacific countries? For one thing, the Asian–Pacific countries are politically stable, compared to other parts of the world, and are generally blessed with an abundance of food, energy and natural resources. We can identify a number of other factors at work in promoting the Asian–Pacific region. One factor might be Confucianism, which encourages hard work and frugality. In the Asian – Pacific region, Confucianism seems to play the role that the Protestant ethic is said to have performed for Western capitalism.

Another factor, hardly recognized, which I believe is of crucial importance to the recent dynamic development of certain Pacific countries, is America's involvement in the Vietnam War. The US involvement in Vietnam continues to be widely perceived by the American public as probably the worst error ever made by the US government in its long history. Despite this negative evaluation, however, it is worth noting the large impact American intervention and its attendant infusion of money, men and material had on the economies of certain other countries of the region.

America's defeat in the Vietnam War did not lead to the communist takeover of all of Southeast Asia as predicted by the domino theory. However, the large sum of the war money infused by the US led Southeast Asian countries to an economic breakthrough. This is not to suggest that the economic problems of the region have been solved, but at least in Thailand, Malaysia, Singapore and Indonesia, the standard of living has improved considerably since the end of the war.

Because of the increasing affluence in the Asian–Pacific, higher education and overseas studies at prestigious Western institutions, which have previously been the privilege of only a handful of the rich elite, are now becoming more and more available to the middle and the upper middle class. For example, in 1982 Thailand sent 6300 to study in the US; 3481 Indonesians were at West German institutions and 1820 at American; Malaysia sent 9085 to the UK and 3282 to Australia, respectively.

In the business sector, we can observe many instances of the first generation entrepreneurs, who succeeded by using traditional business practices, being replaced by the second generation of aggressive business leaders who are increasingly adopting modern management concepts and tools as a result of studying at Western management schools.

In considering the economic development of the Pacific region, we should also turn our attention to the role played by the military, which is very often neglected. Frequently, the military is almost the only organization in developing countries that has administrative as well as training capabilities. The military plays a generally unnoticed but significant role as a source of young business managers and skilled labourers in many Asian countries. Many discharged Asian officers are now serving as prime contributors to the management-side of their economies. Soldiers, on the other hand, are trained as car mechanics, bulldozer and truck drivers and telecommunications operators. When discharged from military service, they are the ones with skills indispensable for sustaining the forceful progress of their economies.

The improvement of managerial as well as engineering skills has helped to facilitate massive transfer of technologies from the US and other industrially advanced nations to Asian–Pacific countries. In recent years, American corporations appear to have come to consider Japan and Asian NICs as the best possible and most efficient places to obtain high quality, yet inexpensive, parts and components, to be incorporated into their products to enhance their price competitiveness in world markets. Whether the country of origin be the US, Japan, Korea or Taiwan, they carry out their purchasing strategies irrespective of national boundaries. Just as the free flow of goods and services across state frontiers is taken for granted in the US, it appears that the strict sense of nationality has lost its significance on the international business scene.

A short while ago, a tanker burned in Spain. The ship was carrying oil from the Middle East and was about to anchor at a Spanish port, the ship owner was an Italian, the ship was registered in Panama, the ship's captain was Japanese and the crew was Korean. In the same way, televisions with a Sony brand are made in USA at the Sony plant in San Diego. Likewise, IBM heavily relies on pieces made overseas for production of its personal computer in the US. The *Business Week* magazine recently revealed that of its total manufacturing cost, which amounts to $860, $625 is expended on purchasing parts and products from Japan and Asian NICs. The US has stopped manufacturing colour TV sets domestically on a full scale, let alone radios and black and white TVs. Colour TVs are now manufactured at subsidiaries of American companies in the Asian NICs and re-imported for domestic consumption. As for hi-fi stereo sets and desk-top calculators, American consumers now rely on Japanese makers.

All types of American corporations, from merchandise distributors such as Sears, to major American machine tool and electronics makers, are buying, on their own initative, large numbers of parts and original equipment manufacturer (OEM) products from not only Japanese makers (both Japanese companies and Japanese subsidiaries of American companies), but also from the other Asian economic 'dynamos'. It is increasingly becoming difficult today to identify the nationality of products.

In the strategically important electronics sector, parts which American companies imported on their own initiative from Japan comprised almost 25 per cent of total Japanese parts production in 1984. Kodak, the leading US camera maker is buying videos from a Japanese consumer electronics manufacturer on an OEM basis. Customs statistics indicate that 52 per cent of the videos manufactured in Japan were exported to the US under OEM agreements last year. The figure for tape recorders was 50 per cent.

In the politically sensitive area of automobile imports, Chrysler, which had so vociferously opposed ending the export quotas on Japanese automobiles, plans to increase its purchases of cars manufactured by Mitsubishi Motors for resale through its domestic dealers from the 87 000 of last year, to 140 000 this year. GM, likewise, disclosed its intention to triple its purchases of Japanese-made cars to 140 thousand this year. In 1984 American car manufacturers bought $3.2 billion worth of auto parts, including engines, from Japanese manufacturers.

A similar situation applies to integrated circuits (ICs), Large Scale Integrated Circuits (LSIs), and super LSIs, which have become indispensable parts (or 'rice' as they are often called by the Japanese) of electronics products. In the area of integrated circuits, Japan demonstrates its remarkable prowess by dominating the 16K, 64K and 256K dynamic RAM markets, with world market shares of 40 per cent, 70 per cent and 90 per cent respectively.

Leading US computer makers are gradually shifting from in-house production of LSIs to purchasing from Japanese manufacturers. They are even asking for samples of Japanese-made LSIs so as to make necessary adjustments in the early phase of product design.

US corporations are also busy entering into formal venturing arrangements with Japanese or Korean counterparts. Fairchild Industries and Texas Instruments have built factories for production of ICs and LSIs in Japan. Last year, several of the US multinationals have gone into joint venturing with Korean corporations in the fields of automotives and electronics. The establishment of a trilateral joint venture consisting of US, Korean and Japanese corporations for manufacture of window glass specifically for automobiles, is underway. The list could go on and on.

Currently the US is running considerable trade deficits with the bulk of its trading partners. Much has been said or written about a mushrooming US –Japan trade imbalance. In the US, the manufacturing industries currently account for roughly 20 per cent of its total GNP. A substantial number of items in its product line, including high-tech products, are gradually losing their international competitiveness. That being the case, persistence in buying low-cost high-quality products from countries running a chronic surplus such as Japan, simply means leaving its domestic manufacturing industries in the lurch.

Given this situation, it is essential that the US refine its policy somewhat from a national security point of view; and the revitalization of its domestic manufacturers should be established as a national priority. The erosion of the American edge in the manufacturing sector is an important issue, not just for the US alone, but also for the other Pacific countries, as it affects, or has the potential of affecting, overall economic growth of the Pacific region.

What measures can be recommended for revitalizing the US manufacturing industries? First and foremost, the overvalued dollar must be corrected so that US imports are made more expensive and exports made cheaper and hence more attractive in foreign markets. At present exchange rates, US competitiveness in manufactured goods is sapped and industrial revitalization efforts will not bear fruit. According to the Federal Reserve Board, the US dollar depreciated at the rate of 57 per cent in the course of the last four years. The chairman of Westinghouse has suggested that Japan should purchase $20 billion worth of goods and services from the US to balance out the huge trade deficit. However, during a recent discussion with the executive director of Nippon Telephone and Telegram Corporation, which was denationalized in April this year, it was argued that it is illogical, from the commercial point of view, to pay $157 for a product which only has an actual value of $100.

Economists estimate that money flowing freely across national borders is nearly twenty times the amount involved with the international transaction of goods and services. Given this figure, it is much more effective to do something about the transborder flow of money than about the goods economy.

Secondly, let us now shift our focus to r&d efforts of our two nations. The US excels in r&d of highly innovative, technology-oriented sectors such as defence, aerospace, optical fibres, computers, nuclear energy, new ceramics, biotechnology and oceanography. In the US the largest portion of r&d spending is allotted to the defence industry. In sharp contrast, Japan's r&d spending last year on the defence industry was 1 per cent of that of the US, which totalled $40 billion.

While a majority of capable engineering graduates find employment in private manufacturing companies in Japan, the bulk of their US counterparts go into defence or aerospace industries. Of course, these sectors are crucial from the national security point of view. However, for the sake of revitalizing its manufacturing industries, the US should not neglect the importance of r&d in more consumer-oriented sectors.

Generally speaking, American engineers and scientists are well versed in basic research which is high-risk in nature and intriguing to the intellect, whereas Japanese counterparts are strong in applied research, namely, the manufacturing of high-quality durable products, which call for less creativity but have clearly defined attainable goals. This partly explains why Japan has successfully dominated the world LSI market; all they had to do was to concentrate their r&d efforts towards the attainable goal of surpassing the degree of integration of a transistor.

Competition for VCRs also ended in grand victory for Japanese makers.

Although the American company Ampex developed the original technology for VCRs, it failed to remain competitive when the company immediately sold its technology to Japanese makers and failed to enter the consumer market. Whereas Ampex simply concentrated on production of VCRs for business purposes, such as those used at TV stations, and sold them for $8000, the bulk of Japanese consumer electronics manufacturers focused their r&d efforts on home-use VCRs with the firm commitment to install VCRs in every household. They eventually succeeded in commercializing the product which sells at a price below $400.

From these observations, it its highly advisable that the US not only concentrates on basic research, but also makes positive efforts to conduct applied research, particularly in the consumer-oriented sectors, to revitalize its manufacturing industries.

Thirdly, it is advisable for US management radically to change their concepts of running a company. For one thing, it is more reasonable to evaluate a Chief Executive Officer (CEO) over the period of a minimum of three to four years: a company president should be given a second chance even after having failed to attain the revenue target for once, just as a presidential term is guaranteed for four years.

What is more, US management should take another look at the long-cherished ethic that employees are mere raw materials, to be processed and used just as if they were nuts and bolts. Such treatment was inevitable on the part of management in olden days when a large portion of labour consisted of illiterate immigrants. However, in order to bolster the corporate environment, management needs to pay special attention to the human side of management, which they have for long set aside in their pursuit of rationalism. I would like to recommend that they make positive efforts to attend to their employees with compassion and assign, as much as possible, self-fulfilling tasks.

It is extremely difficult to change course abruptly, but it is important for US management to recognize the significance of placing the interests of their employees before the interests of their shareholders when formulating corporate policy. US Steel acquired Marathon Oil for $2 billion, rather than utilizing the capital in renovating its steel mills; RCA acquired Hertz in an attempt to diversify its operations. Mergers and acquisitions, typical examples of the so-called 'Money game', are everyday occurrences in the US corporate world. Yet, would not investment in plant and equipment prove to be more effective in the long-term perspective?

The US already has the infrastructure, educated workforce and entrepreneurial climate needed to successfully revitalize its manufacturing industries. In so doing, the only thing the country needs is the political consensus. But what if the political consensus for doing so cannot be built? An alternative, although it requires much endeavour, may be totally to realign the commercial sector under the system of division of labour among Pacific-rim countries, with each held responsible for whatever it excels in and whatever is justifiable from the viewpoint of eradicating trade imbalances on a macro-level. Under such a system, the US, for instance, can concentrate on r&d without fear of competition and export its technologies at a high enough price to cover all r&d spending with considerable markups. In turn, quality-conscious countries such as Japan and Asian NICs may pay royalties to American firms for the imported technologies and devote themselves to full-line production, or assembly of parts and products, based on these technologies. Such a scheme could well be an important test case of the Pacific Economic Community concept.

Technology transfer: an economic development tool

F. Timothy Janis, Glenn Roesler
Indianapolis Center for Advanced Research, Inc.

When we think of technology transfer in the United States, quite often we think of the modern era; in particular, the period of time following the Space Act of 1958. It was in this act that a formal federal programme was legislated to transfer aerospace technology to the non-aerospace industry. Nathan Rosenberg, in his *Perspectives on Technology*,[1] discusses at great length the transmission of technology in the nineteenth century. Suffice it to say that technology has been transferred since technology was first generated.

Definitions

What exactly is technology transfer? A review of the literature indicates that the definition of technology transfer has been tailored to fit the author's needs. According to Webster[2]:

> Technology: The totality of the means employed by a people to provide itself with the objects of material culture.
> Transfer: The carry-over or generalization of learned responses from one type of situation to another.

James and Kenkeremath[3] describe the many perceptions of technology transfer, ie, information flow, knowledge diffusion, moving r&d from the laboratory to end-use, acceleration of secondary applications. The plurality of the definition is reflected in almost every paper published on the topic. This plurality makes evaluation quite difficult since the outcome tends to shape the definition and the success of the process.

Whatever definition is chosen, it is incorrect relative to measurement. Other than possibly Rosenberg's nineteenth-century studies, measurement has not so much been performed upon the efficacy of the transfer process (the process of taking it from the developer to the user, as depicted in Figure 5), but upon the assimilation and subsequent utilization of the technology by the user. Technology transfer, as popularly viewed, is truly technology acquisition and utilization. Thus, to review technology transfer as an economic development tool, one must assess the development process, the transfer mechanism, and the assimilation capacity. To do so accurately the process must be viewed from both perspectives.

For the purposes of this paper, technology transfer will mean 'the process by which developed technologies are diffused, assimilated, and utilized'. This definition presumes that the innovation process, responsible for the develop-

Figure 5 Simplified technology transfer process

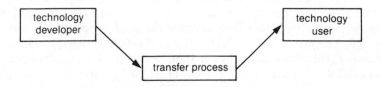

ment of a technology, is a distinctly separate process which does not necessarily direct the transfer and utilization process. Quite obviously, as r&d
expenditures decrease and/or innovativeness decreases, the available resources decrease, thus impacting the transfer process. Likewise, the state of the
economy has a significant impact upon the process. In this paper these factors
will be considered as constants rather than variables.

Historical perspectives

During the nineteenth century as the industrial age was emerging, the transfer
of technology was important to successful industrialization. Rosenberg[4]
suggests that this transfer occurred through the movement of a small number
of highly skilled individuals rather than the transfer of technological skills.
Thus, the belief that technology transfer is based upon successful communication was not true in the early years of the subject.

The development of the formal subject matter on technology transfer can
probably be traced to the Space Act. Formal interest began when John F.
Kennedy announced plans to land on the moon 'in the next decade'. A multi-
billion dollar aerospace industry was created, and 'spinoff' became
synonymous with transferring technology for uses other than those for which
the technology was intended.[5]

Throughout the 1960 and 1970s, the NASA Technology Utilization Program was the primary federally sponsored transfer mechanism. With the
exception of the Agricultural Extension Service, which will not be a topic of
this paper, most other federal programmes were modelled after the NASA
programme. NASA's primary objective was to bring about secondary
applications in industry through the transfer of technology developed as part of
the space programme. This led to the US Congress' definition (1967) of
technology transfer as '. . . the use of knowledge to serve a purpose other than
the one for which the R&D was undertaken'.[6]

In 1975 a small group of individuals involved in technology transfer became
the nucleus of a new society, the Technology Transfer Society. In its August
1977 newsletter, the purpose of the society was stated as:

> The commonality of ASME and AIAA and kindred groups is engineering. This
> is a connotation the Technology Transfer Society is trying to avoid. We want to
> be representative of consumer groups, economists, futurists, financial people,
> attorneys, politicians . . . to name a few categories. We need especially those
> familiar with assessment and forecasting. We need to learn what's going on in
> these fields as it applies to technology transfer and utilization.

A new profession was born, and at its first annual meeting in Los Angeles,
approximately two dozen people attended. Today, the society is still small, with

approximately five hundred members, 61 per cent of whom are from the private sector. This is small compared to medical, legal, and other technical societies. However, a steady growth has occurred, and the society is poised on entering its second decade to advance the field of technology transfer.

On 21 October, 1980, Public Law 96–480, officially called The Stevenson-Wydler Innovation Act of 1980, was signed by the President. The Act focused its attention on the subject of technology transfer. Among many provisions, the law required increased emphasis on transferring the resources and knowledge of the federal laboratories to state and local government and the private sector. The Law was the result of extensive study which yielded many findings. Those of particular significance to technology transfer were: many new discoveries and advances in science occur in universities and federal laboratories, while the application of this new knowledge to commercial and useful public purposes depends largely upon action by business and labour; no comprehensive national policy exists to enhance technological innovation for commercial and public purposes; and it is in the national interest to promote the adoption of technological innovation to state and local government uses.

The remedies proposed, for the most part, followed the traditional path of dissemination. Certain novel aspects such as laboratories providing staff to fulfill the Act based upon total r&d budget, were included. This Act greatly increased the number of professionals in the field of technology transfer. An historical analysis of the Act's impact on the Navy is more carefully examined in an article by David Allison.[7]

In almost every programme conceived, implemented, and written about, the design has been to facilitate the transfer. Any mechanism that would enhance communications was viewed as important. The definition of 'transfer' supports this notion. Furthermore, many found that this could be accomplished through the use of an intermediary. Figure 6 depicts the simple linker model as defined by Jolly.[8]

Figure 6 Simplified linker concept in technology transfer.

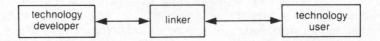

What about evaluation? Again, according to Webster,[2] evaluation is 'the process of determining the significance or worth of something by appraisal and study'. In 1982, Timothy O'Keefe reported on the evaluation results of a programme in forestry. The conclusion he reached was that evaluating a technology transfer programme is not a simple process. Even in a narrowly defined industry (forestry), O'Keefe found it difficult to isolate key elements that could be used to characterize successful and unsuccessful projects. The only common variable (which is an independent and uncontrollable one) was time. He stated that, '. . . there is no single way to develop an evaluation'. O'Keefe further noted that the tendency is to evaluate the technology as opposed to the transfer process. Thus, the evaluation of the transfer process must not only include the transfer, but also the assimilation and utilization processes.

Scope

This paper grew out of a desire to learn more about the technology transfer process and, in particular, its economic impact and concommitant use as a tool. The literature describing technology transfer has been increasing enormously. Milliken[10] stated that the Denver Research Institute has been gathering research information for the past twenty-two years, and has compiled a library comprised of over 3500 specialized documents. Recently, Creighton, et al.[11] published a document entitled *Technology Transfer: Concepts With Supporting Abstracts*, containing over 150 citations selected on the basis of key contributions to the field. Upon reviewing this selected set of materials, it was noted that:

Numerous publications exist on:
1. historical foundations
2. technology transfer approaches
    documentation
    dissemination
    organization
3. models
4. federal sector role
5. case studies.

Fewer publications exist on:
1. policy
2. applicability
3. transferability.

Limited publications exist on:
1. assessment
2. economic measurement
3. theory

In 1984, the US Department of Energy sponsored a conference[12] entitled 'A synthesis of technology transfer methodologies', whose objective '. . . was to reconsider the approaches to technology transfer taken by previous programs on the subject during the 1960s and 1970s for the insights these approaches would provide current Federal program managers.' The proceedings of the conference include a cross-section of papers elucidating definitions, approaches, experience etc. However, even from the impressive gathering, little was contributed to the quantitative understanding of the economic impact of technology transfer. The remainder of this paper will be devoted to examining the issue 'Technology transfer: an economic development tool', both as a statement and as a question.

Process

Two major theories appear to be primarily operative in technology transfer.[5,13] One relates the process to a sociological system; the other to the innovation process. In the former case, communication becomes the key variable, and the process tends to be market-pulled. In the latter case, management integration is probably the key variable, and the process may be either a technology-push or a market-pull, depending upon the nature of the developing firm. For example, mission-oriented firms, federal agencies (DoD, NASA, etc) tend toward technology-push because the market and the technology are synonymous. A typical innovative private sector firm would tend to be more market driven.

The literature and the primary practice of technology transfer tends to follow the communication process. The so-called 'integrated innovation' process, defined by Robbins,[5] is almost absent from the literature. The probable cause is that the primary sponsor of technology transfer programmes is the federal government, which supports mission-oriented activities. Thus, the spinoff technologies are dependent upon communication of their availability. It is this process that will be examined.

Communications

D. G. Christopherson[14] identifed four problems that are the apparent crux of technology transfer: How does one ensure that results of research, the general advance of science, is in fact fully exploited in industry? Whose responsibility is it to consider what practical application a particular addition to knowledge may possibly have? What sort of network of communications can ensure that the new information does, in fact, reach the people who will make most use of it, without at the same time overwhelming them with a host of irrelevancies? How much of our total scientific and technological resources ought to be devoted to the task, not of advancing science, but of disseminating it; of spreading knowledge and understanding of significant research in the quarters where they are most needed?

To be a good communicator requires not only the ability to write and speak, but also the ability to listen. A fifth question, therefore, is who is listening? The questions Christopherson raises require answers. The federal government, with the Stevenson–Wydler Act, answered; they were listening, but not comprehending, because the answers lie in the development and implementation of a national policy. As stated so clearly by Robert Solo.[15]

> ... necessarily, the communication of significantly new insights, new ideas, new techniques, even between two individuals face-to-face, is difficult and rare. But how infinitely more difficult it is when such communication is not from man to man, but from group to group, from company organization to company organization, from industry to industry ... from nation to nation ...

Thus, without clear statements of objectives to accomplish the goals of a policy, measurement becomes aimless. Such is the case in technology transfer.

Most models utilized have adopted various principles for effective transfer. Those suggested by Robbins[5] are: ready access; translatable information; face-to-face interaction; adaptable solutions; and market drives. Casting these principles into a transfer process can produce economic growth. Such a process is depicted in Figure 7. In the highly complex process depicted in the figure, communication is critical throughout. But how is success measured? Is it solely bottomline (increased output)? Unfortunately, not superimposed on the figure is a time axis. If one examines the history of the diffusion of innovations, two characteristics are noted: its apparent overall slowness, and the wide variation in the rate of acceptance of different innovations. In Table 1 a few examples are given of some major innovations and their acceptance. In a study performed by John Enos,[16] he found the arithmetic means for the interval between invention and practice to be 13.6 years.

Figure 7 Technology transfer and economic growth. Source: American Economic Review, May 1966.

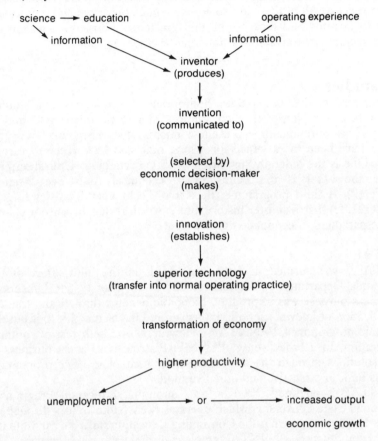

Table 1 Innovation acceptance

Technology	Start date	Realization	Duration
Pacemaker	1928	1960	32 years
Hybrid corn	1908	1933	25 years
Magnetic ferrites	1933	1955	22 years
Transistors	1940	1950	10 years
Oral contraceptives	1951	1960	9 years

(*Source*: Battelle study 'Interactions of science and technology in the innovative process', 1973).

Economists have pursued the rationale for these differentials, and have proposed many theories as explanation. One that is logical is that old technologies which are to be replaced by superior technologies (Figure 7) continue to improve. The point is that, although the technology transfer model commonly utilized is the communication process, it is very apparent that the timetable of the innovation process is often at work. Thus, measurement becomes difficult, if not impractical, in most cases. Alok Chakrabarti[17] found that the tracking of 'tangible' technologies (eg, product, process) as opposed to intangible technologies (eg, information) was easier to measure. In the Experimental Technological Incentive Program (ETIP), the following three criteria of success were identified: information success in reducing key uncertainties (technological, cost, demand, institutional and externalities); application success; diffusion success. All of these are socio-economic criteria which are normally difficult to quantify and measure by the transferer. Thus, the question remains: is technology transfer an economic development tool?

Case studies

Before rendering a final opinion, it is appropriate to review a few case studies. The literature is replete with such studies. Almost all are programmes of relatively short duration, or represent a microscopic viewpoint. Two programmes have been in existence for a long time and have received careful scrutiny. One is the federally supported NASA Technology Utilization programme; the other is the Pennsylvania Technical Assistance Program (PENNTAP). A third programme, the Ohio Technology Transfer Organization (OTTO), has a shorter history, but is worth review because it is built upon the paradigm of economic development.

PENNTAP

PENNTAP[18] was formed in 1965, the result of the joint effort of the Pennsylvania Department of Commerce and Pennsylvania State University. The express purpose was to produce economic benefits through the transfer and application of known scientific information. One of the oldest, if not the oldest state programmes, PENNTAP is now in its twentieth year of continuous operation. In a broad sense, PENNTAP's role is to assist business in finding solutions through the dissemination of technology. The programme functions both in a reactive and initiative mode.

PENNTAP is operated through the Continuing Education Program of Pennsylvania State University, which operates twenty-four offices throughout the state. Its marketing arm is the Continuing Education staff. To carry out the dissemination function, PENNTAP employs several technical specialists. The specialists' principal source of information is the Pennsylvania State Library Information System, which has access to state and university created data bases, and also all commercial data bases. PENNTAP also has access to faculty and to a network of technology transfer specialists.

PENNTAP is guided and evaluated by an active fifteen-member Advisory Council appointed by the President of Pennsylvania State. It has been stated that 'PENNTAP firmly believes that the success of any dissemination information can be measured only by the results produced'. To ascertain these results, PENNTAP has established an evaluation system consisting of a client instrument with follow-up. In a recent report,[18] it was stated that a client response of 37 per cent to 40 per cent was obtained. Based upon these returns and other information, PENNTAP officials reported that over 18 000 inquiries were made with over $69 million of benefits resulting during the period 1971–80. These benefits were in the form of new/saved jobs, enhanced profitability, etc. These benefits were achieved from operating expenses of just over $4 million for that same period.

OTTO

The Ohio Technology Transfer Organization (OTTO)[19] was established in 1978 by the Ohio Board of Regents. Its mission was to broker expertise and supply information to Ohio's business firms. The system that was established differed somewhat from the PENNTAP model. Full-time agents were placed at each of Ohio's community colleges; the agent is a full-time, non-faculty member whose role is to carry out the transfer process.

In 1983, OTTO became part of the state's Deparment of Development to inttegrate it fully into the economic development activities of the state. The administration is totally delocalized with only overall policy and evaluation issues emanating from the Department of Development. Ohio State University's OTTO staff act as a central resource to all a agents. Individual agents' territory and activity are confined to the region covered by his or her community college. After the start-up year, OTTO has progressed to a demand driven system which has occurred through the success of the services it provides.

In 1982, over six hundred firms utilized OTTO services. Clients obtained over 10 000 hours of business and technical assistance for more than seven hundred projects. During this same period, over two hundred hours of training were provided. Based upon evaluation information gathered, it was reported that OTTO projects realized $800 000 in increased sales, and projected greater sales in 1983. Cost savings in excess of $250 000 were also recorded. Finally, over three hundred jobs were reportedly created as a result of OTTO efforts.

NASA Technology Utilization Programme

In 1963,[10] NASA's Technology Utilization (TU) programme, was formed in response to the mandate placed in the Space Act of 1958 that NASA was to disseminate the results of its space r&d. In the 1960s and 1970s, the TU programme was largely an experimental one. Different programmes were created, tested, implemented, revised, etc. In the early 1960s, the Denver Research institute (DRI) began the now twenty-four-year-old programme of research and evaluation of NASA's technology transfer activities. During this period, over 1000 case studies of the transfer process have been made. In excess of 3500 documents on technology transfer have been accumulated at DRI. Of all formal technology transfer programmes, the NASA efforts have been the most reviewed.

Since 1963, NASA has had an average annual funding of $10 million (1984 dollars) for the TU programme. Various mechanisms were established by TU to carry out the dissemination function. Nine Industrial Applications Centers, two State Technology Applications Centers, and a computer software management centre were formed. Their role was to disseminate information primarily on a face-to-face basis. Technical applications teams were formed to carry significant developments from the early research stage to the pre-market stage. Funds were also available for applications projects defined by technology utilization offices at the various NASA flight centres.

In a recent publication, Gordon Milliken[10] reported that the benefits independently gathered and analysed by DRI demonstrated that client benefits exceeded cost. His conclusion was that, on balance, the NASA programme has been a definite success. Milliken stated:

Table 2   Critical success determinants in developing an evaluation framework for immediate and intermediate outputs

Programme elements	Measures*	Operational measures and indicators	Instrument or method
Identification of user needs and matching of federal r&d technology	Responsiveness, quality, timeliness of the matches to user needs.	Number, type and scope of requests/user needs received; frequency of repeat requests; timeliness of response to user queries; user perception of information usefulness/frequency of adaptive assistance needed.	Programme files and records; system user survey.
Personnel exchanges/fellowships/technical liaison	User support continuity/expansion; quality and number of fellows/personnel exchanges and cooperation with ORTA's; utility of assessment information provided by fellows/personnel exchanges/technical liaisons to users.	Nature and magnitude of support by public and private sectors; public and private sector participants; fellow background/expertise; number of fellows; ORTA and fed. lab./fellow interactions; fellow technology assessments and utilization plans; use of assessment information.	Fellow assessment reports; interviews with: public and private sector personnel, federal lab. personnel/ORTA, and supervisor of fellow.
Technology information system(s)	Appropriateness of design, quality and usefulness of the information provided by the system(s); use of information transferred/user.	Compatibility/interface with existing data sources/information systems; number of requests, frequency of requests, use of information (how much of it was used and for what purposes); impact on users.	Programme files and records; user survey.
Audio-visual materials, reports, publications	Use by industry, state, local governments; nature, number and quality of materials prepared and their valuation and use by the public and private sectors.	Number distributed and number of people reading/viewing; effect on user decision making.	Programme files and records; user survey.

Conferences, seminars and workshops	Public and private sector participation, valuation and use of the information provided; levels of public/private sector interest.	Scope of conference, number held, number of attendees, stratification of participants; reported use of information transmitted at conference; response to published proceedings; number of information requests generated from target groups.	Programme files and records; public and private sector survey/questionnaire.
Networking and cooperation	Effectiveness of agency networking and cooperation; extent of agency commitment.	Level of agencies' cooperative efforts to meet private sector/state and local government needs; nature, scope and frequency of federal technology transfer activities/interactions/meetings.	ORTA and programme records, federal agency surveys, reports by ORTA's and fellows; FLC files/records.
Institutionalization of technology transfer	Nature and degree of agency commitment; levels of communication/cooperation with industry/state and local governments; levels of interagency cooperation.	Agency and ORTA/technology transfer activity funding levels; numbers/quality of agency reports; levels of interagency resource sharing; frequency of direct contact with users/other transfer mechanism use; type and frequency of adaptive assistance provided/resources required/matches achieved; information transferred/mechanism use impacts on users/on agency decision making; impacts on federal government.	Agency budgets, ORTA reports, files and records, interviews, case studies.

*Measures of programme results should be used as a constructive feedback mechanism to the programme manager and to others regarding the degree to which successful or other outcomes are obtained and as a guide to where adjustments in programme focus need to be made for improving future technology transfer programme efforts.

(Source: *Journal of Technology Transfer*, 6(1), 1981)

The NASA Technology Transfer program has made many valuable contributions to national productivity through technological advance, whose benefits exceed costs; contributions to the world's pool of knowledge regarding the technology transfer process . . .

The question still remains: is technology transfer an economic development tool? Certainly, in two of the three cases cited, the mission and outcomes would seem to so signify. NASA's mission in technology transfer has been much broader, but the Denver Research Institute's results indicate those initiatives have been successful and have had significant economic impact.

It would appear that the answer to the question is 'yes, but relative', relative to the mission, point of view, constituent, etc. In their article published in 1981, O'Brien and Franks[20] described the critical success determinants useful in developing an evaluation framework. The essence of their comments are summarized in Table 2.

The programme elements defined by O'Brien reflect various programmatic approaches to technology transfer (eg, identification of need, personnel exchanges, materials). The measures suggested are logical (eg, recording number of requests, user perception), and would lead to a useful data base of information. However, in this more definitive study, no direct measures of the economic impact of the process is truly defined. The authors suggest that to perform a more analytic analysis will require quantification of the independent variables. It was suggested that critical to successful evaluation of technology transfer will be: access to and maintenance of data bases of evaluation information; establishing and implementing tracking systems; developing methodologies to better quantify long-range impacts.

The data exists, at least in part, for the NASA TU programmes. Analysing it still fails to establish whether the process is a tool or not. Quite possibly then, it is in the definition of 'economic tool' or possibly in the lack of a definitive policy on measurable outcome.

Conclusion

It was intended to demonstrate that, 'Technology transfer: an economic development tool', was a fact. During the review process, however, it became apparent that one could vacillate between fact and question. It is apparent that technology transfer is popularly viewed by economic development specialists, federal, state and local government officials, and many other as a tool. Quantitative, analytical information corroborating this belief is lacking. That is not to say that vast amounts of evaluation information do not exist. For example, within the programmes conducted at ICFAR, the acquisition and analysis of benefits information is a critical programme element. Each year documents summarizing annual performance are prepared and submitted to sponsors (eg, NASA Benefits Analysis[21]). The results on the programme level point out the successful results of the programme. The indicators may be customer satisfaction to dollar savings and/or jobs saved/created. The attempt to cross-correlate published results of various programmes, however, is not possible. The reasons found are: no universal variables other than time were identified that could be compared; data for the innovation process that the use became engaged in prior to adoption, was either not available or comparable; programme goals and corresponding objectives varied widely from programme to programme; thus, data generated was not comparable.

The conclusions reached in this review are subjective, and thus are suspect. The following observations are offered: that technology transfer is still more an art than a science; that technology transfer is synonymous with economic development; that the US Congress is supportive of technology transfer as an effective and necessary mechanism for secondary uses of federally developed technologies; that published results demonstrated that, for the most part, benefits obtained have exceeded the cost of various programmes; that the measurement of benefits is done individually, and cross-comparison is not possible; and that the statement that technology transfer is an economic development tool in the universal sense is subjectively made, but it is filled with conjectures.

Recommendations

The economic utility of technology transfer has been demonstrated and reported upon in many publications. Its universality as a tool, however, has not been verified. All reported activity indicates that this may be extremely difficult to accomplish. The following recommendations are steps that, if implemented, should enhance the technology transfer profession and its utility as an economic tool. A national task force should be created and charged with producing a policy statement on technology transfer, establishing a set of measurable goals, and establishing a comparable set of programme data to be collected and maintained in a data base. Resources sufficient to do long-term tracking of projects should be included in federally funded programmes. The importance of the technology transfer profession should be enhanced through increased funding. Finally technology transfer should be institutionalized so that policy, operation, and measurement can be monitored, reviewed, revised, implemented.

References

1 Rosenberg N. 1976 Factors affecting the diffusion of technology, *Perspectives on technology*. Cambridge University Press.
2 *Webster's Third New International Dictionary*, G. C. Merriam & Co, 1976.
3 James A. and Kenkermath 1984 Technology transfer: a synthesis of the workshop proceedings. In *Proceedings, a synthesis of technology transfer methodologies*. Dept. of Energy.
4 Rosenberg N. 1976 Economic development and the transfer of technology, *Perspectives on Technology*. Cambridge University Press.
5 Robbins D. 1984 Technology transfer as a process: lessons from the past. In *Proceedings, a synthesis of technology transfer methodologies*, Dept. of Energy.
6 Cropsey V. 1985 Editorial, *J. of Technology Transfer* 9 (2): 2.
7 Allison D. K. 1982 Technology Transfer in the Navy: An Historical Analysis. *Historian of Navy Laboratories* May.
8 George P., Jolly J. A. and Creighton J. W. 1982 The linker's contribution to technology transfer. *J. of Technology Transfer* 6 (2): 53, 57.
10 Milliken J. 1984 The NASA program in technology transfer. In *Proceedings, a synthesis of technology transfer methodologies*. Dept. of Energy.
11 Creighton J. W., Jolly J. A., Bailey C. L. and Blanchette R. A. 1984 *Technology transfer: concepts with supporting abstracts*. Naval Postgraduate School.
12 *Proceedings, a synthesis of technology transfer methodologies*. Dept. of Energy, 1984.
13 Johnson F. 1983 Technology transfer – a view of what works. *J. of Technology Transfer* 7 (2): 1–4.
14 Christopherson D. G. 1962 The Exploitation of Research, *Advancement of Science* p 276, November.

15 Solo R. A. 1966 The capacity to assimilate advanced technology, *American Economic Review* pp 91–7, May.
16 Enos J. 1962 Invention and innovation in the petroleum refining industry. In *The rate and direction of inventive activity*. Princeton University Press.
17 Chakrabarti A. 1984 An integrated approach to measuring effectiveness of federal technology transfer programs. *Proceedings, a synthesis of technology transfer methodologies*. Dept. of Energy.
18 Marlow L. H. Another perspective on technology transfer: the PENNTAP experience. *Proceedings, a synthesis of technology transfer methodologies*. Dept. of Energy.
19 Bailey R., Cooper L. E. and Kramer L. 1985 The Ohio technology transfer organization OTTO: an experiment in academia assisting business. *J. of Technology Transfer* 9 (2): 9–27.
20 O'Brien T. C. and Franks L. M. 1981 Evaluation framework for federal technology transfer initiatives. *J. of Technology Transfer*. 6 (1): 73, 86.
21 Gaugh B. and Janis F. T. 1984 Aerospace research applications center benefits analysis. ARAC Report. November.

Innovation and the smaller firm[1]

Roy Rothwell
Science Policy Research Unit, University of Sussex

For many years economists have debated the contribution small firms make to industrial innovation and economic growth. While some economists, perhaps most notably J. K. Galbraith (1957), have argued for the importance of large size and monopoly power others, such as E. F. Schumaker (1973), have placed their feet firmly in the opposing camp. Similarly the attitudes of national governments to small firms have varied considerably. In the United States, for example, the argument in favour of protection of, and assistance for, small business has been very strong and is summed up succinctly in the following extract from the US Small Business Act of 1953:

> The essence of the American economic system of private enterprise is free competition. Only through full and free competition can free markets, free entry into business, and opportunities for the expression and growth of personal initiative and individual judgement be assured . . . Such security and well-being cannot be realized unless the actual and potential capacity of small business is encouraged and developed. It is the declared policy of Congress that the Government should aid, counsel, assist, and protect as far as possible the interests of small business concerns in order to preserve free and competitive enterprise.

In most countries in Europe small firms have, for much of the postwar era, not had the public support enjoyed by their American counterparts, and public policies have very much favoured the large firm. During the 1960s in particular, company mergers were encouraged and facilitated in order to create major national 'flagship' companies capable of competing in world markets, and the dominant ethos during this period could be said to have been 'big is beautiful'. From the mid-1970s onwards, attitudes changed and government policies towards technological and economic development began increasingly to favour the smaller firm (Rothwell and Zegveld, 1981). This shift in attitude was based on a growing belief that the small firm is a more than averagely potent vehicle for the creation of new employment, for regional economic renewal and for enhancing national rates of technological innovation (Rothwell and Zegveld, 1982). Today, throughout Europe, the dominant ethos can be said to be 'small is beautiful'. Indeed, 1983 was designated by the European Commission in Brussels the European Year of the Small Firm.

In Japan small firms traditionally have been thought of as being economically inefficient (Takigawa, 1974). Large diverse corporations in Japan have been the major vehicle of economic growth and they have shown themselves to be remarkably flexible and technologically adaptive across a wide range of industries and technologies. Small Japanese firms have, nevertheless, played an important, if indirect, role in the dramatic industrial and economic transitions that have taken place in Japan during the past forty years or so. In their traditional role of 'tied' subcontractor small firms have provided the major corporations with an effective source of cheap labour, the ability to specialize in the capital-intensive final phases of production and great employment and financial flexibility (Twaalfhoven and Hattori, 1982).

More recently, both in Europe and in Japan, governments have become increasingly concerned with the creation of new small technology-based firms, which is reflected in the growing number of public sector schemes designed to stimulate the flow of venture capital. In the UK, for example, the government has put considerable resources into a loan guarantee scheme for small firms and into its Business Expansion Scheme (Rothwell, 1986), and in Japan MITI has taken steps to increase venture capital availability. In addition, in the UK, France and Japan, secondary stock markets have been established to facilitate equity investments in small unquoted companies and to provide an exit mechanism to enable venture capitalists more readily to realize a gain on their investments.

The advantages and disadvantages of small firms in innovation

Before going on to address the issue of the innovatory role of small firms, we will first list a number of advantages and disadvantages generally ascribed to small and to large firms in innovation. The following comments are culled from a variety of studies undertaken in a number of countries; they are presented in the form of simple statements or generalizations and they relate to ten aspects of firms' activities.

Marketing   Small firms have the ability to react quickly to keep abreast of fast-changing market requirements in their particular market segments, but for small firms market start-up abroad can be prohibitively expensive. Young small firms in particular can become overdependent on local markets, which may be one reason why small firm formation and small firm innovation are often 'local' phenomena (Rothwell, 1984).

Large firms generally possess comprehensive distribution and servicing facilities and they can enjoy a high degree of market power in existing markets. Large firms are well able to tackle overseas markets.

Management   In small firms there is little bureaucracy and dynamic, entrepreneurial managers react quickly to take advantage of new opportunities. Entrepreneurial managers are willing to accept risk. Technical entrepreneurs, however, often lack management, marketing and financial skills.

In large companies professionally trained managers are able to control complex organizations and establish coherent, long-term corporate strategies. However, large firms can suffer from an excess of bureaucracy and they are often controlled by accountants who can be risk-averse. Large firm managers can become mere administrators who lack dynamism with respect to exploiting new product-market opportunities.

Internal communication   Small firms enjoy efficient and informal internal communication networks. This affords them a fast response to internal problem solving; it provides them with the ability to react rapidly to changes in the external environment.

In large firms internal communication is often formal and cumbersome, which can lead to slow reaction to external threats and opportunities.

Qualified technical manpower   Small firms often lack suitably qualified technical specialists and they are often unable to support a formal r&d effort on an appreciable scale.

Large firms are able to attract highly skilled technical specialists and they can afford the establishment of a large r&d laboratory.

External communication   Small firms often lack the time and resources to enable them to identify and use important external sources of scientific and technological expertise and advice.

Large firms are able to 'plug-in' to external sources of scientific and technological expertise. They can also afford to subcontract r&d to specialist centres of expertise and they can purchase crucial technical information and technology from external sources.

Data on the sources of major initiating knowledge inputs to some 2200 important innovations introduced by British industry between 1945 and 1979 throw some light on this point. Table 3 shows, for small firms (employment less than 200) and large firms (employment greater than 10 000), the percentages of innovatory ideas deriving from internal and external sources for the periods 1945–69 and 1970–79.

Table 3   Source of major initiating knowledge inputs to 2200 important innovations introduced in the UK between 1945 and 1979

	Firm size in 1945		Firm size in 1979	
	(Employees)			
	<§200	>‡10 000	<§200	>‡10 000
Inhouse	83%	58%	68%	77%
External	17%	43%	32%	23%

It can be seen that during the earlier period small firms were indeed very much more introspective than their larger counterparts, just as predicted by conventional wisdom. During the latter period, however, the situation changed and small firms obtained a greater percentage of their innovatory inputs from external sources. Interestingly, while small firms obtained an average of 7 per cent of their external ideas from other companies during the period 1945–69, this had increased to 25 per cent during the 1970–79 period.

Finance   Small firms can experience great difficulty in attracting capital, especially venture capital although, as stated before, this situation does appear to be changing rapidly in Europe and Japan. Major innovation can represent a disproportionately large financial risk to small firms and they generally are unable to spread risk over a portfolio of products. Large firms are better able to borrow on capital markets. They can spread their risk over a portfolio of products and can fund diversification into new technologies and new markets.

Economies of scale and the systems approach   In some areas scale requirements form substantial entry barriers to small firms, and small firms are unable to offer integrated product lines or systems.

Large firms enjoy the ability to gain scale economies in r&d, production and marketing. They can offer a wide range of complementary products and can bid for turn-key projects.

Growth   Small firms can experience difficulty in acquiring external capital necessary for rapid growth, and entrepreneurial managers sometimes are unable to cope with expanding and increasingly complex organizations.

Large firms have the resources to enable them to finance expansion of the production base and to fund growth via acquisition and diversification.

Patents   Small firms can experience problems in coping with the patent system and they cannot afford the time or costs involved in patent litigation.

Government regulations   Small firms often cannot cope with complex regulations and the unit cost of compliance for small firms is often high.

Large companies can fund legal services or specialist departments to enable them to cope with regulations, and they can spread regulatory costs. They are also able to fund the r&d that is sometimes necessary for regulatory compliance.

Two points are immediately obvious from the above list. First, innovatory advantage is unequivocally associated with neither large nor small firms. Second, the innovatory advantages of large firms are associated with the relatively greater financial and technical resources available to them, while the advantages of small firms are those of flexibility, adaptability and responsiveness. In other words, the advantages of large firms in innovation are seen to be mainly material, while those of small firms are in the main behavioural.

Large firms that succeed in combining both are, of course, in an extremely strong position, and it is a fact that many large firms, particularly in the United States, have attempted to establish, internally, small-firm-type structures to enhance their innovativeness. More recently in the United States there appears to be a trend towards establishing large firm–small firm collaborative ventures, perhaps most notably in the area of biotechnology.

The role of small firms in innovation

While a number of studies have been pursued which have highlighted the contribution of small firms to technological innovation and economic growth in the United States (NSF, 1976; Morse, 1976; NSF, 1979), within Europe there have been few really systematic and comprehensive studies of this type. A notable exception can be found in the systematic innovation data-collecting activities of the Science Policy Research Unit during the past fifteen or so years. The SPRU data base contains details on some 4400 important innovations introduced into commercial use by British companies between 1945 and 1983 (Robson and Townsend, 1984).

Table 4, compiled from the SPRU innovation data base, presents aggregated data showing the percentage of innovations by size of firm for eight time periods beteen 1945 and 1983. It shows that the share of total innovations taken by firms employing less than 500 (SMFs) has averaged 26.4 per cent during the thirty-eight-year period covered, and that it has increased significantly since 1975. Whether or not the dramatic increase between 1980–83 is due to the influence of the plethora of government policy initiatives introduced to assist small firms and to the greatly increased availability of private sector venture capital for small firms since 1980, is not known. The marked decrease in share by firms in the size category 1000–9999 appears to be partly the result of structural industrial shifts caused by a series of takeovers and mergers, although as we shall see later shifts in relative innovative efficiency have also played a part.

Table 4 Innovation share by size of firm in the UK, 1945–83

Time period	Size of firm							No. of innov's.
	1–199	200–499	500–999	1000–9999	10 000–29 000	30 000–99 999	100 000+	
1945–49	16.8	7.5	5.3	28.3	13.7	18.1	10.2	226
1950–54	14.2	9.5	4.5	32.3	18.4	12.0	9.2	359
1955–59	14.4	10.1	9.1	24.9	16.3	13.2	11.9	514
1960–64	13.6	9.2	6.0	27.8	16.2	14.5	12.7	684
1965–69	15.4	8.2	8.5	24.7	15.6	14.9	13.2	720
1970–74	17.5	9.0	6.3	20.7	17.1	15.4	14.0	656
1975–79	19.6	9.6	7.5	16.2	14.1	18.6	14.5	823
1980–83	26.3	12.1	4.3	14.9	14.6	12.1	15.2	396
Number of innovations	744	411	299	1004	690	660	670	4378
Average percentage	17.0	9.4	6.8	22.9	15.8	15.1	13.0	100

⟶ *adds to 4478*

Table 5 presents aggregated time series data for innovation share, not by size of innovating firm as above, but by size of innovating unit, ie, subsidiary, division, central laboratory, etc. This shows a marked shift in share of innovations towards small and medium-size units (SMUs), from 27.9 per cent during 1945–9 to 49.8 per cent during 1980–83. As Figure 8 suggests, this is again the result of changes made by subsidiaries of larger companies. To some extent this pattern might reflect, at least implicitly, attempts on the part of larger companies to marry the

Table 5 Innovation by size of innovating unit in the UK, 1945–83

Time period	Size of innovating unit							No. of innov's.
	1–199	200–499	500–999	1000–9999	10 000–29 000	30 000–99 999	100 000+	
1945–49	18.6	9.3	8.8	48.7	11.5	0.9	2.2	226
1950–54	20.1	13.6	6.1	46.8	9.2	2.8	1.4	359
1955–59	17.9	14.0	11.5	39.7	11.9	2.7	2.3	514
1960–64	17.4	12.7	10.2	41.8	11.7	3.4	2.8	684
1965–69	21.4	14.2	11.4	37.9	9.2	3.3	2.6	720
1970–74	24.5	14.0	12.2	34.0	10.1	2.9	2.3	656
1975–79	31.3	13.6	13.0	29.8	8.3	2.7	1.3	823
1980–83	32.1	17.7	10.1	29.3	6.8	2.8	1.3	396
Number of innovations	1025	605	480	1625	427	125	91	4387
Average percentage	23.4	13.8	11.0	37.1	9.8	2.9	2.1	100

resource-related advantages of large firms to the behavioural advantages enjoyed by smaller firms, listed earlier. What the SPRU data also indicates is that large firms have tended to acquire smaller firms to facilitate their movement into new areas of activity, ie, they have frequently diversified through the process of small firm acquisition.

Figure 8   Innovation share by status of innovating unit

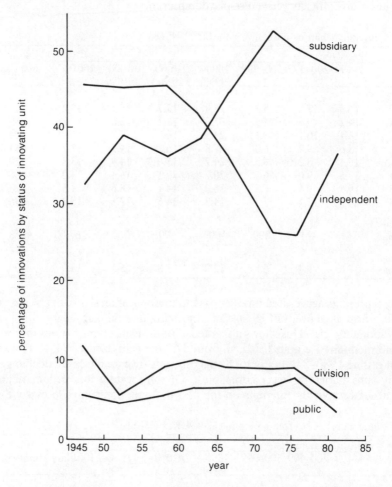

It was suggested earlier that the innovatory potential of firms of different sizes is likely to vary considerably between sectors, and the disaggregated SPRU data has confirmed this to be the case. In the scientific instruments industry, for example, SMFs have been consistently innovative and they enjoyed an average of 58.5 per cent of total sectoral innovations between 1945 and 1983. This is an area in which entry costs are relatively low and in which there exist many specialist market niches suitable for exploitation by SMFs. Small firms in specialist machinery areas have also made an important innovatory contribution.

In pharmaceuticals, in contrast, SMFs share in innovations averaged only 14 per cent over the thirty-eight-year period, and it has been zero since 1974. Pharmaceuticals is an r&d intensive area in which development costs are high and in which the introduction of a new ethical drug involves considerable regulatory costs and sometimes uncertainties (Rothwell, 1979).

The case of electronic computers is interesting since it illustrates clearly the necessity for adopting a dynamic approach to the question of firm size and innovation. For most of the period up to 1970, SMFs share of innovations in this area was relatively small or zero. Between 1970 and 1983, however, SMFs' share has increased dramatically from 36 per cent during 1970–74, to 47 per cent during 1975–79, to 64 per cent during 1980–83. During the 1950s and the 1960s UK production was composed almost entirely of mainframe computers with associated high r&d, manufacturing and servicing costs, which effectively debarred SMF participation on an appreciable scale. With the introduction of the integrated circuit and more significantly of the microprocessor, entry by SMFs became possible, and they rapidly became involved in the production of mini- and micro-computers and peripherals to satisfy the many new market segments that emerged. The rapidly developing field of biotechnology might similarly open up niche opportunities for SMFs in pharmaceuticals and related areas. Thus, while one type of technology might effectively prevent significant participation by SMFs, another can present them with many new product-market opportunities.

Simply counting innovation shares, of course, tells us nothing about the relatively innovative efficiency of firms of different sizes measured as innovations per unit of employment; nor does it provide any indication of relative r&d efficiency measured as innovations per unit of r&d expenditure. This issue has been dealt with in some detail by Wyatt (1984), whose results will be only briefly summarized here.

Utilizing the SPRU innovation data and employment statistics published by the UK Business Statistics Office, Wyatt has derived time-series data on the ratio of innovation share/employment share, for firms in five employment categories. This analysis, using aggregated data, shows the following results. An increase over time in the relative innovative efficiency of firms with employment between 1 and 199, from 0.46 in 1955–59 to 0.53 in 1975–80. An increase over time in the relative innovative efficiency of firms with employment between 200 and 499, from 0.66 in 1955–59 to 0.82 in 1975–80. A decrease over time in relative innovative efficiency of firms with employment between 500 and 999, from 0.76 in 1955–59 to 0.46 in 1975–80. A more marked decrease over time in the relative innovative efficiency of firms with employment between 1000 and 9999 from 0.83 in 1955–59 to 0.45 in 1975–80. A consistently greater-than-unity relative innovative efficiency of firms with employment greater than 10 000, eg, a ratio of 2.02 in 1955–59 and a ratio of 1.91 in 1975–80.

On the basis of this data, Wyatt concludes that the fact that firms with employment less than 500 have maintained their share of British innovations more successfully than those with employment between 500 and 10 000 reflects not only structural industrial shifts, but also changing patterns of innovative efficiency. While the aggregate data indicates that it is firms in the largest size category that have attained the highest levels of relative innovative efficiency, the disaggregated data, as we might expect, indicates considerable variation between sectors, and small firms show relative innovative efficiency levels of greater than unity in plastics, textile machinery, mining machinery, radio, radar and electronics capital goods and scientific instruments.

Turning to relative r&d efficiency of innovation, Wyatt's data paints a rather different picture. In 1975, firms with employment between 100–499 enjoyed 2 per cent of total national manufacturing r&d expenditure; between 1969 and 1980, they produced 20.6 per cent of total innovations, yielding a relative r&d efficiency ratio of 10.3. The comparable figures for firms in the largest size category (employment greater than 10 000) are 80 per cent and 43.4 per cent respectively, yielding a relative r&d efficiency ratio of 0.54. Thus, on the basis of this data, r&d efficiency is very much higher in the smaller firms. A possible explanation of this, and one favoured by Wyatt, is that there is a lower degree of functional specialization in small firms with a higher proportion of in-novative activities occurring outside of what is formally defined as r&d, a point emphasized by Segal and Quince (1985) in their study of new small firms in Cambridge. This would imply, however, that the informal r&d performed in small firms is very considerable indeed. For example, even if we ascribe a 20 per cent share of total r&d to the smaller firms – a factor of ten increase – their relative r&d efficiency would still be almost double that of the largest firms. Whatever the case, given the overwhelming concentration of r&d resources in the largest sized firms, it is hardly surprising that they have produced the bulk of British innovations. From the viewpoint of the health of the small firm sector in Britain, perhaps the most promising feature is the increasing in-ovative efficiency of SMFs. Given their relative lack of r&d resources, they have performed remarkably well.

The role of small firms in the emergence of new technologies[2]

Up to this point we have dealt largely with the role of small firms in intro-ducing new product innovations. Below we shall adopt a more dynamic view and describe the role that new technology-based firms (NTBFs) have played in the emergence of new technologies and new industrial sectors based on these technologies.

In 1959, Fairchild Camera Corporation exercised an option to buy a majority interest in Fairchild Semiconductor. The latter grew rapidly from sales of $0.5 million in 1960 to $27 million in 1967 to $520 million in 1978. During the next few years there was considerable spinoff from Fairchild Semiconductor of both people and technology, and many companies were formed by people formerly with, or associated with, Fairchild. This process has been described by Mason (1979):

> The first spin-off was in 1959, when Baldwin, not from the original Shockley team, left Fairchild to form Rheem Semiconductor, *collecting on the way people from Hughes Aircraft*. In 1961, four of the originals left to form Amelco and one of these, Hoeni, left in 1964 to form Union Carbide Electronics; moving on in 1968 to Intersil. Of . . . interest . . . was another event in 1961, when Signetics was formed. This was formed by four people who were a significant part of the Fairchild Semiconductor team. . . . *They managed to get venture capital backing from the Dow-Corning group for this move.*

At the same time that new technology-based small firms were being spawned in Silicon Valley, Bell Labs (a subsidiary of AT&T), continued with its vigorous inventive and innovative activity, although all AT&T's output (via Western Electric) was produced for its own use in order to avoid antitrust litigation. Bell Labs, along with other major companies have, between them accounted for a high percentage of all major innovations in semiconductor technology.[3] Interestingly, since 1976, major Japanese companies have made an increasing contribution to technological advance in semiconductors: Sharp's automatic bonding on exotic subtrates in 1977; Mitsubishi's vertical injection logic and V-MOS in 1978; Fujitsu's 64-K bit in 1978 (Dosi, 1981).

Despite the initial dominance of large companies in basic invention in the semiconductor field, new technology-based small firms played a key role in commercial exploitation, especially during the earlier stages in the US semiconductor industry's development.

What, in fact, occurred during the evolution of the US semiconductor industry was a classical example of the dynamic complementarities that can exist between large and small firms. Existing large firms provided much of the basic, state-of-the-art technology, venture capital and technically skilled personnel which were essential to new technology-based firm start-up; the new technology-based firms provided the risk-taking entrepreneurial drive and rapid market exploitation.

From the late 1960s onwards, the output of the US semiconductor industry began increasingly to be concentrated in the top ten or so companies. Production economies of scale grew in importance (and plant size increased), as did production learning, and firms began actively to seek rapid movement down the production learning curve. The importance of price in competition increased as the unit cost of semiconductor component production decreased. According to Sciberras (1977), the prime motive for rapid cost reductions was to deter new entrants by creating significant scale barriers to entry in addition to technological entry barriers. This might at least partially explain why semiconductor technology was exploited in Europe by large existing electronics companies: Europe entered the race at a late date, by which time existing scale and technological barriers largely precluded entry by new small firms.

Thus, in the development of the US semiconductor industry, we see an example of Schumpetarian industrial evolution from the entrepreneurial model of the newly emerging industry, to the managed model of the mature international ologopoly of today. Nowadays, the main opportunities for new entrants appear to be not in semiconductor production itself, but rather in the application of semiconductor devices to the production of new products, notably in the general area of information technology, currently mooted as the new industry of the next decade.

The evolution of the computer-aided design industry

A second example of industrial evolution that indicates an important role for NTBFs can be founded in the case of the computer-aided design (CAD) industry. The data below is drawn from the work of Kaplinsky (1981, 1982), who has identified four main phases in the development of the CAD industry: pre-1969 (industry origins); 1969–74 (dynamic new firms); 1974–80 (the trend to concentration); post-1980 (maturity).

During the first phase development was concentrated in established large companies in the defence, aerospace and aeronautical industries in collaboration with mainframe computer manufacturers, and in the late 1960s General Motors entered the field with the development of its Design Augmented by Computers programme.

In summary, therefore, during this early period there was hardly any 'market' for CAD, with most developments occurring to assist own-use by large, technically advanced engineering corporations in the US and (to a lesser extent) in the UK. (Kaplinsky, 1981).

The second phase was characterized by the emergence of the new small spinoff firms in the US (from both CAD producers and electronics companies) which played the primary role in the rapid diffusion of CAD devices into the electronics industry. Several of these firms grew extremely rapidly to become, along with IBM, today's market leaders. In Europe, in contrast, the major existing electronics firms developed CAD equipment for their own use.

In summary, therefore, this second period of industry development saw the emergence of new, independent firms and the rapid diffusion of the technology out of the defence, aerospace and automobile sectors to the electronics sectors. (Kaplinsky, 1981)

The third phase saw the rapid diffusion in use of CAD across manufacturing, a process in which the newcomers played a key role. During this period of extremely rapid market growth, the industry became increasingly concentrated, 93 per cent of US market share in 1980 being held by eight companies and most notably Computervision with 33.2 per cent of the total. At the same time patterns of ownership began to change and there was a series of takeovers by major corporations of several of the fast-growing newcomers.

To summarize, therefore, this third phase of industry development was associated with the growing size of CAD firms, the growing organic trend towards concentration within the sector, and a tendency for formerly independent CAD firms to be swallowed by existing trans-national corporations. (Kaplinsky, 1981)

At the beginning of the current phase in development, the market was dominated by turn-key suppliers supplying either mainframe systems (user entry costs of about $500 000) or mini-computer systems (user entry costs of about $200 000). From 1980 onwards, as the user base has broadened, a market niche has emerged for dedicated systems. These are based not on a comprehensive and flexible package of software applications, but on limited software packages for specific applications. A number of microcomputer based companies, founded by spinoffs from existing CAD suppliers, and using mature application programmes developed by these suppliers, have begun to emerge, offering systems for as little as $30 000 each.

to summarize, therefore, this most recent stage of industry development has seen two divergent trends – a continued tendency to concentration and an opposing tendency for the entry of new small firms selling limited capability dedicated systems. (Kaplinsky, 1981)

In the UK, it has been estimated that US firms held a 62 per cent share of all CAD systems installed up to mid-1981 (Arnold, 1982). Of the remaining 38 per cent share of installations, 17 per cent were held by subsidiaries of large electronic companies established in the late 1960s, 12 per cent by spinoff companies, 5 per cent by a public body (essentially a software house) and 4 per cent by other companies.

From the above brief descriptions of the evolution of two high-technology industries we can draw out a number of significant factors: Established large US corporations played a crucial initiating role in invention and innovation both in semiconductors and CAD technology. In both instances the early inventive and innovative activity was geared towards 'own use'.

In the case of semiconductors, much of the dynamic growth and market diffusion came about as a result of the formation and rapid expansion of NTBFs. In the CAD industry, NTBFs similarly played the key role in the rapid diffusion of CAD systems to electronics and other areas. In both cases, the technological entrepreneurs often came from established corporations, bringing a great deal of technological and applications know-how with them, and in both cases, established corporations and venture capital institutions played an important part in funding the start-up and growth of NTBFs. The industries rather quickly became highly concentrated and subject to external takeover. Finally, in both cases, as the industries matured, scale economies[4] became increasingly important in the mainstream activities and strong oligopolies were formed, leaving only specialist market niches for new and small suppliers.

It is clear from the description of the evolution of the semiconductor and CAD industries that it is necessary to consider the interactions between small and large firms if we are fully to understand the evolutionary dynamic of technologies and industrial sectors. In both instances existing large corporations played the major initial role in invention, producing new devices largely for in-house use only. The major role in the initial rapid market diffusion of these new devices, however, was played by new, small but fast-growing companies founded by technological entrepreneurs. Moreover, the technical know-how, the venture capital and the entrepreneurs themselves very often derived from the established corporations, as well as, in the case of the latter two, from major companies operating in other areas. A spinoff firm appeared to be the most suitable organizational form for types of innovation where (the application of) new technologies are involved. Thus, we see a system of dynamic complementarity between the large and the small: both had their unique contribution to make; both were necessary, the former to the initiation of the new technological paradigm, the latter to rapid market diffusion and general commercial exploitation.

What our discussions suggest is that established technology-based large corporations can be extremely effective in creating new technological possibilites; they are highly inventive. While they are adept at utilizing the results of their inventiveness inhouse (*new* technology for *existing* applications), they are less well adapted to the rapid exploitation of their inventions in new markets (*new* technology for *new* applications). It appears that new firms, initially, are better adapted to exploit new techno-market regimes, breaking out from existing regimes within which established corporations, for historical, cultural and institutional reasons, might be rather strongly bound. Referring back to the discussion of innovatory advantage and disadvantage, it appears that during the early phases in the evolution of a new industry the behavioural advantages of small scale are crucial; as the industry evolves, technological possibilities become better defined and market needs become increasingly well specified, the advantages of large scale begin to dominate. Comparative advantage shifts to the larger firms and the industry develops towards a mature oligopoly, a situation characteristic of the semiconductor and CAD industries today.

At this juncture it might be worthwhile summarizing briefly a number of differences in the mode of evolution of the semiconductor industries in the

United States, Japan and Europe, in order to indicate the respective roles played by firms of different sizes in these countries.

United States   Leading-edge r&d was performed in established large corporations who innovated mainly for 'own-use'. High rates of spinoff coupled to vigorous entrepreneurship and access to venture capital led to rapid growth and diffusion. Large companies continued for many years to play a major role in basic invention. The US rapidly gained market leadership and maintained a strong technical lead. Military r&d funding and procurement played key roles, especially during the early years of the industry. The system of large–small firm complementarities was peculiarly well adapted to the creation of *new* techno/market regimes.

Japan   Late entry was followed by the coordinated acquisition of technology (mainly from the USA) on an industry-wide basis, in which process MITI played a key role. Large companies with considerable inhouse r&d resources demonstrated high technological adaptability. High levels of 'directed' r&d in major public/private collaborative development programmes enhanced the technological learning and adaptation processes. Technological adaptation, coupled to highly efficient production sequences utilizing 'total quality control' techniques, led to a rapidly growing market share. The Japanese system has proved itself well adapted to rapid catching up in 'determinate' technologies and markets, ie, to moving within *established* techno/market regimes.

Europe   Europe possesses considerable basic scientific and technical strengths, but is hampered by laggard innovative behaviour in technology, manufacturing and marketing. Inhouse attempts at catching up by established electronics companies have been inadequate, and because of laggard behaviour by established large companies, the possibilities for NTBF formation are small since US companies were already well down the learning curve. Inadequate public r&d funding and procurement activities and, little r&d coordination at the national level are further disadvantages.

Cultural and economic factors are not conducive to spinoff and entrepreneurship.

Continued technological and market backwardness.

Turning now to 'new wave' biotechnology, the economic potential of this infant industry is immense, and many new firms have been established within this area – most notably in the US – during recent years, frequently being closely linked to university-based research (ie, in this instance the state-of-the-art knowledge is vested in the academic system). It is interesting that, when it became generally realized that biotechnology is still in its research intensive phase, the commercialization of biotechnological products on a large scale being a thing of the late 1980s onwards, independent venture capitalists began to have second thoughts concerning their investments in the newcomers. Increasingly, established large corporations stepped in to fill the venture capital gap. In fact, we can today see synergistic interactions occurring between a number of large firm/small firm combinations. Dow Chemical and Monsanto, for example, while pursuing their own research and development programmes, are investing also in smaller companies; Biotechnology General, an entrepreneurial newcomer in the US, is negotiating for venture capital with three large firms to help finance the development of three new agricultural products; Bio Isolates of Swansea is now setting up a joint venture with Dunlop; Grand Metropolitan has invested more than $4 million in Biogen, a new Swiss-based biotechnology company; and so on. The point is, whether or not any of the new small biotechnology firms become the giants of the future or whether they act as a technical resource for existing large firms is, today, less important than their role in stimulating widespread interest and greatly increased investment in biotechnical r&d, ie, they have played a crucial initiating role.

Finally, in the emergence of the new-wave biotechnology industry, we can again see a number of important differences between the mode of development of new industry in the USA and its counterpart in Europe (specifically, the UK), and these are illustrated in Figure 9. As stated above, the main carrier of the new industry in the United States has been a swarm of NTBFs spinning off from state-of-the-art research centres in universities. In the UK, in contrast, state-of-the-art university research is being transferred into industrial use (to large firms) mainly via the contract research mechanism either privately, or through the publicly formed company Celltech. In other words, in Europe we see once again a relative paucity of entrepreneurial activity (Rothwell, 1985), which contrasts with the situation in the USA.

Figure 9　The 'new wave' biotechnology industry

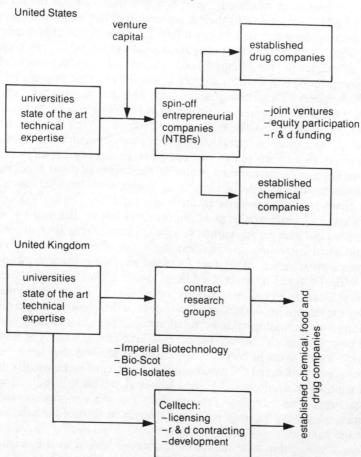

Discussion

In this section an attempt will be made to pick out one or two of the more important issues that have arisen from the previous discussions. In the first place, the firm size/innovation data for the UK has highlighted two important points. First, generalizations regarding the role of small firms in innovation can be misleading and any analysis should proceed on a sector-by-sector basis. Second, dynamic analysis of this issue clearly is necessary since, as illustrated in the case of the UK electronics computer industry, small firms' role can alter significantly over the industry cycle.

An important and related point is that the small firm sector is highly heterogeneous, and to talk about 'innovation and the small firm' in general terms is meaningless. The traditional small firm, for example, operating in long-established areas such as textiles, garments, leatherwear and metalworking, is unlikely to be involved in the production of product technological innovations, and the technology utilized in such firms is likely to be exogenously produced by materials and equipment suppliers. Modern, niche-strategy small firms, in contrast, utilize product-embodied technology to afford them the ability to compete in specific market segments through the provision of innovative, often custom-built devices. As we have seen, such firms in the scientific instrument and specialist machinery areas have made a signficant innovatory contribution in the UK. NTBFs are a special category of small firm, which operate in newly emerging and fast-moving areas of technology. They are highly innovative and their membership of the small firm category is often transitory since this type of small firm has exceptional growth potential.

In addition to the three categories already described, which are clasasified largely acording to the degree and nature of product technological embodiment, there is a fourth category of small firm, that of parts and sub-assembly suppliers. This class of small firm does not manufacture complete products, but rather supplies inputs to the products produced by firms of all sizes and operating across the technology spectrum. Often they will perform little r&d of their own, but produce to precise user specifications established on the basis of r&d efforts in the user company. In this respect, their potential for innovation may be determined mainly by the nature of these specifications. In other cases, for example in electronics components and sub-assemblies, supplier firms may be innovative in their own right.

The final, and perhaps the most important point, is that small and large firms do not exist in separate worlds. On the contrary, there are complex flows of technological know-how and finished innovations between firms of all sizes and across a great variety of sectors. As noted above, for example, during the period 1970–79 small firms in the UK obtained a quarter of their external innovatory ideas from other – mainly large – companies, and Figure 10 illustrates the flow of product innovations between different sectors in the UK.

In addition to technological inter-relationships, there exist a variety of other types of complementarity between small and large firms. A study of new small technology-based firms in Sweden, for example, showed that large Swedish firms frequently supported the newcomers in a variety of ways, usually through the provision of technology and skilled labour (Utterback, 1982). Moreover, the large firms often acted as early markets for the newcomers, and pre-payments were among the most important sources of finance for half the small firms in the sample.

A second study, this time in the Netherlands, looked at the relationship

Figure 10 Innovation flows between manufacturing product groups in the UK

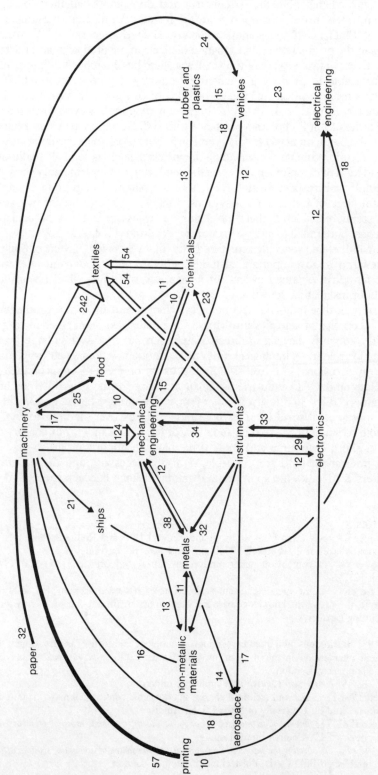

between spinoff firms and their parent company (van der Meer and van Tilburg, 1983). It showed that both the parent firm and the spinoff benefited through cooperation, often involving support from the former. An illustrative example is the case of Philips and the spinoff company, B & B Electronics BV, which specializes in the production and installation of electronic scoreboards and related products. These activities were of too small a scale to be of interest to Philips, and B & B were able to produce a qualitatively equivalent product at lower cost. Philip's support consisted of the provision of technical information and appropriate labour to B & B. The most important support, however, consisted of obtaining orders from Philips and assistance with B & B's export activities. Philips included the (complementary) B & B products in quotations to its customers, thus enabling it to offer complete installations for projects such as football stadiums.

A second kind of complementarity was the rendering of supplementary services by the spinoff with respect to the products of the parent firm, a good example being in the area of traffic control systems. Philips, a large producer of traffic control systems, considered their installation a necessary but not particularly advantageous undertaking, and a firm spun off from Philips to specialize in installation and related servicing activities. In the first years of its existence, Philips was the new firm's most important customer. The benefit to both companies was clear: the new firm obtained orders for its services and Philips had no further worries about installation activities.

The reality is that industrial technological change and industrial production comprise a complex of activities involving firms of all sizes. Sometimes firms act in concert, frequently they act in direct competition; in some sectors large firms play the major role in technological innovation, in other sectors small firms lead the way; on occasions – as we saw in the cases of the US semiconductor, biotechnology and CAD industries – small and large firms play different but complementary roles in the evolution of new, technology-based sectors; the relative importance of small firms in innovation can vary over the industry cycle; and the role of small firms in innovation can differ significantly from country to country. In short, both large and small firms have an important part to play in industrial innovation; both are desirable, both are necessary, and the trick for policymakers is to strike the appropriate dynamic balance between the two.

References

1 This chapter is largely taken from Rothwell and Zegveld 1985 and Rothwell 1985.
2 This section is taken from Rothwell 1984b and Rothwell and Zegveld 1985.
3 In excess of 60 per cent of all major innovations introduced between 1951 and 1971 (Webbink 1977).
4 In the case of CAD the most significant scale economy has been accumulated software expertise, ie, the size of the knowledge base is a much more significant barrier to entry than manufacturing capacity.

Dosi G. 1981 Institutions and markets in high technology industries: an assessment of government intervention in micro-electronics. In Carter C. F. *Industrial policies and innovation*. Heinemann London

Galbraith J. K. 1957 *American Captialism*. Hamilton London

Kaplinsky R. 1981 Firm size and technical change in a dynamic context (Mimeo). Institute of Development Studies, University of Sussex, UK, August

Kaplinsky R. 1982 *The impact of technological change on the international division of labor: the illustrative case of CAD*. Frances Pinter London

Mason D. 1979 *Factors affecting the successful development and marketing of innovative semiconductor devices*. Unpublished PhD thesis, Polytechnic of Central London

Morse R. S. 1976 *The role of new technical enterprises in the US economy*. Report of the Commerce Technical Advisory Board to the Secretary of Commerce, January

National Science Foundation 1976 *Indicators of international trends in technological innovation*. NSF-6889, Washington, DC, April

National Science Foundation 1979 NSF small business innovation research program. Washington, DC, April

Robson M. and Townsend J. 1984 Trends and characteristics of significant innovations and their innovators in the UK since 1945 (Mimeo). Science Policy Research Unit, University of Sussex, UK, August

Rothwell R. 1979 *Government regulations and industrial innovation*. Report to the Six Countries Program on Innovation, c/o Policy Studies Group TNO. PO Box 215, 2600AE Delft, The Netherlands

Rothwell, R. 1984a Technology-based small firms and regional innovation potential: the role of public procurement. *Journal of Public Policy* **4** (4)

Rothwell R. 1984b The role of small firms in the emergence of new technologies *OMEGA* **12** (1)

Rothwell R. 1985 Venture capital for the development of new technologies and the creation of companies. OECD, Paris, June

Rothwell R. 1986 Venture finance, small firms and public policy in the UK. Paper prepared for conference on Venture Capital and Public Policy, University of Pisa, 6th July *Research Policy*.

Rothwell R. and Zegveld W. 1981 *Industrial innovation and public policy*. Frances Pinter London

Rothwell R. and Zegveld W. 1982 *Innovation and the small and medium sized firm*. Frances Pinter London

Rothwell R. and Zegveld W. 1985 *Reindustrialization and technology*. Longman London, (Published in the USA by M. E. Sharpe, Inc, New York)

Segal and Quince Partners 1985 *The Cambridge phenomenon*. Segal and Quince Partners, Cambridge

Schumaker E. F. 1973 *Small is beautiful*. Harper and Row London

Takizawa K. 1974 A comparative study on the problems of small business in the USA, the UK and Japan *The Economic Science* **21** (3). Nagoya University, Japan

Twaalfhoven F. and Hattori T. 1982 *The supporting role of the small Japanese firm*. Indivers Research, Netherlands.

Utterback J. M. 1982 *Technology and industrial innovation in Sweden: a study of new technology-based firms*. Centre for Policy Alternatives, MIT, Cambridge, USA

Van der Meer J. D. and van Tilburg J. J. 1983 *Spin-offs uit technisch kommerciele infrastructurenentrepeneur*. Van der Meer and van Tilburg, Enschede, the Netherlands

Webbink D. W. 1977 *The semiconductor industry; structure, conduct and peformance*. unpublished staff report to the US Federal Trade Commission, January

Wyatt S. 1984 The role of small firms in innovative activity (Mimeo). Science Policy Research Unit, University of Sussex. (To be published in *Economia and Politica Industriale*, 1985)

Part 2　　Public policies

Government initiatives to encourage technical innovation[1]

Walter Zegveld
Netherlands Organization for Applied Scientific Research

The benefits currently accepted to be associated with technical change and industrial innovation are such that governments in most industrialized countries feel that they cannot do without explicit technology and innovation policies. The pressures to construct such policies have grown as a result of a number of factors, including the worldwide deterioration of the economic climate during the 1970s, changes in the international economic order, balance-of-payments problems, competitiveness of industry, and last but not least, the general acceptance of the case long argued by many economists that innovation and often related technology play key roles in stimulating economic development.

Implicit in the title of this paper is the assumption that the current development of economic activities is in some way linked to the emergence of technological possibilities; that existing industries can in some way be regenerated through technological change and that new industries can be created in a similar way. Reindustrialization can be defined in this context as 'the structural transformation of economic activities into higher added value, more knowledge-intensive product groups, and the creation of major new technology-based industries and products serving new markets'.

Technical change and economic development can neither be separated from a larger societal context nor from the micro level, that of the individual firm. After describing differences in industrial development between the United States, Japan, and Western Europe, the issue of technology policy related to economic development is treated at three different but interrelated levels: society at large, the individual firm and the national economy.

Differences between the United States, Japan, and Western Europe

One useful way of approaching the question of the relationship between industrial development and technology is to consider some of the significant differences between the United States, Japan, and Western Europe concerning their technological and industrial development during the past thirty years. In terms of the introduction of new technologies, the overriding impression is that in the United States the new postwar, technology-based leading sectors came into being sooner and grew more rapidly than elsewhere. In Western European industry, with some exceptions, the strategy mostly seems to be that of a follower, at least as far as commercialization is concerned. In Japan the strategy clearly has been one of rapid catching-up based on the adoption and adaption of foreign technology, coupled to highly efficient and quality-orientated mass production. In order to support this impression, a number of economic and technological indicators can be used to illustrate the differences between these countries. Among other things, substantial shifts in international trade have taken place during the past twenty years, particularly in the area of high-technology goods. In general, economic development since World War II has shown rapid growth in Japan and in a number of Western European countries, while the development within the United States has been much slower, although still at a relatively high level. An initial illustration of trade shifts between a number of economic blocs is given in Table 6, which shows the shares of total exports in international trade between 1963 and 1980 of six major trading blocs or countries. The figures demonstrate that, after rising from 41.5 per cent to 45.0 per cent in the period 1963–73, Western Europe's share in international trade subsequently dropped to 41 per cent in 1980. The United States' share dropped to 10.6 per cent in 1980, after a slight increase in the 1960s. Striking features of this data are the gradual rise in Japan's share from 3.4 per cent in 1963 to 6.6 per cent in 1980 and the increasing share gained by newly industrializing countries.

Table 6   Shares in world exports, 1963–80 (in % of total)

	1963	1968	1973	1980
Total world trade (in milliards of $)	155	238	574	1973
Total, of which	100	100	100	100
EC (9 countries)	33.8	34.6	36.6	33.3
(of which intra-EC trade)	(15.2)	(16.4)	(19.3)	(17.6)
Other West European countries	7.7	8.0	8.4	7.7
United States	13.4	14.6	11.9	10.6
Japan	3.4	5.6	6.4	6.6
Comecon	12.1	11.3	10.0	9.0
Developing countries including newly industrialized countries	20.6	18.4	19.2	27.5

Source: GATT, International Trade

The differences between the United States, Japan, and Western Europe (EEC) become clearer, moreover, if we look on a lower level of aggregation, in other words at the export figures for each product group separately. While it can be seen from Table 7 that the EEC is the largest exporter in the OECD, Japan nevertheless proves to have achieved a greater increase in its share in the period 1973–80. The figures, show, furthermore, that while Japan occupies a relatively weak position in the product groups (grouping I) relating to agricultural products and raw materials, in other product groups where there is greater emphasis on industrial articles and goods, Japan's position shifts considerably towards greater export shares. In the manufactured-products group the respective OECD export shares of the EEC, the US and Japan are 38.6 per cent, 22.3 per cent and 19 per cent. However, in the period 1973–80, Japan achieved a considerable improvement of 2.6 per cent, while during the same period the EEC's share dropped 0.4 per cent. This improvement in Japan's position is even more pronounced in the machinery, equipment and transportation grouping of manufactured products (grouping III, by far the

Table 7 Changes in shares of OECD exports 1973–80

	OECD exports* in 1980 billion US$	Per cent	Shares of OECD exports* in 1980			Changes 1973–80		
			Japan	USA %	EEC*	Japan percentage	USA points	EEC* difference
Total products	852		15.3	25.1	37.2	2.25	0.09	1.82
I Food, beverages, tobacco	75		2.3	42.8	33.3	−0.6	−1.1	7.6
Agricultural products	27	21.5	0.7	55.8	9.4	−0.1	6.5	−0.8
Mineral fuels	41		1.2	19.4	47.5	0.3	−1.4	11.2
Metals unworked	18		4.1	33.1	13.1	2.5	13.1	2.6
Other raw materials	22		1.0	16.3	40.0	−0.5	0.9	5.7
Manufactured products of which:	668		19.0	22.3	38.6	2.6	0.8	−0.4
II Non-met. min. products	31		13.0	18.2	44.4	0.9	2.9	−2.1
Iron and steel	46		34.2	7.5	38.0	2.2	−0.4	−3.6
Metal products	22	20.8	15.7	16.1	44.5	−0.0	−0.9	2.8
Basic materials	45		9.0	28.8	44.4	0.9	3.3	−1.8
Chemical products	24		4.8	25.1	47.5	0.5	2.2	−1.2
III Agricultrual machinery	9		10.3	34.8	39.7	3.4	−2.7	−0.5
Electrical machinery	40		22.3	23.0	40.1	7.7	−3.8	−2.0
Power gen. machinery	20		17.1	27.5	40.9	3.8	−0.1	−4.4
Other machinery	90	42.0	13.3	23.9	45.4	4.2	0.2	−4.0
Office and telecom. equipment	42		34.6	27.2	25.7	2.1	2.6	−1.4
Optical, clock, photo	31		24.4	26.6	30.8	7.5	0.2	−3.6
Road vehicles	89		32.5	16.4	32.7	14.8	−5.0	−4.7
Other transport equipment	37		14.6	43.2	33.8	−9.5	11.8	−9.0
IV Textiles	24		22.0	15.2	39.9	−1.2	4.2	−3.2
Clothing	9		3.7	12.1	48.1	−7.0	4.5	3.7
Leather, shoes	8	16.7	4.9	9.7	51.3	−1.8	3.3	−0.0
Paper	32		3.5	19.0	16.3	· 0.5	2.9	0.9
Wood furniture	9		3.3	12.7	41.3	−2.8	−1.3	11.8
Plastic, rubber	31		15.1	20.7	47.5	−0.9	−0.4	0.2
Other manuf. products	30		14.7	29.4	45.1	−1.4	−3.8	6.1

*Not including intra-Community trade.

Source: E.E.C. The competitiveness of European Community industry, March 1982, p 10.

largest of the manufacturing groupings). While it is true that the US and the EEC account for the greater part of total exports in most of these products, Japan has been able to improve its share considerably in almost all the product groups in this category. The US share, and to an even larger degree that of the EEC, fell in a number of product groups over the period 1973–80. In the last category of product groups (grouping IV), which are primarily basic consumer goods, eg, textiles, leather, etc, the EEC's position is dominant. The decline in Japan's share in the period 1973–80 in OECD trade in these traditional, low-technology groups is marked. It can also be seen that in the 1970s Japan improved its position in the technically more advanced groups of machinery and equipment manufacturing and, most notably, in road vehicles. Indeed, while between 1962 and 1977 the US share in OECD exports in technologically intensive manufactured goods declined from 28.3 per cent to 18.9 per cent, the share enjoyed by Japan increased from 4.2 per cent to 16.1 per cent (Aho and Rosen, 1980). Another way of approaching the differences in trading patterns, and one which has become generally accepted, is by using the so-called 'export specialization coefficient'. This has some methodological shortcomings, in particular if it is used for a comparison between larger economic blocs, but nevertheless gives some indication of changes in specialization. The export specialization coefficient refers to the relationship between the export share of a given sector in the total exports of a country or group of countries and the corresponding figure for a control group. The formula is:

$$S_{jk} = \frac{X_{jk}}{X_{jt}} : \frac{X_{nk}}{X_{nt}}$$

where X is exports, j the exporting country, n the control group, k the sector or the product category, and t the total products of the industry. (See: EEC, *The development of industrial sector structures in Europe since the oil crisis*, Brussels 1979). Table 8 shows the export specialization coefficients for the EEC, the USA and Japan in the years 1963, 1973, and 1980; the control group is made up of the combined OECD countries. The figures, therefore, indicate the extent to which the exports of the three separate blocs depart from the trend in the OECD as a whole.

Since the figures in Table 8 largely speak for themselves, it can be remarked that the EEC has apparently only been partially successful in increasing its specialization in trade in products in grouping III. This would also seem true of the United States, although to a lesser extent. Japan has been able dramatically to improve its position in the equipment sector in the past few years. The table also shows that as early as the 1960s Japan has reduced its specialization in traditional product groups like textiles and clothing. Patterns of trade specialization today for Japan, the US and West Germany are shown graphically in Figure 11, which confirms the pattern suggested in Table 8 (*Economist*, 9 July 1983).

We will now take a closer look at the role which technology and the production of high-technology goods have played in the development of the three blocs. In Table 9 specialization coefficients are given again, but this time for the category, high-technology products. From this it can clearly be seen that the EEC's position worsened in the years 1963–80. Next to the EEC the US also shows a decline, but to a lesser extent. Japan, on the other hand,

Table 8 Specialization coefficients EEC, US and Japan, 1963, 1973, 1980

	Community*			USA			Japan	
	1963	1973	1980	1963	1973	1980	1963	1973
Iron and steel	0.99	1.01	0.96	0.42	0.35	0.3	1.72	1.85
Metal products	1.08	0.99	1.11	0.84	0.74	0.70	1.06	0.89
Basic chemicals	0.99	1.12	1.08	1.05	1.13	1.22	0.60	1.57
Chemical products	1.21	1.25	1.23	1.14	1.07	1.14	0.38	0.26
Agricultural machinery	0.80	1.03	1.10	1.83	1.74	1.69	0.07	0.42
Electrical machinery	1.16	1.06	1.06	1.03	1.24	1.07	0.75	0.88
Power generating machinery	1.15	1.03	1.15	1.20	1.43	1.35	0.52	0.89
Other machinery	1.07	1.32	1.27	1.24	1.16	1.17	0.39	0.57
Office, telecommunications equipment	0.95	0.74	0.71	1.31	1.23	1.32	1.55	2.12
Optical clock, photo	0.78	0.93	0.84	1.11	1.30	1.27	0.95	1.09
Road vehicles	1.31	0.96	0.84	1.00	1.00	0.73	0.47	1.08
Other transport equipment	0.78	0.77	1.04	1.43	1.79	2.33	1.32	1.78
Textiles	0.94	0.95	0.87	0.43	0.44	0.58	2.47	1.22
Clothing	0.99	0.79	0.83	0.27	0.25	0.37	2.05	0.45
Shoes	1.05	1.16	1.06	0.38	0.27	0.35	1.22	0.36
Paper	0.51	0.55	0.56	0.80	0.79	0.76	0.35	0.25
Wood, furniture	0.65	0.62	0.84	0.45	0.54	0.45	1.64	0.30
Plastic, rubber	0.98	1.01	1.03	1.11	0.82	0.79	0.90	0.81
Other manufactured goods	0.86	1.03	1.22	1.82	1.68	1.39	1.07	1.06
Total manufacturers	1.00	1.00	1.00	1.00	1.00	1.00	1.00	1.00

*Extra-EC trade
(*Source*: EEC, 1982, p 18)

dramatically improved its position with respect to high-technology products which resulted in a rise in the specialization coefficient from 0.56 in 1963 to 1.41 in 1980. The data presented above indicates a significant shift in patterns of international trade during the past twenty or so years. The dominant position of the US in technology-intensive trade has eroded significantly, while that of Japan has undergone marked improvement.

Table 9 Specialization coefficients for high-technology goods

	1963	1970	1980
EEC	1.02	0.94	0.88
USA	1.29	1.27	1.20
Japan	0.56	0.87	1.41

Control group: Total world trade in industrial products.

(*Source*: EEC, 1982, p 19)

It is not, of course, technology per se that affords a nation its competitive advantage in world markets, but rather the ability of companies in that nation effectively to translate technological advantages into marketable goods. The data presented so far relate more to the embodiment of technology in goods rather than to the technology itself. There does exist, however, a set of data which concerns trade in technological know-how rather than in technology-embodying goods: these are the statistics on international flows of patents, inventions, processes and copyrights.

Although the differences between Japan, the United States and Western

Figure 11 Trade specialization: Japan, US and West Germany. *Export (import) specialization (ie relative share) = share of product group in country's exports (imports) relative to product group's share in total OECD exports (imports) (*Source*: OECD, MITI. Taken from : *The Economist* 8 July 1983.

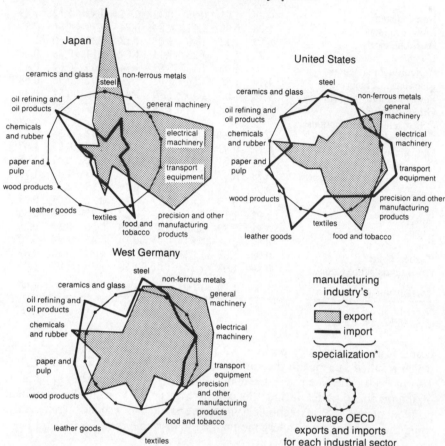

Europe can be illustrated fairly simply on the basis of statistical material, this does not mean that these differences in technological and economic development are easy to explain. Too many factors – cultural, social, managerial and economic – are involved. Moreover, a factor which appears to have a positive influence on technological development within the social context of one economic bloc or country may have a negative effect in another bloc or country. For example, the lack of worker-mobility in Western Europe may be contrasted with the large mobility in the United States which, again in contrast with Europe, has resulted in a great deal of 'spin-off' entrepreneurship in the USA. One of the most striking characteristics of the social structure in Japan, on the other hand, is the great immobility of the labour force in large firms. This fact does not seem to have negative effects on the acceptance of new technologies in that country. On the contrary, Japanese workers in larger firms, with life-employment expectations, have little to fear and much to gain from the acceptance of new technology. Any explanations of the differences between Japan, the United States and Western Europe must, therefore, be highly speculative. Possible or partial explanations of the differences that have developed between Japan, the United States, and Western Europe are reproduced in tabular form in Table 10.

Table 10   Differences between Japan, United States, and Western Europe

Japan	United States	Western Europe
strictly coordinated export policy	'market-pulled' innovation	long tradition of scientific research
politico-economic infra-structure with interweaving of state, banks and industry	great personal mobility and competitiveness. Many new technology-based firms formed	lack of entrepreneurship and the formation of new technology-based firms
aggresive industrial policy, long-term public and private sector strategies	legislation and education directed towards entrepreneurship	emphasis on supporting traditional sectors
coordinated policy towards the acquisition of technology	support for strategic sectors in connection with position as a superpower (defence, aerospace)	relative weakness in product development and marketing. Lag in the commercial exploitation of new technologies
strong emphasis on efficient mass production and on total quality control	rapid growth of new industrial sectors based on radical technologies	
home market which demands innovation	high availability of venture capital	paucity of venture capital
	large home market which demands innovation	

Source: R. Rothwell and W. Zegveld 1985 *Reindustrialization and Technology*. Longman, London; and M. E. Sharpe Inc., Armonk, New York.

Society and change

Following an initiative by the government of Japan, a research project was executed within the framework of OECD to study 'the future development of advanced industrial societies in harmony with that of developing countries'. The primary purpose of the project was 'to provide OECD member governments with an assessment of alternative patterns of longer-term world economic development in order to clarify their implications for the strategic policy choices open to them in the management of their own economies, in relationships among them, and in their relationships with developing countries'. The final report of the study was published in 1979 under the title *Interfutures; facing the future; mastering the probable and managing the unpredictable.*

Although Interfutures' position in OECD and its terms of reference, made the project's approach predominantly economic, an effort has been made to appreciate the systematic relationships between economic phenomena and other aspects of physical and social reality. Above all, in considering the way in which the world economy works, the project never lost sight of a number of essential elements: the national societies, the social groups which coexist in their midst, and the governments of the nation states which represent them politically.

Similarly, since the strategies of the actors involved depend very much on the way in which relations between groups and individuals are organized, the importance was recognized of institutions and structural elements such as markets, decision-making processes, public services and government administrations. It can be assumed that in the course of the remainder of this century, these institutions and structural elements will undergo substantial change – some will develop, others will have to contend with mounting difficulties and still others will survive by adapting. Some may also be changed or transformed by governments wishing to use them in order to find better answers to longer-term problems. While Interfutures was mainly concerned with future-oriented research on economic phenomena, it tried not to neglect political struggles, social conflict, value changes and institutional developments which are inseparable from them. The main theme in the societal, economic, technological and industrial development process can be coined as 'change'. It is our capacity for change, at all levels, that is the most important factor in the process of structural adjustment.

Based on Interfutures' approach a simplified framework can be constructed describing the capacity for change at the level of society. This framework consists of the following three interrelated elements: values, institutions, and the level of social, economic and technological development. These three elements, and a certain minimum relationship between them, would determine the capacity of evolutionary change. The level of disequilibrium between the development of the three elements would constitute the rate of conflict in society in accommodating change.

It was Schumpeter in *Business Cycles* (1939) who first advanced the notion of radical innovations as a major factor in the recurrent crises of structural adjustment. Schumpeter thereby pointed to such important exogenous factors as wars and harvest failures facilitating rather drastic value changes. Our present day challenge is to change in the absence of such important exogenous factors.

With respect to values it can be stated that these have changed considerably over time and will continue to do so. Emancipation in a broad sense and individualization at large have become important factors. The often-quoted relationship between values and technological change in the case of 'the pill' has been succeeded by a case like the decentralization of decision-making with respect to the introduction of modern production technology.

Present institutions often temper the pace of technology and that of the societal change process. Institutions have been established in different eras and often for different purposes. For example, the traditional role and structure of the European with respect to telecommunication is not necessarily advantageous from a present-day standpoint with respect to the development of the telecommunication industry. The structure of centralized electricity generation, distribution and pricing does not necessarily facilitate the introduction of decentralized total energy systems. The role of the labour unions cannot but differ in a period when the role of workers-councils is increasing. Decision-making processes have changed and will continue to change drastically over time; one of the main problems being the level at which decisions are made. On the one hand nuclear energy decisions can hardly be other than centrally taken. With respect to the introduction of modern production technology on the other hand a decentralized decision-making process is required, both from a standpoint of values as well as of bare necessity.

The institutional framework of many of the structural elements in Europe is, compared to the USA, tied to, or part of, the public sector under government control. For Europe this means that the capacity for change is lower than that in the USA due to the fact that the political process plays a major role in decision making.

Change and the individual firm

The individual firm is confronted with numerous external and internal changes. Basically, the individual firm went through a process of strategic positioning along the lines of the manufacturing of products, the realization of product-market combinations and the operationalization of these product-market combinations within the framework of a social and physical environment. Technology is becoming more and more a strategic factor in establishing the overall development of the firm.

It should be kept in mind that Ansoff's *Corporate Strategy* was first published only in 1965 and pointed at two interrelated elements; diversification and the so-called product-market matrix. Diversification by way of introducing new products serving new markets has not always been successful. A trend is presently discernible for firms to concentrate more on the core of their business. The latter development is frequently taking the form of selling out the diversified part of the operation or placing it at the periphery of the core activities in such a way that it is in a position to operate largely independently. When considering product-market-technology combinations a different matrix now appears. Technology in this case is to be considered as a strategic element of the firm; either in the form of production technology or in the form of product quality in a broad sense.

In the USA, technical entrepreneurship in small- and medium-sized firms and especially in new technology-based firms (NTBFs) plays a much more dominant role than in Europe. This factor most probably is of utmost importance with respect to industrial employment and flexibility in industrial production.

Change and the national economy

During the past three decades, at least up to the end of the 1970s, macro-economic policy in the Western world has concentrated mainly on the maintenance of full employment largely through the control of financial flows and through demand management. Postwar economic development up to the mid-1970s can be characterized as an era of continuous economic growth accompanied by minor fluctuations about the growth path. By the time the outflow of personnel, first out of agriculture and later out of industrial production, could no longer be absorbed in the other sectors (recently mainly the collective-service sector), the changes in the relationship between production and employment have become more generally manifest. In the agricultural sector this development was accompanied by a manifold increase in agricultural output. In industrial production, European Community countries on the whole, doubled their output over the period 1960–80. Both in agriculture and in industrial production, employment decreased in absolute terms; in agriculture over the period 1945–80 to about 20 per cent; in industrial production over the period 1960–80 to about 85 per cent.

It is important to stress here the structural character of the present economic situation. In the late 1960s, a large number of postwar industries simultaneously entered the maturity and market-saturation phase of their life cycles. A Dutch study by Geldens published in 1979 showed, for example, that no less than 75 per cent of Dutch industrial value-added was generated in industries in the saturation and declining phase of the industrial cycle. In this phase of the cycle, key words are: rationalization and growing automaticity, growing manufacturing unemployment and price competition. Under these conditions innovation is necessary in order to initiate new products and to enable industries to enter the first phase of a next generation of growth cycles.

It would be difficult, if not impossible, to present a case in which an increase in present production would solve the unemployment and economic problems. The implication, however, of the structural interpretation of the present crisis is that it should not be tackled by traditional demand management policies alone, but by adding a different kind of policy: reindustrialization and technology policy. While an adequate macro-economic stabilization policy is indeed necessary to create a favourable climate for technological change and reindustrialization, it is, by itself not a sufficient condition to induce the necessary innovative activity that constitutes a primary element in economic and social development. Poor macro-economic conditions are not favourable to radical innovation and weak aggregate demand and uncertainties about the future both have their negative repercussions regarding investment behaviour in general, and investment in new product and process technologies in particular. Such poor conditions would mainly lead to further automating existing industries.

With respect to the size of (future) innovative efforts, it is more than probable that reduced manufacturing profitability and subsequent reduction in real company r&d outlays diminish the sources of future innovations and hence the opportunities for future economic growth. Uncertainty concerning future economic developments may give rise to risk-averting behaviour, consisting of a shift to less radical projects with short-payback periods, thus influencing the nature of the innovative efforts: a tendency towards incremental innovation to the detriment of radical technological change.

A balanced and integrated reindustrialization and technology policy contains three primary and interrelated elements determining the innovative potential of the industrial sector. The three elements are: technological opportunity; structure of the industrial sector (including finance); size and structure of market-demand.

It is apparent that in an approach towards reindustrialization defined as 'the structural transformation of industry into higher added value, more knowledge-intensive sectors and product groups, and the creation of major new technology-based industries serving new markets', science and technology are necessary, although not sufficient elements: in other words they are primarily enabling factors. On the supply side, the technical and scientific infrastructure should obviously be aligned with the industrial sector. This means that not only is the structure of the industrial sector itself of great importance to reindustrialization, but also its coupling with the infrastructure. Markets are obviously of foremost importance to the industrial sector and should be looked at not only from a more traditional standpoint of access, size, and tariff-barriers, but also from a more dynamic and cultural technology-led viewpoint including such concepts as 'leading markets' and 'public acceptance' of new products and services.

The three elements determining the innovative potential are now described below in more detail.

Technological opportunity

An essential element in reindustrialization and technology policy is the generation and the transfer of scientific and technological knowledge. In an effort to enforce product development activities industry should be stimulated to execute more r&d of its own. Next to this, there is the transfer problem. 'Knowledge' as an input-factor to industry is transferred in two main ways: first, knowledge is incorporated in the labour supply of industry via the labour market. The currently perceived importance of education and training can well be illustrated and measured by the considerable financial allocations to this area; the financial means in question represent a significant share of overall government budgets. At the same time, relatively little attention is being paid to the development of coupling mechanisms, interfaces, between the educational system and its 'clients', an important client being industry.

The high cost, waste, and demotivation of the educational system in many industrial countries is such that adjustment of coupling mechanisms as well as of curricula deserves high priority. The second main technology transfer path consists of direct knowledge and hardware transfers to industry from the technical and scientific infrastructure; mainly wholly or partially publicly funded r&d institutions including universities and industrial research institutes.

An important development in the r&d system in industrialized societies is that the volume of r&d in industry is rather rapidly increasing over that in the university. In the Netherlands the industry/university ratio is 2:1; in Japan the ratio is 6:1. The continued growth in this ratio has caused the leading edge in a number of scientific and technological areas to be now located in industry. It is the challenging task of industry, universities and government to devise structures to transfer knowledge from industry to the university necessary for the education of students. In Japan and in the USA this phenomenon has led to the establishment of accredited 'universities' as part of industrial firms. Not only is this the case with respect to the beta sciences (Wang University), a recent announcement by Anderson to establish a university implies that this is now also the case in the area of accountancy.

Within the framework of reindustrialization and technology policy, it is clearly important to restructure the pattern of allocation of public funds, skilled manpower supply and public r&d facilities in such a way that they better match the requirements of the market sector. To achieve this, of course, it is equally clear that industry needs to establish as precisely as possible, its perceived set of current and future needs. Incentives should thus be provided to the orientation of these resources to answering the pressing scientific and technical requirements of the market sector. This stronger orientation to the problems of the market sector may be achieved not only by changes in the methods of funding infrastructural research, but also by establishing new and different relationships between industry and infrastructure.

Structure of the industrial sector

In a model of postwar industrial evolution the changes in industrial structure can be described as associated with the maturization of a set of techno-economic combinations. Also, the often described role of new technology based firms (NTBFs) in the emergence of the semiconductor and CAD industries in the United States presents clear evidence of the availability of rapid diffusion processes. These points suggest that the emergence of new techno-economic combinations is often associated with the innovative and/or funding endeavour of large corporations coupled to vigorous entrepreneurial activities of NTBFs. More recently the emergence of the new wave biotechnology industry (started by spinoff entrepreneurs from universities) again illustrates the importance of NTBFs during the early phases of industrial evolution. In addition, it demonstrates the increase in small firm/large firm complementarities taking place in the infant biotechnology industry. These points suggest that from a standpoint of industrial structure, an important feature of the emergence of new combinations is the system of dynamic complementarity established between small (new) and large (established) firms. Thus, an important feature of reindustrialization policy lies in stimulating the appropriate complementary dynamism between large and small firms.

Complementarity and collaboration can, of course, exist throughout the industry life cycle; for example between 'colleague' suppliers operating in the same market, a form of collaboration which varies from joint development to joint production and sales. Complementarity may also take the form of contacts between manufacturer and user or between manufacturer and supplier(s). It is clear, moreover, that these contacts should be stronger the more technically sophisticated and complex is the product involved.

In Japan, in contrast to the United States, the role of NTBFs in the remarkable structural transformation that has taken place since 1945 has been very small. Large, conglomerate corporations and trading firms have demonstrated remarkable corporate flexibility and dynamism during the rapid technological catching-up (and subsequent overtaking of Europe in some areas) achieved by Japanese industry. Even here, however, a system of many 'tied' subcontractors, has provided the industrial giants with a great deal of flexibility in certain aspects of their operations, mainly in production.

An important element of the structure of the industrial sector is the financing system. Just as European governments have begun to provide special funds to support r&d activities of existing small- and medium-sized firms, such as the Instir system in the Netherlands, so also have they taken steps to increase the flow of venture capital to stimulate the establishment and growth of NTBFs. Venture capital schemes in Europe have taken a number of forms: both wholly public or private and public/private mixes. The traditional risk-avoiding financing institutions, including pension funds, are now getting more and more involved in the venture capital business. Although the present schemes would still need considerable development, venture capital is now available and adds an important and necessary element to the structure of the industrial sector.

In the more generic field of finance, three broad areas of policy should be regarded.

Finance for r&d. This includes orienting finance of infrastructurally-based r&d towards stimulating developments in main priority areas and in facilitating transfers to industry. It also includes utilizing government grants to orienting industrial r&d towards reindustrialization projects and achieving complementarity between the industrial and infrastructural streams of technological development.

Finance and industrial structure. This involves influencing financing systems (both public and private) towards achieving the appropriate industrial structural dynamism. In general, it means increasing the availability of 'patent' money for long-term restructuring programmes in firms and venture capital for new technology-based start-ups.

Overall fiscal climate. This involves establishing an overall climate conducive to private investment in reindustrialization projects by favourable tax regimes, directed public expenditures, moderate interest rates and so on.

To function effectively, cooperation between firms must at least partly rest on social organization, eg, networks. A second form is the system of industrial standardization, a major problem in a not united Europe. There are four basic types of industrial standards: Information standards provide terminology and test and measurement methods for evaluating and quantifying product attributes. Compatibility standards specify properties that a product should have in order to be compatible with a complementary product or system. Variety reduction standards limit the product to having only a certain range of allowable characteristics such as physical dimensions. Quality standards ensure an acceptable level of product performance along several dimensions including reliability, durability, efficiency, safety, and environmental impact.

Each of these standards reduces the cost and uncertainties inherent in market transactions, allows firms to specialize their product portfolios (since they can more readily rely on independent suppliers for inputs and complementary products), and thus achieve economies of scale in production and distribution. They also facilitate the entry of new firms into the activity by encouraging the development of independent sources of input and equipment supply (which reduces the capital costs of entry) and by limiting the technical uncertainty confronting potential buyers.

Size and structure of market demand

Size and structure of the demand side are also key elements in determining innovative performance. Consideration of market structures and dynamics is thus an important element in reindustrialization and technology policy.

Compared with Europe, the USA and Japan both have large internal markets which adapt easily to, and indeed help to create a technically sophisticated supply. Firms in these countries have to compete successfully in their national markets because of the severe levels of internal competition existing there. In the effectively fragmented markets in Europe, fierce competition on more than a national basis is often lacking, largely because of the existence of many non-tarrif barriers. Even within the EC, many obstacles prevent the functioning of one 'common' market; technical and administrative barriers to trade, and subsidies to industrial and agricultural firms all distort competition in the internal market. Trade liberalization, including the harmonization of standards within Europe, and abolishing non-tariff barriers, is a major avenue for European reindustrialization and technology policy and provide a sensible framework for achieving greater competitiveness in world markets.

The significance of the size and structure of 'local' respectively 'national' demand in determining the innovative performance of a particular region should not be underestimated. In lesser developed regions, firms are confronted with a mostly 'traditional' demand structure, which often is exerted by a small number of buyers. Policies aimed at improving the indigenous technological potential of a region should make development regions less vulnerable to the consequences of their currently one-sided and mostly traditional production-structure. This may in turn generate a qualitatively higher demand in terms of technology.

An important element of such policies is the creation of an innovation-oriented public procurement system. For a large variety of products governments provide substantial markets and are hence in a position to exercise their market-power in influencing the direction of supply towards higher valued-added, technologically more innovative products. Thus, public procurement policy can be considered an effective instrument to promote innovation and as a consequence to general new employment.

Procurement policy fits well with a description of the present economic situation. One of the primary aims of reindustrialization and technology policy must be the identification, stimulation and diffusion into use of the new technologies on which future economic growth can be based. The more traditional public policies of support, encouragement, experiment, and adaptation of new technologies should be complemented by more ambitious long-term, technology-stimulating procurement strategies. It is, however, clear that there is a great deal of tension between the requirements of innovation-oriented procurement strategies and the current policies of many Western countries which are primarily directed at reducing government deficits and are thereby reducing the deliberate market role of governments.

The success of reindustrialization and technology policy depends to a large extent on the acceptance of new products and services by society at large. Information programmes and awareness programmes for different target groups, including managers as well as the general public, should be strongly considered here. In this respect there is an obvious link with the educational system.

There exist strong relationships between the demand-side on the one hand, and the scientific and technological infrastructure on the other. Existing needs in society may influence or even force the scientific and technological research institutions to try to pave the way (in scientific or technological terms) to the fulfillment of these needs, ie, existing needs may establish the research agenda. On the other hand, it may be that the market becomes aware of previously unspecified needs as the result of the emergence of new technological opportunities, ie, technological opportunity determines the nature of a new set of market needs. Taking these interactions into account, the main factors determining innovative performance can be summarized in Figure 12.

Clearly reindustrialization and technology policy must simultaneously tackle all three elements of the above model. In addition, governments must provide a suitable regulatory framework in which all three elements can develop effectively.

In conclusion, it can be stated that at the level of the national and inter-

Figure 12   Factors determining innovative performance

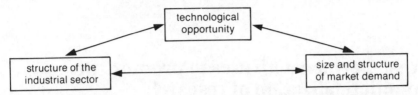

national economy governments generally realize the importance of technology for social and eocnomic development. At the same time it should be recognized that the technological potential can only be made effective in a framework incorporating the industrial structure and the volume and nature of markets.

Government initiatives to encourage technical innovation can hardly be expressed in numbers. It is the adjustment of the general environment favourable to innovation as well as the establishment of a number of specific measures that are required. Since both these generic and specific policy measures have to fit the social, economic and cultural environment of the countries involved, any superficial comparison would oversimplify the issue and could lead to misinterpretation of the factual situation.

References

1 This chapter is based on Rothwell R. and Zegveld W. 1985 *Reindustrialization and Technology*. Longman, London and M. E. Sharpe Inc., New York.

Aho C. M. and Rosen H. F. 1980 Trends in technology-intensive trade with special reference to US competitiveness *Science and Technology Indicators Conference*. OECD, Paris, 15–19 September.

Schumpeter J. A. 1939 *Business Cycles*. McGraw-Hill, New York.

West German activities to promote the commercialization of research

Gerhard Bräunling
Fraunhofer-Institut für Systemtechnik und Innovations Forschung

The support of new technology-based firms in the context of national innovation policies

In any attempt to portray systematically the development of technology and innovation policy in the Federal Republic of Germany, as in most industrialized countries, four (ideal) approaches can be identified, each of which is based on a different set of institutional, procedural and policy critera.

The first approach centres on the promotion of big science and large-scale technology (nuclear energy, aerospace). These large-scale technological programmes often focus on large-scale experimental or testing equipment, and have been carried out at government research establishments and in large corporations.

Technology transfer and support of commercialization in large-scale technical development must be seen on two levels: Primary transfer (or primary utilization) is achieved if the public sector or semi-private bodies (electricity supply industries, for example) procure and use the large-scale technical systems developed. Secondary technology transfer (ie the secondary utilization of research results) for further industrial fields of application has been considered very important in public discussions. The attempts at secondary transfer, which were most advanced in the USA in the context of the space programme (where they have acquired a marked justificatory function), have been extended to include systems for information transfer using data-base supported information and documentation systems.

The second approach to technology promotion is determined by the promotion of key technologies, such as electronic data processing or information technology, production, automation, microelectronics, new materials, or biotechnology. This approach is concerned in the first instance with efficient and technologically capable medium-sized firms and institutions which, both in the private and semi-private sectors, carry out contract r&d for industry. Forms of support of technology transfer and commercialization which are particularly typical of this approach are r&d contracts and the systematic utilization of research results.

In the third approach the emphasis in technology and innovation promotion is on support for the early diffusion of new technologies and for industrial modernization and rationalization schemes, which mainly relate specifically to small- and medium-sized companies. State aid is strongly concerned with the expansion and improvement of the scientific and technical infrastructure.

Transfer instruments appearing for the first time in this approach are technology and innovation advisory services and specific transfer of staff from research establishments to industry.

There is a fourth approach in innovation policy which focuses on the support of the creation and development of new industries. The starting point for public support is the entrepreneur in his attempt to commercialize technologically based products or services.

In the Federal Republic, the distribution of public funds for innovation clearly demonstrates a 'coexistence' of all four approaches. The Federal Government is mainly involved in the support of big science and key technologies, whereas state and regional bodies focus their promotional activities on assistance to firms and entrepreneurs.

The design and implementation of the experimental programme 'Support of New Technology Based Firms' (NTBFs)

In launching the experimental NTBF-scheme in 1983, the Federal Ministry for Research and Technology (BMFT) took a step towards a completely different philosophy of innovation promotion: for the first time, the object of the BMFT's support switched from 'r&d-projects' to 'entrepreneurs' who are about to start or have just started high-tech companies.

The NTBF-scheme pursues four aims: to create an atmosphere encouraging the founding of more new technology-based firms; to elaborate and test effective consultancy tools, services, and promotional instruments specificly tailored to the needs of NTBFs by means of an experimental programme; to stimulate financial institutions and venture capital companies to engage in the early stages of the financing of the NTBFs; and last but not least, to support directly the start and early development of NTBFs.

There are three types of possible beneficiaries of this scheme: people with technical background and technological capabilities intending to start a NTBF in manufacturing; existing NTBFs that are younger than three years, have less than ten employees, and are not majority owned (ie less than 50 per cent of their shares belong to another company whose aims differ from those of the new technology based firm); and engineering or consultancy firms which want to shift from services to manufacturing. Applications have to meet certain requirements in order to be accepted.

The innovation level of the new venture in question has to be so high that the development can be characterized in terms of 'new technology' or at least as the launching on the market of a very intelligent application of a new technology in terms of a new product or a new service. The entrepreneurs have to affirm that the new firms do not only want to develop the new product or service, but also intend to produce and sell it. Finally, the applicants must meet the requirements of one of the four specific approaches of the programme. The regional approach is confined to six regions where the publicly funded technology advisory centres selected are located, which provide extensive counselling services for NTBFs. The nation-wide approach is restricted to NTBFs applying microelectronic technologies or commercializing biotechnological developments. The science park approach extends the regional approach to firms located in fifteen selected incubator centres proposed by the States of location. The venture capital approach tries to stimulate and support the cooperation of NTBFs with venture capital companies and applies to NTBFs in which at least 25 per cent is financed by a venture capital company.

The present implementation of the experimental programme, which has been supplied with a budget of DM 325m for the years 1983–86, relies mainly on existing organizations and administrative procedures: selected regional innovation consultancy offices which had been built up five years earlier under the experimental scheme 'technology transfer and innovation consultancy'; the VDI Technology Centre, which has been in charge of microelectronics promotion and advisory scheme; the BMFT's traditional grant schemes for r&d projects which are administrated by the BMFT's promotional units; the Lastenausgleichsbank, a state bank which runs credit and guarantee schemes for business starters in general; and the Institute for Systems Analysis and Innovation Research (ISI) which is experienced in administrative and managerial back-up services, as well as in the monitoring and evaluation of innovation promotion programmes.

To ensure an efficient and fast execution of the new scheme, the experiences and capacities of these institutions have been used to assist in the implementation of the NTBF-scheme. The basic philosophy behind the promotional instruments of the scheme is a phase model of the development of a NTBF: in the founding phase, a business plan is drawn up (Phase I); in the development phase the young company develops a new product (Phase II); in the production phase the firm prepares and starts up its production and at the same time organizes the sales of the new product (Phase III).

Depending on the stage of development of a new technology-based firm, three different promotional instruments are applied. If there is no feasibility concept for the new firm, grants can be given to reduce the costs of consultants or experts engaged to assist in drawing up the business plan, doing market surveys, assessing the technological feasibility etc. These grants can be up to 90 per cent of the costs of consultancy but usually do not exceed DM 54 000. The work of the consultants should aim at sound records and expert's reports to allow an assessment of an innovative firm. The implementation of this socalled Phase I is performed by the innovation consultancy offices selected.

To support research and development projects, grants up to 75 per cent but not exceeding DM 900 000 can be given to young firms. In addition, guarantees by the Federal Government can be granted for bank loans needed to finance r&d projects. The guarantee may cover up to 50 per cent of the loan, but may not exceed a total of DM 150 000. Application and granting procedures for Phase II support are similar to BMFT's procedures for r&d grants. State guarantees will also be provided for bank loans needed to finance expenses for production start-up and market introduction costs. The guarantee covers 80 per cent of a bank loan for a maximum of DM 2 million. The Lastenausgleichsbank administrates the guarantees in Phase III.

Support under the experimental programme has to be applied for at every phase. However, it is not necessary to participate in every phase of the programme. As long as the requirements are met, a firm can enter the programme at any phase.

As we have seen in the United States, as well as in other European countries and in Japan, venture capital does not usually engage in early-stage financing. In the Federal Republic, however, the experimental programme tries to stimulate the venture capital market in three ways. First, by extending the programme and thereby opening up Phase I for venture capital companies, a didactic 'objective' is pursued. In the first twelve months, up to 80 per cent of the external consultancy expenses will be covered by governmental grants; in the subsequent twelve months, the percentage rate will be reduced to 60 per cent and after twenty-four months to 40 per cent. In this way venture capital companies should get used to evaluating NTBFs in their early stages. Second, the programme transfers to the venture capital companies the know-how regarding start-up counselling and specification of technology and marketing problems, which has been gained by the institutions engaged in implementing the programme. Last but not least, the stimulation and – direct and indirect – support of the development of a market for professionals skilled in the assessment and managerial assistance of NTBFs should create an environment in which a venture capital company can refer to experienced consultancy in fields in which it does not possess the required know-how itself.

Finally, a remark should be made on the role of the Fraunhofer Institute for Systems Analysis and Innovation Research (ISI). The ISI has been charged with the task of a programme support unit that does not deal with administrative matters. ISI work concentrates on the following main support activities. For the Federal Minister for Research and Technology the ISI acts as consultant on the further development of the experimental programme, produces progress reports about the implementation and effects of the programme, and monitors other public and private activities supporting NTBFs.

Furthermore, the ISI organizes the exchange of experiences between counsellors of the technology advisory agencies, the managers of incubator centres, and venture capital companies concerned with the programme; it also produces back-up services for the consultants in respect of managerial tools and the assessment and controlling of new ventures. The characteristics and development of the NTBFs are monitored by the ISI for the purpose of evaluating the programme. Finally, the Institute acts as information clearing house in NTBF matters, by issuing a NTBF newsletter, organizing seminars with banks and commercial consultants and by publishing the results of the NTBF programme.

Interim assessment

An assessment of the NTBF-programme will need information on the characteristics and development patterns of the NTBFs assisted as well as comparative information on a control group of non-sponsored NTBFs. It will also require information on the operations of the various institutions engaged in implementing the programme, and on changes in institutions and organizations dealing with NTBFs.

In the following sections we have to restrict ourselves: to describing some major characteristics of the entrepreneurs and ventures assisted, to comparing the results obtained so far with the goals set initially, and to assessing indirect effects on intermediate institutions dealing with NTBFs.

Some characteristics of the new firms and their founders

Initially, there were only vague ideas on the kind of innovations and the type of entrepreneurs to be supported. There was a widespread belief that young scientists from universities and research establishments with new products in the fields of microelectronics or biotechnology, needing assistance from technology consultants, would be the major group benefiting from the scheme.

An interim assessment which we performed recently showed a more differentiated picture. In Phase I (assistance in drawing up the business plan and its assessment), consultants were engaged (and sponsored) to perform the following jobs: market surveys (58 per cent); technological feasibility studies (43 per cent); working models (23 per cent); patent search (14 per cent); and business plan assessment (12 per cent). The average cost of an expert's report or service by a consultant was DM 30 000; almost 60 per cent of all firms supported so far (174) received grants to engage two or more experts.

The firm's founders and firms receiving support were concentrated in the electronics industry. The general dominance of microelectronics-based firms is reinforced by the fact that the NTBF-scheme has no regional limitations for applications from these firms:

Information and communications	50 per cent
measuring, analysing, testing instruments	23 per cent
data processing, software	17 per cent
communications technology	3 per cent
consumer electronics	3 per cent
electronic components	4 per cent
Mechanical engineering and mechatronics	26 per cent
machinery & tools	7 per cent
pumps, engines	4 per cent
traffic and transport technology	4 per cent
robotics	4 per cent
medical instruments	4 per cent
laser	3 per cent
Process engineering	21 per cent
process & systems engineering	20 per cent
biotechnology	1 per cent

Most of the entrepreneurs supported are experienced professionals, not youngsters. Their average age is thirty-eight years (only 12 per cent of them are thirty or younger.) Before they started their own company, they had held positions mainly as follows: in industry (51 per cent); at a university (15 per cent); at a research establishment (6 per cent); and in their own (service) company (11 per cent). On average they have eleven years of professional experience, not only in research posts (60 per cent), but also in management (22 per cent) and marketing positions (15 per cent). More than one quarter of them had previously been self-employed and most of them hold a university (66 per cent) or engineering college (21 per cent) degree.

NTBFs started by a 'team' have grown in importance. Initially, about one third of all new firms supported were founded by a team, and in the last six months, every second new firm was started by a team.

The entrepreneur candidates or firm founders plan to develop products, mainly investment goods (81 per cent). About half of these products may have wide applications, the others are to be sold in market niches or small market segments. Almost two-thirds of the new companies try to sell these products directly, the remainder will engage in original equipment manufactured (OEM)-products. More than half of the products will cost more than DM 10 000, and more than one sixth with a unit price in excess of DM 100 000.

Goal achievement

When comparing the effects of the programme observed so far with the initial goals, the following assessments can be made.

The first goal was general motivation and encouragement of technical people to entrepreneurship, especially in high-tech companies. The programme has contributed to a large extent to the creation of a broad public interest in entrepreneurship and has stimulated entrepreneur candidates to elaborate their product and business ideas. One must also realize, however, that the programme has been 'marketed' intensively by the regional consultancy offices, banks, incubator centres etc. Also the programme has been regarded as meeting the widespread reorientation in employment away from the public sector and large corporations towards smaller firms and self-employment, and the belief that entrepreneurial venturing in high tech offers the most profitable business opportunities.

To some extent the programme has facilitated the development of a public belief that the support of young high-tech companies could make a significant contribution to reducing unemployment, or to generating new industries. Though there is no empirical evidence to support these expectations, the widespread belief in NTBFs has created a general awareness of the roles and problems of new firms, and stimulated, or even forced, other public or semi-public actors (such as financial institutions, regional or local authorities, research establishments etc) to implement support actions for young entrepreneurs.

The second goal was the development and testing of appropriate and effective forms of assistance to NTBFs. After one year of implementation, the NTBF scheme has been revised and extended. The major changes are the extension of Phase I grants to venture capital firms to motivate them to engage in early stage financing, and the extension of the regional approach to include selected science parks. Formal and informal procedures in assessment, consulting, granting of subsidies and controlling of NTBFs have been steadily developed and improved.

According to a 'catalyst' concept of the experimental scheme, information and experiences in NTBF support (eg NTBF-newsletter, seminars, workshops) are exchanged on a regular basis with other institutions dealing with NTBFs (banks, state and local authorities, chambers of commerce and crafts, consultants). Thus these institutions are participating in a learning process and will be able to acquire the know-how necessary to take over elements of the NTBF-scheme after its termination.

The third goal involved the stimulation of banks and venture-capital companies to engage in early stage financing of NTBFs. On a formal level, this goal has been achieved already, one year after the scheme started. Until 1983, only one venture-capital company was operating in Germany, whereas today about thirty venture-capital companies are in business. These companies have been founded by management consultants, banks and large companies, banks and property management companies, savings banks and insurance companies. The capital announced and the fund volumes envisaged amount to a total of approximately DM 800 million. These venture-capital companies, however, failed to invest in more than forty NTBFs in the last two years, concentrating on early growth and second round financing.

About ten major savings banks provide risk capital in the form of so-called 'innovation loans', characterized by limited liabilities of the borrower in case of failure, the provision of commercial advice by the bank or an associated consultant, and various forms of commercial monitoring and controlling during the term of the credit.

The fourth goal was the direct support of NTBFs. At the moment, it seems to be too early to assess the commercial potential of the NTBFs promoted. The reasons for failures which will definitely occur (our estimate: 35 per cent) have yet to be analysed in detail. There are no empirical indications so far to support the argument proposed by critics that the NTBF scheme is 'seducing' candidate entrepreneurs into founding an NTBF and taking high-development risks (a pre-condition for support under the NTBF scheme), instead of starting a soft company which would have provided a sounder basis for business development.

Impact on the innovation infrastructure
The NTBF scheme not only has a direct impact on the firms assisted, but also facilitates longer-term changes in the so-called innovation infrastructure (ie the totality of actors offering information, consultancy, knowledge and know-how, capital and business opportunities to innovative firms, and the interaction structure between these actors).

Because of the high acceptance of the NTBF scheme and the funds allocated to it, other actors dealing with NTBFs have a chance to respond to it. They are doing so mainly by extending or intensifying existing NTBF-related activities; by offering new services or assistance activities; by coordinating or integrating existing efforts. A good example of the latter is provided by regional and local incubator centres, which are organized and financially assisted in joint actions by various acts (such as banks, chambers of commerce, local authorities).

Another important impact on the innovation infrastructure can be seen in the education and training of a significant number of people engaged in the operations of the NTBF scheme such as counsellors from the regional offices, commercial consultants providing expertises, bank managers and consultants assessing firms applying for risk bearing capital. Thus, learning costs associated with the development of an efficient assistance to NTBFs, and profitable cooperation and business relations with them, are covered by the NTBF scheme to a larger extent than merely direct assistance.

When looking at the infrastructural impact of the NTBF programme, a new role for government appears. The traditional role of promotion by financial assistance becomes less relevant, with more emphasis on the new role of catalyst. This is realized by taking on the risks of experiments and initiatives, by providing a forum for the exchange of information, experiences and opinions, by assisting in consensus' formation and by initiating and supporting cooperation between the various actors of the innovation infrastructure.

It is this role of catalyst that some authors ascribe to Japan's MITI. In West Germany, it is not yet well understood, accepted and performed by governmental officials. It requires more acceptance of risk-bearing, more imagination and less use of money and authority by the governmental institutions concerned, and it provides less visible results in cases of success.

Government initiatives to encourage technological innovation: the Ben Franklin Partnership Initiative

Walter Plosila
US Department of Commerce

In an increasingly complex and technology-driven society, higher education is being recognized as a critical asset for improving a state and local economic base. The assets higher education institutions provide range from the more traditional function of educating a future workforce to providing an environment to stimulate technological innovation, or to performing a direct entrepreneurial role. Each of the differing objectives, along with alternative activities, based on these objectives, to build business/higher education/government partnerships in support of economic development will be discussed in this paper.

Objectives

In the United States, different localities, regions and institutions are approaching the development of business/higher education/government partnerships, with varying and in some cases, multiple objectives. Some partnerships focus simply on development of better relationships and communications between the private sector and higher education, in expectation of additional funding support for the institution. Other partnerships focus on improving basic and fundamental knowledge in the sciences. Some are used to help secure additional support to build and equip new facilities with the objective of producing better educated students. And still others contain multiple objectives: ensuring that research and development leads to commercial applications which helps to diversify the economic base through new firms and jobs and an improved competitive position for existing firms. The multiple objectives of these partnerships affect the types of relationships and the activities to be undertaken by a higher education institution in support of economic development.

Background

The impetus for the increased focus on government/business/higher education partnerships are multiple in nature. One factor is that we are going through a major explosion of our knowledge base in this country. It is important to recognize that knowledge is moving rapidly out of the laboratory, whether a university laboratory or a private sector laboratory, and into the market place. If that transfer has appeared rapid in the last five to six years, it will be even more rapid in the next ten years. This is very important, because it indicates where our job growth will be and the kind of industries which will dominate the economy in the future. It will affect what and how we produce.

The second important factor is that 90 per cent of the workforce in the year 1990 is already working today and 75 per cent of the workforce in the year 2000 is in the workforce today. We not only face a rapidly changing technology but we must recognize that much adult education and retraining will be necessary, because so much of the future workforce is already working.

The third factor is that technology will affect all occupational groups. There is a widespread myth that says 'we should not worry too much about high technology' because it will not create very many jobs. If you define high technology narrowly, it is true that the absolute number of jobs created in those fields is not large according to most projections. However, states have not focused their efforts and plans on just high technology. The historical example of a broader view is the California situation. California had a very large job growth in the 1970s; however, most of that job growth was not in the Silicon Valley firms which made the computers, chips or whatever. Most of the new jobs were in other industries such as trade, wholesale, and other service sectors which purchased and used technology. The rate of technological change and its effects on the workforce suggest that we must also be concerned about adapting technology to our existing industries so that they can be modernized, be competitive, and stay in business, if not expand. All workers regardless of skill or title, in some way, will be users of technology.

The fourth factor is that to maintain our competitive edge and meet the needs for employment of our citizens, we must encourage entrepreneurship. Most of the job growth in the nation will come from small firms. And, as the National Science Foundation has noted, most of the technological innovations in the last fifty years have come from small firms. This will most likely continue to be the case.

Activities

The past five to ten years have seen a significant increase in the number of higher education/business/government partnerships in support of economic development in the United States. Much of the impetus is based on the widely known successes of the Silicon Valley/Stanford University area of California and the Route 128 development complex associated with the Massachusetts Institute of Technology in Boston, Massachusetts. More recently, the Research Triangle in North Carolina has received similar attention. However, its successes have generally been in attracting the r&d operations of major corporations rather than having its faculty and students start up their own businesses in the area. Many areas in the United States are attempting to emulate these three success stories but in different ways.

Some are attempting this through the development and building of new research parks which may contain as their initial core-tenant a 'centre of excellence' research institute. These efforts are focused on attracting into an area new firms and industries with the centre of excellence serving as the magnet. This approach may simply represent a response to changes in the US economy from an industrial and manufacturing to a service and information based one. The result is research parks with multiple-tenant facilities rather than traditional parks composed of single tenant manufacturing operations.

In contrast to the emphasis on research parks, a number of higher education/

business/government partnerships tend to be entrepreneur-oriented, resulting in an alternative to the bricks and mortar physical manifestation – what are termed 'small business incubators'. Similar in design and operation to those in parts of Great Britain and elsewhere in Europe, they represent a more formal expression of efforts of higher education and business partnerships to replicate the Stanford University and MIT experiences. Entrepreneur approaches tend to focus on home-grown entrepreneurship, that is, on start-up firms locally, rather than attracting into an area firms from the outside. While not receiving the same public media attention as the research park, they are relatively inexpensive approaches, usually relying on rehabilitation of older buildings. Route 128 and the Silicon Valley, according to most knowledgeable observers, represented the accumulation of an extensive number of individual entrepreneur decisions. Higher education entrepreneurship efforts, combined with development of nearby incubator space, attempt to replicate this pattern, but with greater structure and direction.

Models for business/university/government partnerships
There is no one model approach in the United States for higher education institutions' involvement in economic development. In fact, in recent years, flexibility and experimentation seem to be the key words, with a wide variety of approaches being undertaken by American higher education institutions in concert with state and local governments and the private sector.

One major approach has been to establish centres of excellence within certain fields by a higher education institution or consortium of institutions. Such centres are felt to be effective magnets leading not only to the spinoff of new technologies and firms but also serving to attract development. Home to four of the top fifty graduate research universities in the United States, Pennsylvania had not experienced the entrepreneur benefits over the past several decades that had occurred in California or Massachusetts.

In an effort to serve as a catalyst or facilitator for local economic development, the Commonwealth of Pennsylvania initiated a programme called the Ben Franklin Partnership. Proposed by Governor Dick Thornburgh in February 1982, four Advanced Technology Centers were established in March 1983. The Centers are located at the Pennsylvania State University in University Park; a joint Center of the University of Pittsburgh and Carnegie-Mellon University in Pittsburgh; Lehigh University in the Allentown-Bethlehem area; and the University City Science Center (which includes the University of Pennsylvania, Drexel University and Temple University) in Philadelphia.

The Ben Franklin Partnership features a decentralized approach which relies on local initiative to identify critical technologies, develop entrepreneurship efforts and redirect existing education and training programmes to the workforce needs of the future. While the four centres are based at research universities, they are operated by policy boards that represent consortiums of the region's colleges and universities, business, labour, local government, and other groups and organizations. In total, 123 of the state's higher educational facilities and 1700 private sector firms have been involved in projects at one or more of the centres.

Each of the four centres is required to provide assistance in three areas: joint research and development with the private sector, with an emphasis on applied research; education and training; and entrepreneurial development. State funding is provided on an annual competitive basis among the four centres based on past performance and proposed programmes for the succeeding year. Each of the centres selected four r&d centres of excellence in which it focuses its efforts, based both on faculty expertise and private sector interest. State funds are distributed on the basis of individual projects rather than for each r&d area. A set of identified projects between specific private firms and college and university faculties make up each of the four research centres of excellence.

Private sector firms must signify interest in pursuing a given project, must provide sufficient matching funds first, before government funds are released, and must have received a guarantee of the college's or university's involvement based on the project's technical merit. Education and training projects are directed at providing new services or filling gaps in existing education and training programmes. Entrepreneurship activities range from providing management and business services to incubator tenants to providing engineering graduate or law school students services to start-up firms.

Pennsylvania's Ben Franklin Partnership is one of the few comprehensive approaches to linking higher education and economic development. It includes project funding, centres of excellence, technology transfer, and entrepreneurial development support. This is not the usual approach found in the United States for business/higher education/government partnership in support of economic development. For example, both Ohio and New York emphasize centres of excellence; Alabama emphasizes technology transfer; Texas and Arizona focus on entrepreneurial development. In the case of Pennsylvania, it was felt that a singular focus would not take full advantage of all of the higher education assets nor give maximum impetus to diversifying our economic base.

The philosophy of the Ben Franklin Partnership can be summarized as follows. First, the programme depends heavily upon involving, using and working through the private sector. If we move too rapidly and simply spend money on problems, we may end up with traditional university research and development but no real private–public partnerships that will sustain themselves over the long term. Consequently, public funding has increased from $1 million to $10 million to $18 million to $21.6 million over the past four years.

Second, the approach is decentralized into four centres that are operated as consortiums. The centres are located at research universities; however, they are operated by consortiums which include members of business, labour, economic development groups and other organizations. Mobilizing and organizing the consortiums are very important aspects, otherwise the groups would be bidding on the available money without any prospect of working together or being innovative.

Third, the approach is competitive. The funds are not divided evenly among the four centres, whether it is $18 million in 1984 or $21.3 million in 1985. We make the centres compete with each other to attract private-sector involvement, private-sector match, and to create jobs – which is the bottom line of the programme. For example, in 1985 on a competitive basis funding to the four centres ranged from a high of nearly $5.9 million to a low of $4.7 million in state money.

The objective is simple. The Partnership aims to adapt rapidly the research to the commercial marketplace. One way to comercialize research is by having the private sector work jointly with colleges and universities. And as a result, this will help to create private jobs in the Commonwealth of Pennsylvania.

The research and development benefits both research on the leading edge of technology and the application of technology to traditional industries. One university is working in a traditional industry, with a glassmaker, using the university's expertise with CAD/CAM and applying it to glass cutting in order to minimize wasted glass. Very few would consider glass as a high-technology industry; however, when they use technology it helps the firm to stay in business.

In addition, there are projects with the construction industry and the clothing industry. Carnegie-Mellon in Pittsburgh is working with machine shops throughout western Pennsylvania – from Erie to Altoona to Washington County – to apply existing robotics technology to those small machine shops that need modernizing in order to survive.

On the other side of the equation, there is research and development on the cutting edge of technological development ranging from the world's first intelligence construction robot, a portable scanner, use of fibre as an anti-microbial agent, to an epileptic seizure detection apparatus, and electro-chemical sensors for steel making.

Beyond research and development, all of the higher educational institutions, community colleges, vocational and technical schools are being helped to fill gaps in their education and training activities. Money is not being used as a supplement to traditional, categorical grant programmes, rather, to make certain that the curricula and the training opportunities offered by community colleges are what the private sector needs for the future in terms of a skilled workforce. For example, one community college is developing a new course in conjunction with one of the research universities. The research university provides or shares equipment, helps train faculty, and then works with them to actually develop the courses. Another example is an on-site business and education training centre at one of the research parks in which twenty-eight colleges and universities are providing seminars, skill upgrading and training for the employees in that research park. It is the first centre of its kind in the United States.

The third area of activity undertaken by the four Ben Franklin Partnership Centers is entrepreneurial development. Entrepreneurial development efforts attempt aggressively to identify inventors and link them with entrepreneurs. Since the Ben Franklin Partnership programme began linking inventors with entrepreneurs, it has been a priority and has attracted approximately $22 million in venture capital to the projects. In addition, a set of services to firms are provided so that they are able to participate in government programmes – such as securing federal Small Business Innovation Research (SBIR) Act funds – an effort in which Pennsylvania moved into a *fourth* rank among the fifty states this year in SBIR awards made.

Finally, there are or will be incubator facilities in place for each of the centres. Incubators basically have three ingredients: low-cost space and a cloistered environment for start-up firms during their first few months or years; a set of services to assist small firms; and a set of entry and exit policies to assure the facility is used for entrepreneurs, not as a multi-tenement building or professional office building.

An environment is provided in which they can prosper more easily, share expenses with each other, and share some service costs. They have access to secretaries, attorneys, and a whole set of business services. Incubators, in essence, have low-cost and shared operations; they are not simply a professional office building.

There have been some interesting experiences already with the incubator facilities. One firm began two years ago with three employees in an incubator and now has twenty-one employees and has purchased its own building. This is significant growth in a short period of time. One incubator is in a vacant school building that basically is being leased with a low rent rate to the local industrial development authority which manages the incubator space. There are also $17 million in additional funds for incubator facilties which the voters approved in 1984. Basically, this is used for loans for bricks and mortar and equipment as part of an incubator facility. The Ben Franklin Partnership funds are used for services – not bricks and mortar.

The intent of the Ben Franklin Partnership programme is to focus efforts upon a home-grown economic development strategy. It aims to help existing firms to stay in business and expand and start up new firms. In fact, according to some of the national studies, some of the reasons Pennsylvania has not done as well as some of the Sunbelt states is the fact that there is a greater level of absolute number of plant closings (not relocations to Sunbelt) and a much lower 'birth rate' of small firms. Recently, Dun and Bradstreet reported in 1984 that Pennsylvania's birth rate of new firms was above the national rate and the death rate of small firms was lower than the national rate.

Technological innovation programmes such as Pennsylvania's Ben Franklin Partnership should be recognized as long-term programmes. By themselves, these programmes will not determine the community's and the region's economic fate. However, they represent some fundamental shifts in how higher education institutions can and should be involved in economic development in partnership with government and the private sector. And the early results attest to the programme's success.

The Partnership involves all types of higher education institutions in many different roles in local economic development. A small liberal arts college has used funding to establish a new biomedicine technician programme and attracted venture capital as a result of its biomedical research. One university has shown it can assist a traditional industry by applying CAD/CAM to the clothing industry. Twenty-eight colleges and universities in the Greater Philadelphia area provide courses and certificate programmes, on-site, to over eighty firms and thousands of employees in a new technology and research park outside Philadelphia. Another university is developing new training programmes for displaced steel workers in the Mon Valley of Western Pennsylvania.

The private sector has developed new, sustained relationships with higher education institutions. The Ben Franklin Partnership requires $1 of matching support from the private sector, university and other sources. In the current year, every $1 of state funds is being matched by $3.80 in private and other funds. $21.3 million in state funds this year is being matched with over $80 million. Since the programme began, $50 million in public funds has leveraged a match of nearly $170 million, the most leveraged and largest annual state technological innovation programme in the United States.

The programme is attracting new financing to assist start-up firms. Accounting, legal and other firms provide donated services to start-up firms. Venture capital is being attracted to funded projects and totals over $22

million in the first twenty-six months of the Ben Franklin Partnership programme. The r&d centres of excellence at each of the four Advanced Technology Centers are serving as a new type of magnet – for venture capital. And
in just over two years, the four centres have assisted in the start up of 184 new
firms and the expansion of 121 existing firms, contributing to more than 1600
new jobs while assisting 127 firms to retain 834 existing jobs.

More focus is being given to existing firms and start-up firms by local
economic development groups, in contrast to their previous focus on attracting
firms from outside the state. The Ben Franklin Partnership has assisted fifteen
of the twenty small business incubators currently operating in the Commonwealth. By providing low-cost space and a set of management and business services, incubators create a nurturing process for firms that otherwise
might not even be in business. In addition to developing the largest number of
operating incubators of any state in the United States, Pennsylvania's Ben
Franklin Partnership funds innovative entrepreneur assistance programmes
such as the Enterprise Corporation of Pittsburgh. This local economic development group works in close association with the two research universities
in Pittsburgh to help start up firms obtain financing, fund entrepreneur
education courses and seminars, and otherwise help develop business plans,
etc. Pennsylvania's incubators also include the Homer Research Laboratory in
Bethlehem, donated by Bethlehem Steel; three vacant school buildings; a
former post office, and a former zipper plant.

The Ben Franklin Partnership has contributed to new relationships among
local government, local economic development groups, and their counterparts
within a region and between regions of the state. In Philadelphia, Ben Franklin
Partnership support has helped capitalize seed venture-capital funds with
three local organizations, two of which are city agencies – a new local government role. Similarly, in Philadelphia, five medical colleges and several
universities pooled for the first time their faculty to secure designation as a
National Aeronautics and Space Administration (NASA) Center for
Bioprocessing and Pharmaceutical Research. In many communities, incubator
services to tenants have brought groups and organizations together that previously worked separately. The Lehigh Center even provided training to
elected local officials on the dynamics of technological innovation and its
implications for local decision making. And finally, in 1983 and 1984, all of
Pennsylvania's research universities, government officials and business communities united behind a successful effort to locate the new US Department of
Defense Software Engineering Institute at Carnegie-Mellon University in
Pittsburgh.

Conclusion
The Ben Franklin Partnership represents but one approach in the United
States to higher education/business/government partnerships in support of
economic development. Universities in the United States are increasingly
recognizing the need to devote more attention to such relationships. In so
doing, the historic and traditional patterns are changing. A more active, direct
and entrepreneurial role for the higher education sector is emerging.

There are several issues that must be addressed as these new roles emerge.
University administrator attitudes may be critical to the success of these
ventures. Colleges and universities have as a fundamental mission the

education of a student. Their reward structures, including tenure, do not always encourage involvement in such government/education/business relationships. There are activities the university should not and probably cannot perform, such as direct product development. But there are a wide variety of relationships that can be developed, depending on the attitudes of the institution, its strengths and the needs and desires of the business community.

Both business and higher education must reach accommodation as to what their respective objectives are and how they can be achieved. With government representing a third party in such relationships the result may be additional objectives. These objectives will help determine the activities to emphasize – whether they be centres of excellence, technology transfer, entrepreneur education and training, project grants, a combination of these such as Pennsylvania's Ben Franklin Partnership, or some other approach. The physical manifestation of these activities generally results in varying emphasis on research parks and/or incubators.

Comparative advantage is a critical factor in developing a higher education role in economic development. Colleges and universities vary in relative strengths. R&D emphasis, in particular should build on such strengths. But it also should be recognized that higher education r&d includes capabilities to assist traditional and existing industries, such as through application of process technologies such as sensors, computer and robotics.

In many cases, local, regional, and state government officials can play an important facilitator or catalyst role in business–higher education partnerships. While such subnational involvement in the promotion of technological innovation is relatively recent; subnational governments in the United States are critically situated to encourage and facilitate the process of technological innovation.

Subnational government policies, support for education and training, full development of university and industry research linkages and technical and management support to small business are part of many state and local economic development strategies. In Pennsylvania, not only the state's, but both Philadelphia and Pittsburgh's strategies, build upon one of their comparative advantages – higher education. Higher education institutions of all kinds in the United States, from major national research universities to liberal arts colleges to technical institutes, are demonstrating that they can contribute meaningfully to economic development efforts through effective partnerships with the business community and public agencies.

References

Doyle H. and Brisson C. 1985 *Partners in growth: business–higher education development strategies.* Northeast-Midwest Institute, Washington.

Technology and growth: state initiatives in technological innovation. Final Report of the Task Force on Technological Innovation of the National Governors' Association, 1983.

Johnson, L. G. 1984 *The high-technology connection: academic/industrial cooperation for economic growth.* ASHE-ERIC Higher Education Research Report No. 6. Association for the Study of Higher Education, Washington, DC.

Innovation and entrepreneurship initiatives in Australia

Norbert Nimmervoll, L. A. Balzer
Royal Melbourne Institute of Technology

Australia's manufacturing sector has largely had a history of hiding behind protectionist walls to produce products for the local market either under licence or copying overseas successes. Entrepreneurs have generally stayed away from manufacturing and looked to areas such as mining, land speculation and the media. Many indicators of the malaise of the Australian manufacturing sector could be given. Examples are: employment in the electronics industry halved over the ten years from 1970 to 1980 (this may be unique in the world!); Australia's total computer related exports did not match its computer hardware imports from Ireland in 1982; the software industry, seen as one of the few success areas in high tech in Australia, exported less than 5 per cent by value of its product in 1982; gross expenditure on research and development by industry continues to decline from an already very low base (government expenditure on research and development is eight times as great as that of private industry). Private sector employment in research and development declined 5 per cent from 1978–79 to 1981–82.

Because Australia has traditionally looked to primary exports and lately to the mining sector for wealth generation, there has been little government interest in making manufacturing competitive until the 1980s. It was not until 1982, at the height of recession and high unemployment that it was realized that manufacturing was important after all. One result of this has been an interest in new policy areas to promote innovation and new technology business.

Before considering these policies, it is necessary to point out that the Australian system of government is a federal one, with six state governments as well as the national or commonwealth government. The various state governments have considerable independence and local flexibility to carry out initiatives. The Commonwealth government on the other hand is often constrained by having to appear evenhanded with each state when attempting to develop new programmes.

Innovation related initiatives

For innovation development to occur and develop into a significant economic and social phenomenon appropriate conditions need to exist in three areas: access to adequate funding, mechanisms for fostering new ideas, and an appropriate support infrastructure.

Funding

Funding issues are, firstly, adequate access to equity funding, ie, venture capital and the ability to trade in equity, ie, a secondary board market. Also necessary is access to loan funding appropriate to technology businesses (eg, against future business activity and not current assets) and the minimization of the cost burden of developing a new business or product through appropriate taxation and government grant initiatives. As has been demonstrated by the Australian experience, correcting the funding issues is the most straightforward of the three environmental factors for innovation growth.

Venture capital   The Commonwealth government introduced a scheme whereby investors could claim 150 per cent tax deductibility for investments placed in licensed Management Investment Companies (MIC) in August 1983. The most important consequence of this initiative was that it caused financial institutions in general to consider venture capital (to determine whether an MIC licence was worth having), and a significant level of venture capital activity has resulted at little cost to the public purse.

In addition, the Commonwealth and state governments have themselves moved into becoming venture capital providers in varying degrees and generally at arms length through development corporations. For example, the Australian Industries Development Corporation (AIDC) is a Commonwealth government statutory authority able to raise funds in the capital market. In the past much of its activity was mining and related to large companies. It is now involved in equity investments in biomedical engineering, biotechnology and new materials technology.

Secondary board market   The public servants responsible for the MIC programme immediately recognized the need for a mechanism to trade in equity without having to seek full stock exchange listing and encouraged the development of a secondary board market. In this they were helped considerably by the high level of rivalry which exists between states and hence state governments, the smaller states being keen to break the financial dominance of Sydney and Melbourne. A secondary board was first established in 1984 in Perth, where trading in technology stock is already brisk.

Loan funding   Traditionally banking in Australia has been extremely assets-oriented and thus conservative when considering new business ventures. Most manufacturing companies therefore had to rely on retained earnings and overdraft facilities for meeting cash requirements.

Since 1982 state governments in particular have made a significant impact on freeing funding for industry development through providing loan guarantees and, where necessary, loans. For example, the Victorian Economic Development Corporation (VEDC) in Melbourne changed from a government mechanism for funding decentralization in 1981, to loaning 42 per cent of its funds to technology-based companies in 1983, and being a major guarantor for loans from banks for such companies. It is interesting to note that the VEDC has been extremely successful financially as a consequence.

In addition, the Australian government has recently deregulated the banking industry, allowing the entry of a number of new foreign banks. An immediate consequence has been that all banks have had to broaden their business base, becoming more flexible in their policy towards business loans.

Conclusions about funding for innovation   In the short space of three years Australia has been able to move from a situation of a lack of funding for new ventures to one where the limitation is suitable investment opportunites. As a consequence a number of doubtful investment risks are already beginning to appear on secondary boards, and a shakeout is inevitable. However, in the short time indicated sufficient success stories have already been established for this type of investment to be a permanent part of the Australian financial scene. For example, a company with a new paint-curing process achieved listing on the main stock exchange board and its shares moved from $0.50 on listing in November of 1983 to $13 by February of 1984. Labtam, a local computer company, has been able to grow at a rate of approximately 300 per cent over a year with venture capital injection, and so on.

Fostering new ideas
The development of new products and services requires the encouragement of individual inventors and of r&d throughout industry. These are much more difficult areas for government to influence through policy change because success depends on modifying attitudes.

Inventors/innovators assistance   The Commonwealth government has had an Assistance to Inventors Scheme in place for the last five years. This scheme was largely the result of pressure from the inventors association and until recently provided up to $10 000 in assistance for prototype construction. As could have been predicted, the results of the scheme have been marginal. Because funds were limited, careful screening of applications was required causing long processing delays and hence discouraging applications (self-regulating but not discriminating for quality). Single inventors rarely have the capacity or resources to take an invention from concept/bread board stage to a prototype likely to lead to commercialization. Furthermore, market assessment was lacking.

Recently there has been an attempt to address the final point by having innovation centres provide an independent delay in the approval process. The scheme is now under review, one option being canvassed is to fund the innovation centres in each state to administer it.

Assisting inventors is, of course, made difficult by the certain knowledge that the vast majority of ideas will not be commercialized. The trick is to pick the few inventions with commercial potential (a non-trivial task!) and to deal with the remainder of the inventors in a way which avoids them from feeling cheated.

Encouranging industry r&d   As already indicated, Australia has a poor record of industrial r&d and its performance has continued to decline. Government funding of r&d is eight times that of industry. In fact, funds from overseas companies (and most large companies in Australia are) halved from 1978–79 to 1981–82. Government encouragements for r&d has, until very recently, been based on a grants system with a commencement grant component (for first-time applicants with a high likelihood of success) and project grants.

Companies generally perceived the system as a way of 'getting back some of their taxes' and looked to maximize their grant for minimum real r&d. The government has recently bowed to industry pressure and introduced a 150 per cent tax deduction for r&d in addition to retaining the grants.

For the majority of local manufacturing industry, the decision is whether or not to stop being a manufacturer and increasingly become a re-seller of imports (generally a better and more profitable existence). Promoting industrial r&d to managers and stockholders will effectively be a long educational process.

Commercializing government-sector r&d   As government research laboratories, universities and tertiary institutes come under increasing financial pressure, and community demand for a demonstration of 'return-on-taxpayers-investment', such organizations have increasingly looked to ways of generating commercial benefit from their research efforts. Many universities and institutes of technology have established companies for this purpose (in part this is the role of Technisearch, see below). The West Australian Institute of Technology has gone to the extent of being party to the successful application for a licence as a management investment company (ie, a venture capitalist).

Support infrastructure
Critical for Australia today is the rapid development of a support infrastructure for new technology development. Without it, the interest generated in investing in new technology will increasingly look to investing outside the country, and the attitudinal changes necessary to foster new ideas with commercial potential will not occur. Support mechanisms required are, of course, wide and varied and include: helping industry to introduce new methods; reducing the investment cost necessary (in people and time) to use new technologies in products; and increasing the ability of a company to penetrate export markets.

Focusing, however, only on the contributions an innovation centre might make, they are: reducing the cost and development time required to take inventions to innovations with commercial interest. This is a major role for innovation centres. The majority of the commercialization of innovations will occur in existing companies and, hence, the need is for effective information networks to maximize technology/ideas transfer. For innovations leading to business start-ups risk of failure can greatly be reduced by locating them in an environment minimizing start-up costs through shared resources and experiences – an incubator for start-ups. The centres might also increase the pool of individuals interested and capable of promoting innovation and entrepreneurship.

Innovatory organizations in Australia   The first organization established in 1979 to assist in the innovation process in Australia was the Australian Innovation Corporation (AIC), a private company with many of the major corporations as shareholders. The objective of this private company was to 'utilize the r&d capabilities of its shareholders to help inventors commercialize their inventions'. It had failed by 1983 because inventors' access to the laboratories of member companies had to compete with the companies' mainstream tasks and because shareholders demanded short-term results.

In 1982 the Commonwealth government funded the establishment of an innovation centre within the Victorian Chamber of Manufacturers (VCM) in Melbourne, with direct involvement in its management by the Inventors Association. The chamber's motivation was to try to get new products to its members, and the centre began with an open-house policy towards inventors. By 1984 this centre found that it had to use a significant up-front fee to screen inventors to manageable numbers. In addition, the chamber found that its members were not generally looking for untried products, but required a good deal of up-front work (particularly in identifying real customers) before showing interest. The VCM Centre has ceased operation and government funding has been withdrawn.

At about the same time, in 1982, the Royal Melbourne Institute of Technology (RMIT) established the Centre for Innovation Development, an outcome of a concern that the Institutes' research results were not being taken up and commercialized. From the outset the CID restricted itself to try and process only a small number of projects.

Since 1982 the Commonwealth government has sought state government support to establish innovation centres in all other states and this process is now almost complete. Innovation centres in West Australia and South Australia are associated with technology parks, while those in NSW and Queensland are linked to Industry Associations and essentially act as a clearing house, assessing inventions and matching them to likely commercializing companies as quickly as possible.

Although it is too early and, in fact, unfair to pass judgement on individual centres, a generalized conclusion is possible from observing past and present centres' performance. To succeed innovation centres must have a clearly demonstrable capacity to 'add value' to the projects they undertake. Providing a location, as in a technology park, is a very visible example.

A particularly successful initiative, developed with government and industry funding, has been an annual Enterprise Workshop series. First begun in 1979 as a national workshop, and developed and conducted for the first two years by Professor Wayne Brown, the workshops are now conducted each year in every state. Multidisciplinary teams develop a business plan for a real product and compete against each other in presenting their plans to be judged by investors and industry leaders. The best teams from each state participate in a national judging. The workshops have made a major contribution in generating individual awareness of the innovation process. A significant percentage of the staff in the various innovation centres are past workshop participants. The most recent development has been the establishment of a Centre for the Development of Entrepreneurs at Chisholm Institute in Melbourne. The Commonwealth has indicated an intention to support such centres in each state.

Centre for Innovation Development – CID
The Centre was established in 1982 as part of RMIT, the initiative coming largely from within the Faculty of Engineering with some support from the Faculty of Business. Since the beginning of 1985 the CID has been a division of Technisearch Limited, a wholly controlled subsidiary of RMIT. Technisearch Limited is the body through which the Institute carries out all its commercially orientated activities.

RMIT Engineering Departments have a policy of close industry interaction through applied research, consulting and industry orientated student projects. As a result of this interaction, it became evident that there existed a need to improve the climate for the local commercialization of technology-based innovations.

The CID was established with the goals of: assisting production innovation; raising community awareness through (say) innovation related seminars; acting as an industry/government resource through innovation orientated consulting.

In a business sense the Centre saw, and continues to see, product innovation as its long-term mission, using seminars as the promotional vehicle and consulting as the mechanism for short-term generation of cashflow.

A constraint on the Centre at RMIT is that it must be totally self-funding. To enable the CID to emphasize product innovation, from its inception funding support was sought initially via industry sponsorship to a level of A$300 000 a year over five years. A mixture of the economy going into recession in 1982 (from which it is just beginning to emerge), plus a lack of interest in innovation, meant industry sponsorship never reached this level. The CID has, therefore, depended largely on its own ability to generate funds.

The Centre has managed to grow from an initial full-time equivalent staff of two to its present capacity of seven. Government funding support to date has been restricted to specific activities, for example, an incubator programme. However, the Commonwealth government's Department of Industry, Technology and Commerce (DITaC) has undertaken to provide $300 000 over the next three years. This initiative, which began at the end of 1984, is the subject of the remainder of this paper.

The Nascent Technology Ventures Program (NaTeVs)

Experience at RMIT showed that calling support start-up ventures an 'incubator programme' created a negative image; hence, the development of a unique programme name. The objective of the NaTeVs programme is to assist start-up technology ventures by providing space, office support, access to RMIT resources at cost and assistance in managing the start-up phase.

Support is limited to a maximum of two years and the Centre is looking for a fixed payment (typically in the order of A $5000) at the end of each year in the programme and a minority equity participation (a maximum of 10 per cent in the start-up). Because of the nature of RMIT, as a central city institute, the type of real estate available is restricted to office-style accommodation. The NaTeVs, therefore, occupy part of the floor on which the CID is now located, with the space partitioned by movable walls providing flexibility.

The NaTeVs programme currently includes:

1. A company intending to develop a state-of-the-art printed circuit mounting capability (including surface mounting components).
2. An electronics company, formed by four final year engineering students, developing cashflow through a product linked to a telephone system. The intent is ultimately to become involved in commercializing a new and novel optoelectronics product.
3. A company formed by three scientists who left CSIRO, an Australian Government Scientific Research Organization, to develop commercial products in the bushfire prevention, detection and protection areas.
4. A company developed from the research carried out at the Graduate Management School at the University of Melbourne, based on computer analysis of the financial risk profile of commercial companies. The company's Principal is the ex-professor involved in this research.

Over the relatively short time that the NaTeVs programme has existed, experience has shown that the major contribution the CID is able to make to start-ups is credibility. The perceived link with RMIT provides the start-ups with an image of having a broadly based and highly stable support structure. In the medium-term the Centre will also provide start-ups with an extensive contact network in both industry and government. Its long-term objective is to provide a well-developed mechanism for bridging the seed capital gap between the perception of a business opportunity in a technology field, and it being a fledgeling business attractive to investors.

PART 3   Science parks, innovation centres and the role of higher education establishments

The economics of entrepreneurship education

Edward McMullan
Faculty of Management, University of Calgary

Governments are beginning to discover that entrepreneurship education provides an exciting new vehicle for economic development. Britain (Watkins and Morris, 1981), Ireland (Conner, 1985), the State of Oregon, in the USA (Cutler, 1984) have all developed sizeable programmes which include a network of universities and colleges providing educational services for small business owners and entrepreneurs. In addition, the US government has operated the Small Business Institute Program which has paid a stipend for each small business project prepared by university students (Hoy, 1982; Solomon and Weaver, 1983). What makes these programmes interesting is that they represent strategic attempts to use entrepreneurship education for economic development. These programmes are designed not only for the benefit of regular students but also for the benefit of those currently developing new enterprises. In the past, education was expected to have a diffuse, long-term impact upon economic development. Plans were prepared which forecasted the future employment requirements in different fields of study. Entrepreneurship education is different. In addition to the long-term effects, it may also be expected to have a measurable, short-term impact upon venture development and job formation. New manpower plans may be needed to project the future needs not only for employees but for employers as well (Bauman, 1985).[1]

Since David Birch's seminal research (1979) on job creation, governments have become increasingly aware of the significance of new ventures and small-business innovation for job creation and economic development (McMullan and Vesper, 1985). One vehicle after another has been introduced to encourage venture formation and development. On the premise that a lack of venture capital was the main bottleneck, many new programmes have been introduced to increase the amount of available financial capital (Bygrave, Timmons, and Fast, 1984). On the supposition that existing space and service infrastructures were inadequate, governments have more recently emphasized the formation of small-business incubators (Kioratko and LaFollette, 1985). From financial and physical capital, attention has begun to shift more to human capital – to the entrepreneurs who drive the process and to their ability to do the job. According to Peter Drucker the challenge facing educators is a big one:

> Entrepreneurship is 'risky' mainly because so few of the so-called entrepreneurs know what they are doing. They lack the methodology. They violate elementary and well-known rules. This is particularly true of high-tech entrepreneurs. (1985, p 29)

Venture capitalists were some of the first to recognize the shortage of adequately educated entrepreneurs. The professional venture capitalists were only too aware that many of their would-be clients were obviously amateurish. Frequently, they have complained about the numbers of sadly inadequate business plans which they were being asked to review (Rosene, 1979). Even those relatively few entrepreneurs whom they did finance frequently lacked the knowledge needed to successfully develop a venture. Some venture capitalists have maintained that it is management expertise, and not money, which has been their most important service.

Until the eighties, entrepreneurship education has been largely a fifth columnist activity of an assortment of academics within departments that had other mandates and other commitments. From the sixties onward, entrepreneurship educators have had to compete with existing programmes for declining resources. Despite these handicaps, entrepreneurship education has grown dramatically to the point where well over 200 institutions of higher learning are offering relevant courses (Vesper, 1982). Recently, there has been some attempt to measure economic consequences of this type of programming. Early results are promising. It appears to be a time when economic developers are formally promoting entrepreneurship education as one of their battery of weapons in the battle against unemployment.

Education and economic development

Measuring the economic contribution from education is extremely complex. First of all, one must distinguish two types of beneficiaries: those individuals graduating through the formal education system, and the society at large (Mayundar, 1983). A number of studies have been conducted that demonstrate that those with more education not only tend to earn more, but also tend to be unemployed less: 'thus for the individual, extended education not only increases earnings, but it also reduces the likelihood of unemployment and to a smaller extent its duration' (Atkinson, 1983, p 32). Although the financial returns to education tend to justify lost income and other associated expenses, the return on individual investment varies notably with level and type of education (Cohn, 1979). One Canadian study illustrated the wide range of subsequent internal rates of return from twenty-one different university undergraduate disciplines for students graduating between 1961 and 1972. The highest internal rate of return for 1961 graduates was 19 per cent for pharmacy and mining engineering graduates. The lowest return went to social work graduates at 10 per cent. Commerce and business administration was intermediate at 15 per cent. In 1969 the return to commerce graduates went up to 20 per cent; by 1982 it was back down to 16 per cent.

Even though a society may deem it desirable to subsidize the personal betterment of its citizens, the usual justification for social investment should be in the returns to citizens at large. Economics focuses on the returns from education in the form of economic growth and development. Here is where the picture usually becomes very cloudy. A number of attempts involving numerous necessary assumptions have been made to determine the proportional influence of education upon economic growth. E. F. Denison has estimated 'education in the form of the average amount of education held by workers employed in the business sector (USA, 1929, 1969) was the source of 14 per cent of the growth. This manifests itself in the form of increased skills and versatility' (Atkinson, 1973, p 49). Results, however, should be treated as tentative and specific to the data collected:

The conclusions ... must be that it is extremely difficult to calculate the contribution of education to economic growth; the effect varies considerably between countries but is often substantial, and that all estimates must be treated with a great deal of caution. (Atkinson, 1983, p 52)

Those calculations of social returns tend to rely on calculations of additional tax dollars generated by graduates as over non-graduates (Cohn, 1979, p 113). This, of course, is a very limited interpretation of economic benefits arising from education. Denison (1974) estimated approximately one third of US economic growth came from advances in knowledge. Let us not forget that educated individuals become the disseminators of current knowledge. Interpreting and effectively diffusing new knowledge may require relatively high levels of education.

In general, researchers have had serious problems generating economic data which reasonably approximates the real benefits of various levels and kinds of education. Not the least of their problems stems from the artificial nature of some labour markets which require a diploma for entry. Entry to relevant education may be restricted in turn by a profession (ie medicine) thereby keeping remuneration high by an institutional device. The screening, in effect, may produce the higher earnings and not the education: 'In the screening approach, it is just the acquisition of a diploma or a credential. It is argued that education achievement – or the acquisition of training – may not have a significant effect on productivity.' (Cohn, 1979, p 29). Another related problem is that of determining causality. Even if a particular market for graduates freely admits people without degrees or relevant qualifications, one still has the problem of having selected many of the best people into the education system and thereby biasing any subsequent comparisons.

Entrepreneurship education that aims to enhance practitioner capability, and not just to study the phenomenon, is new to educational institutions. Quite possibly it was Dwight Baumann who offered some of the first modern courses in the late fifties at MIT. In 1958, he offered a 'new product design' course that took a broad perspective which emphasized building new companies around new products. A number of the graduates of this and related courses began distinguishing themselves quickly as successful technological entrepreneurs. The early years of the field were marked by a number of pioneering professors scattered about various universities, but there was very little in the way of an identifiable field of activity. After 1979, the year which marks the beginning of the annual Entrepreneurship Research Conference – first sponsored by Baylor and then by Babson College – the field began to coalesce. Contributions from a number of different disciplines were brought together providing a more solid base for course development. Majors or concentrations in entrepreneurship became something more than an odd amalgam of related courses. Students not only took one course, but began concentrating on the subject.

Although calculating social returns to investment in education may be messy in most fields, entrepreneurship education offers unusual potential. First of all, graduates are intended to be not just salaried employees in the infrastructure supporting new venture development; more importantly, they are intended to develop their own businesses and employ other people. Studies of the number of businesses started, their subsequent growth and profitability, should enable calculations to be made on employment, exports, taxes and innovations. One may even choose to look at second generation spinoff companies to determine resulting benefits.

Not only are there likely to be benefits from the graduates of such programmes, there may also be some substantial pay-offs from the process itself, since entrepreneurs-in-training may contribute value-added to community enterprises offsetting the cost of their education. What is more, entrepreneurship programmes can be used to support university technology transfer. Students may be used to develop research projects into marketable products, and some may even choose to champion the resulting ventures (McMullan and Melynk, 1985). Finally, since there is still so little research in the entrepreneurship field, new knowledge is likely to make a large impact. In other words, the marginal returns on this type of knowledge are still very high.

The performance of graduates

Since the field of entrepreneurship is so new, there have been only a few formal studies of graduates so far, although there are several other studies in the planning phase. (Bob Ronstadt of Babson is currently planning a major study of graduates across a number of different universities. Reinson of York is also planning to follow up systematically his graduates as is the University of Calgary.) Those studies which have been done, reflect the impact of both credit and non-credit programmes. As is to be expected, the start-up rates appear to be higher where students are screened and where support is more intensive. Output measures tend to focus upon incidence of business start-ups and numbers of jobs created. So far there are no longitudinal studies of growth rates and profitability of the graduates' enterprises over time.

To date, research has been conducted on five different programmes in an attempt to measure the relationship between the formal study of entrepreneurship and subsequent venture development activity. Hornaday and Vesper (1982) found that Babson College students (both MBA and BComm), who elected to take a single course in entrepreneurship, were much more likely subsequently to start their own businesses (21.3 per cent were full-time self-employed, 12.5 per cent part-time self-employed as against a control group who had not taken the course where only 14.2 per cent were full-time self-employed and 2.5 per cent part-time self-employed). Sixty-six per cent of those who had taken the course prior to starting a business felt the course had affected the direction of their careers. A comparable study at the University of Witchita by Clark, Davis and Harish (1984) found that of 892 non-business owners taking the 'Your Future Business' course, 129) (14.5 per cent) subsequently opened a business. Ninety-eight (66 per cent of the 129) credited the course with either having a 'large effect' or a 'very large effect' upon their decision to start their venture. The Witchita course was directed at both university students and members of the local community, 'with ages ranging from 16 to 75'. A sixteen-week British programme at the University of Manchester (Watkins and Morris, 1981; Watkins, 1982) required participants to spend the first month in residence. Participant selection from a large pool of applicants was based upon judgments of each applicant's potential to succeed. After running this programme seven times, Manchester undertook to measure its success. 'Seventy-six per cent of participants completing a programme initiated a business.' One year after completion the average employment level was eight people per new firm created. An Irish programme

(Conner, 1985) involved 830 young people under 25 years of age. Sixty-seven per cent subsequently became self-employed – one third in manufacturing. The parent programme, which has involved 1600 people (mostly over 25 years of age) since 1978, has seen 42 per cent of the graduates become self-employed – the average business employing 4.6 persons at the most recent measurement. A pilot study of ten University of Calgary MBAs graduating, with three or more courses in entrepreneurship, revealed that eight out of ten had businesses underway and the remaining two were planning to start a business in the not-too-distant future (McMullan, Long and Wilson, 1985). Table 11 provides a summary of these results.

Table 11   Business development by entrepreneurship course graduates

	1	2	3	4	5
Study	Watkins & Morris 1981	Hornaday & Vesper 1982	Clark, Davis & Harnish 1985	Conner 1985	McMullan, Long & Wilson 1985
Type of students	non-credit	credit BComm & MBA	non-credit	non-credit	credit MBA
Types of courses	1	1	1	2 for different groups	3 or more
Number of students	110	520 349 responding	892	830(1) 1600(2)	10 concentrating in entrepreneurship
% self-employed	76%	33.7%	14.5% new 25–40% still self-employed	67% (1) 42% (2)	40% new 40% still self-employed
Employment generated	8/venture (after 1 year)	---	3 full time per new venture & 3.5 part-time employees	4.6/venture	11/venture (1–4 yrs.)

In-process pay-off

Economic benefit may also be derived from the project work which students perform as a part of their education. Entrepreneurship is a practical art. Direct experience working with new ventures is important for effective learning. Entrepreneurship students learn venture development by working with their own and with other people's ventures. The best way to learn how to develop a venture beyond a certain stage is to be party to such a development and personally to contribute as much added-value as possible. For this reason, entrepreneurship education may use mini-internships with various community ventures as part of their pedagogy. Since many would-be entrepreneurs have the technical know-how but not the business expertise, it is evident how talented entrepreneurship students can make a substantial value-added contribution to venture development. When ventures are screened and allocated best to fit the specific requirements of individual classes, it becomes more obvious how contributions may be made. Even when they have the relevant knowledge and skill, entrepreneurs frequently lack the time to effectively study a market or adequately research the tax implications of different types of financial arrangements. Entrepreneurs commonly lack adequate resources for the early stages of venture development. These are crucial stages in which the entrepreneur determines what business to be in; how the product should be designed; what market to target; what strategy to use producing and dis-tributing the product, etc. This is a time when the entrepreneur may be most susceptible to new information and a time when a student may possibly add the most value to an entrepreneurial venture.

The programme at the University of Calgary has relied heavily upon such mini-internships with community entrepreneurs who are seeking this type of support. Programme administrators have set a minimum of 200 hours of work with community ventures as a requirement for a major in the discipline. In this programme during 1984, students and faculty invested approximately 11 000 hours contributing in various ways to the development of 63 different entre-preneurial ventures. It was found that each hour produced a measurable benefit of approximately $215.[2] Since faculty, staff, mentors and other related programming was involved, it is unreasonable that only a portion of the $215 per hour benefits per contact hour be attributed to the students' intervention. Even if only $100 per hour of value contribution is attributed to student contributions to community enterprises, then every student may be expected to add a minimum of $20 000 worth of value to those enterprises which are most in need of such support and least able to pay for it. This type of pay-off should be compared with the costs of educating such students.

Effects on the community infrastructure

As we move towards a competitive world economy which necessitates enterprises to be more sophisticated and more technologically advanced in order to survive, the university has the potential of playing an increasingly prominent role in economic development. Internationally competitive ventures will need to adopt the best ideas from the several business disciplines within an entrepreneurial framework. Moreover, these ventures will need assistance from a number of sectors of the university. Most typically, entrepreneurship programmes have been based either in schools of business or of engineering (Vesper, 1980). Both disciplines have had value to offer the new venture development process. Despite the complementarity of such contributions, universities have usually been hard pressed to engender anything more than nominal cooperation between different schools. In fact, the usual scenario is much worse with conflicts between schools frequently winning over cooperative initiatives within a single faculty or school. Entrepreneurship programmes have most frequently emerged from management, policy, or marketing departments – the soft side of business (Vesper, 1982). Getting useful contributions from finance, management science, and accounting – the hard side – has proven more difficult.

The University of Calgary's programme provides a single case study of the potential impacts of entrepreneurship programmes. As Al Shapero, late scholar of entrepreneurship, noted on a visit to Calgary in December 1983, the courses in the programme offered a laboratory opportunity for each of the functional disciplines in the management school. By allocating community ventures according to their informational requirements across a number of project courses, each faculty member was assisted in the task of getting educational project work for his/her students. Since the entrepreneurs were actively requesting that the work be done, motivation was typically high. Over a number of years, so many faculties became personally involved either with entrepreneurial projects or in teaching new venture courses that the theme of 'entrepreneurial management' is under discussion as the integrating theme for the entire management faculty.

The next programme to be involved was industrial design from the Faculty of Environmental Design. Students were exchanged between programmes and team teaching was initiated. It became quickly apparent that entrepreneurial clients could benefit substantially from the contributions of industrial design students. They not only improved physical product attributes, but frequently also were able to lower production costs in the process. Law was third to become involved. Here again, it became evident that new ventures are in frequent need of legal work which they are unable to afford. Third-year law students in a commercial law practice became valuable contributors, providing advice and direction upon incorporation, contracts, leases, product liability, partnership agreements and the plethora of other legal issues. More recently, faculty members have become active from engineering, computer science and biochemistry.

On a university level a technology transfer office was established. The interdisciplinary talents of the entrepreneurship group have been influential in several aspects of this office, from the selection of key personnel, to the definition of function and the provision of important contacts. On a much larger scale, the university is making plans for a major technology park. Through the entrepreneurship programme, the university is obtaining credibility and additional bargaining power with the provincial government. Instead of advocating a plan in a vacuum, the president of the university should be able to use the community pay-off from the entrepreneurship programme to leverage his application. What is more, the university has obtained the services of a leading entrepreneurship scholar, Karl Vesper, as a consultant to the planned technology park through the contacts of programme members.

On a community level, the programme established a new venture forum, which monthly has brought together sixty to eighty people from the community who are involved in new venture development. Three hundred or more community people have used the forums and other special lectures to make valuable contacts. Researchers and inventors, innovators and entrepreneurs, merchant bankers and venture capitalists, and many others in the new venture infrastructure, have used the university as a meeting place. The forums, presentations and a quarterly newsletter are all structured to provide educational value as well as contacts. Probably most important of all, the university legitimizes everyone's involvement in innovative venture development and, in the process, accumulates substantial credit for itself within the influential business community.

Schwartz and Teach (1984) attempted to measure the impact of related programming at Georgia Institute of Technology upon the 'professional infrastructure for emerging technology start-ups' in Atlanta. 'Through the auspices of Georgia Tech., five major Venture Capital conferences have been convened in Georgia since 1980. A seed capital conference was convened for the first time in early 1983 and has been repeated in 1984. The Technology Development was begun in 1983, under the aegis of the (program)' (p 127). The researchers polled fifteen people from the big eight accounting firms, the largest law firms in Georgia and some of the biggest banks. Nine of the respondents listed the Institute and ten listed the programme as having been 'responsible for creating . . . interest in emerging technology start-up firms' in the community.

One of the highest potential contributions which an entrepreneurship programme may offer a local community is that of efficient networking. As Sue Birley (1985) has observed from her research on 160 new firms in St Joseph County:

> The choice of networks is key in understanding the nature of the subsequent firm, since it is during the start-up the elements of the firm are set. Decisions are made upon what type of resources to use, how to source them and what size the firm should be. In using *only* his business associates and family, the entrepreneur is likely to re-create the elements of previous employment.

Moreover, 'an inefficient use of the formal infrastructure can lead to poor advice and lack of use of the many schemes available'. Birley concluded that an enterprise office can be used as an efficient networking vehicle and in the process encourage small local firms 'to develop strategies for finding new customers and new markets in new fields in the longer term'.

Pay-offs from Entrepreneurship research

Until recently the philosophy of Social Darwinism dominated most people's thoughts about entrepreneurship. The fittest would survive because they were meant to survive. Moreover, since entrepreneurship was the essence of free enterprise, it was a natural process guided by Adam Smith's famous 'invisible hand'. Those that survived and became rich were the entrepreneurs almost by definition. If you failed, you were not meant to succeed since you were not a real entrepreneur. Being a member of the first generation wealthy was the best evidence of entrepreneurial success. The logic was circular and self-serving.

Research on the factors contributing to venture success or failure identified a number of controllable variables (Vesper, 1980) and in the process dispelled the folklore of Social Darwinism. Research on failure rates helped to quantify the risk involved (Shapero and Giglierano, 1982). Research on the relative economic impact of new and innovative ventures has been revolutionizing government's ideas on how to develop economies (Birch 1979; McMullan and Vesper, 1985) as has the research on identifiable entrepreneurial communities such as Silicon Valley and Route 128, Boston. Research on venture capital and on incubator organizations has helped to shape the decision processes around those new institutions. Research on corporate innovation and entrepreneurship has been revolutionizing our concepts of how to organize and run large businesses. Research on the characteristics of entrepreneurs shows promise for their efficient identification. Research on entrepreneurship education has been supporting radical changes in educational planning and values (see Table 12).

Table 12   Some of the important findings to date relate to the following:

- the job creating potential of new ventures and small business (eg Birch, 1979)
- the relative efficiency of research and development in smaller enterprises (eg Cooper, 1964)
- circumstances favouring venture success (or failure) (eg Vesper, 1980)
- the real rates of failure

- the characteristics of entrepreneurs (eg Brockaus, 1982)
- the personal consequences of an entrepreneurial life style
- the process of venture development (eg Churchill and Lewis, 1983)
- the venture capital phenonemon
- the incubator phenonemon (eg Allen, 1985)
- the phenonemon of entrepreneurial regions
- the spin off phenonemon (eg Cooper, 1964)
- corporate entrepreneurship or intrapreneurship (eg Pinchot, 1985)
- the phenonemon of entrepreneurship education (eg Vesper, 1980)
- the factors favouring new venture activity on a personal, social and cultural level (eg Kilby, 1971)

One may well be amazed at the significance of many of the findings in the field of entrepreneurship research given its short history as an empirical scientific discipline. Whereas many fields are advanced only slowly and painstakingly by one research study after another, against a backdrop of hundreds of similar studies, the field of entrepreneurship research appears to be leaping forward – each new realization heralding still more. When Thomas Kuhn (1970) wrote of paradigm shifts, it was likely that he was referencing changes of this magnitude, ie a shift from a managerial to an entrepreneurial society (Naisbitt, 1982). Instead of envisaging the field as a lot of static little businesses (eg the local barbershop) not worthy of professional management attention, the model entrepreneurial venture has become the new high-tech firm (eg Apple Corporation). The challenges of strategic development appear even more complex than the jobs of the middle managers and the staff specialists in large organizations. The gestalt shift involved allowed re-searchers to see the phenonemon in an entirely new light. Attention moved from the maintenance of the old to the creation of the new. Education has shifted from analysis to creativity and from statics to dynamics.

Although a number of important observations have been made, there is much research which needs to be done. Many questions need answering perhaps none more than how to enhance people's entrepreneurial capacities and improve their probabilities of success. There are many findings which need refining, such as what are the real rates of new business failure. In order to develop full-scale educational programmes in entrepreneurship, much more in the way of quality teaching materials will be needed. Furthermore, those performing the research will be developing some of the expertise needed for educating others. Finally, it is through research that we will come to know how better to make investments in this new field. Without scientific findings we are limited to people's educated guesses and experienced intuition.

Conclusions

There are many pay-offs that can result from effective entrepreneurship education. Entrepreneurship education can have a direct and measurable impact on economic development not unlike that of venture capital or of business incubators. Although it may be difficult to demonstrate conclusive causal linkages, this is so with all social phenomena. Allen (1985) reported finding that 92.5 per cent of the entrepreneurs surveyed from forty different incubators say they would have started irrespective of the incubator. This statistic, however, says nothing of the relative likelihood of success.

There is a commonsense element to this exercise. Once we look at the many things that are useful for entrepreneurs to know, it becomes commonsense to realize that entrepreneurs are not born with such knowledge. Nor is it reasonable to expect that all but a few will pick up most relevant knowledge as a part of their daily living. It is commonsense to believe that education (if it encourages creativity) can be used effectively to enhance relevant skills as well as relevant knowledge. Inasmuch as education in general appears positively to affect an entrepreneur's probability and degree of success (eg Vesper, 1980; Cuba et al, 1983), how much more likely it would seem that education dedicated to meeting the needs of technological innovators and entrepreneurs would be even more effective.

The advantages to be obtained from entrepreneurship education complement rather than compete with other vehicles for stimulating new venture formation. It is quite possible that the resources contained in universities, colleges and technical schools could be organized to provide the type of seed capital support which is so difficult to raise from the venture capital community. Instead of cash, potential entrepreneurs may obtain the human and physical resources they need to develop prototypes, prove market feasibility and develop venture plans. At present the Rensselaer Polytechnic Institute on-campus incubator strives to provide this type of early-stage help, in order to develop businesses to the state where venture capitalists are willing and able intelligently to review them as commercial propositions. As these ventures develop and outgrow the limited space available, they have been moving into another incubator in the university research park some distance from the campus. In off-hours, the incubator residents can have access to the university's computer and various university laboratory facilities. Business students are also beginning to be involved in providing appropriate analysis.

The rate at which new programmes are appearing suggests that we are poised on the verge of a massive expansion of entrepreneurship education. Unfortunately, the field is new and ill-prepared for large-scale growth. If the planners are concerned about the effective execution of their plans, they will have to attend to the problem of educating the people they need to efffectively run their programmes. The problems may be large but not in comparison with the likely economic pay-offs.

References

1 Comments by Dwight Baumann at a conference at the University of Illinois at Champagne-Urbana, 1985.
2 Seventy-three per cent of the 11 000 hours of work performed was on fifty ventures. The entrepreneurs leading those ventures claimed a total of $1 750 000 (con) added to their business through this programme (McMullan, Long Graham, 1985). The subsequent estimate of $215/hour was calculated using the formula:

$$\frac{.73 \times \$1\,750\,000}{11\,125 \text{ hours}}$$

Allen D. N. 1985 An entrepreneurial marriage: business incubators and start-ups. *Fifth entrepreneurship research conference.* Babson College, Wellesley, Mass.
Allen D. N. and Nyrop K. A. 1985 An examination of the state's incubator initiatives. *30th annual conference of the International Conference for Small Business.* Montreal, Canada, June, 1985, pp 375–90.
Atkinson G. B. J. 1983 *The economics of education.* Hodder and Stoughton, London.
Birch D. L. 1981 Who creates jobs? *The Public Interest* Fall.

Birley 1985 The roles of networks in the entrepreneurial process *Babson Entrepreneurship Research Conference*. Wharton School, Penn.

Boyd D. and Gumpart D. 1983 The effects of stress on early-stage entrepreneurs. In Hornaday J. A., Tarpley Jr, F., Timmons J. A. and Vesper K. H. (eds) *Frontiers of Entrepreneurship Research*. Babson College, Wellesley, Mass. pp 180–91.

Brockhaus R. H. 1982 The psychology of the entrepreneurs. In Kent C. A., Sexton D. L. and Vesper K. H. (eds) *Encyclopedia of entrepreneurship*. Prentice-Hall, Englewood Cliffs, N.J.

Bygraves W. D., Timmons J. A. and Fast N. D. 1984 Seed and start-up venture capital investing in technological companies. In Hornaday J. A., Tarpley Jr, F., Timmons J. A. and Vesper K. H. (eds) *Frontiers of Entrepreneurship Research*. Babson College, Welleseley, Mass.

Churchill N. C. and Lewis L. 1983 The five stages of small business growth *Harvard Business Review* May/June, **61** (3): 30–50.

Clark B. W., Davis C. H. and Harish V. C. 1984 Do courses in entrepreneurship aid in new venture creation? *Journal of Small Business* April.

Cohn E. 1979 *The economics of education*. Ballinger Publishing Company, Cambridge, Mass.

Conner P. J. 1985 The facilitation and stimulation of entrepreneurship of young persons in Ireland through the Youth Enterprise Programme. *Babson Entrepreneurship Research Conference*. Wharton, Penn.

Cooper A. C. 1984 Contrasts in the role of incubator organizations in the founding of growth-oriented firms. In Hornaday J. A., Tarpley Jr F., Timmons J. A. and Vesper K. H. (eds) *Frontiers of Entrepreneurship Research*. Babson College.

Cooper C. 1964 R and D is more efficient in small companies *Harvard Business Review* June.

Cooper C., Dunkelberg W. C. and Furuta R. 1985 Incubator organization backgrounds and founding characteristics. *Babson Entrepreneurship Research Conference*. Wharton, Penn.

Cuba R., Decenzo D. and Anish A. 1983 Management practices of successful female business owners *American Journal of Small Business* 8 (2) Fall: 40–6.

Cutler S. 1984 Oregon small business development center network: Program information. Lane Community College Small Business Development Center, September, 1985 (manuscript).

Drucker P. 1985 *Innovation and entrepreneurship: practice and principles*. Harper and Row, New York.

Hornaday J. A. and Vesper K. H. 1982. Entrepreneurial education and job satisfaction. In Hornaday J. A., Tarpley Jr, F., Timmons J. A. and Vesper K. H. (eds) *Frontiers of Entrepreneurship Research*. Babson College, Wellesley, Mass., pp 526–39.

Hoy F. 1982 Intervention in new ventures through the SBI versus SBDC. In Vesper K. (ed) *Frontiers of entrepreneurship research*. Babson College, Wellesley, Mass.

Kilby P. (ed) 1971 *Entrepreneurship and economic development*. The Free Press, New York.

Kioratko D. F. and LaFollette W. R. 1985 Analyzing the incubator explosion: the types, the purposes and the services *30th Annual World Conference of the International Council for Small Business*. Montreal Canada, June, pp 411–34.

Kuhn T. 1970 *The structure of scientific revolution*. University of Chicago Press.

McMullan W. E., Long W. A. and Wilson A. 1985 MBA's concentrating in Entrepreneurship. Unpublished paper.

McMullan W. E., Long W. A. and Graham J. B. 1985 University innovation centers and the entrepreneurship knowledge gap. In Vesper K. (ed) *Frontiers of Entrepreneurship Research*. Babson College, Welleseley, Mass.

McMullan W. E. and Melynk K. 1985 University innovation centers and academic venture formation. Invited paper at Conference on Academic Spinoffs, University of Illinois, Champagne-Urbana, June.

McMullan W. E. and Vesper K. 1985 New ventures and small business innovation for economic growth. National Science Foundation, Conference on Economic Development, invited paper. Rensellaer Polytechnic Institute, Troy, NY.

Muyundar T. 1983 *Investment in education and social choice*. Cambridge University Press, Cambridge, England.

Naisbitt J. 1982 *Megatrends: ten new directions transforming our lives*. Warner Books, New York.

Pinchot III G. 1985 *Intrapreneuring*. Harper and Row, New York.

Roitman D. B., Emshoff J. C. and Robinson Jr. R. B. 1984 College-based managerial and technical assistance for small business *Journal of Small Business Management* October.

Ronstadt R. 1983 The decision not to become an entrepreneur. In Vesper K. (ed) *Frontiers of Entrepreneurship Research*. Babson College, Wellesley, Mass., pp 233–54.

Rosene M. 1979 *Business plans that pass the 'Snicker Test' Venture* October: 68–72.

Schwartz R. G. and Teach R. D. 1984 Primary issues affecting the development and growth of a professional infrastructure for emerging technology start-ups: the State of Georgia experience. In Hornaday J. A., Tarplay Jr. F., Timmons J. A. and Vesper K. H. (eds) *Frontiers of entrepreneurship research*. Babson College, Wellesley, Mass. pp 126–35.

Sexton D. and Bowman N. 1984 *Personality inventory for potential entrepreneurs: evaluation of a modified LPI/PRF–E test instrument*. In Hornaday, J. A., Tarplay Jr. F., Timmons J. A. and Vesper K. H. (eds) *Frontiers of Entrepreneurship Research*. Babson College, Wellesley, Mass. pp 513–28.

Shapero 1981 Numbers that lie *Inc.* May.

Shapero A. and Giglierano J. 1982 Exists and entries: a study in yellow pages journalism. In Vesper K. (ed) *Frontiers of Entrepreneurship Research. Babson College.*

Universities and technological entrepreneurship in Britain: some implications of the Cambridge phenomenon

Nick Segal
Segal, Quince and Wicksteed, Cambridge

The Cambridge phenomenon – the burgeoning growth, spearheaded by small and indigenous companies, of high-technology industry in and around Cambridge, England – has attracted attention, nationally and internationally, since publication earlier this year of a study that documented and analysed it and assessed its prospects and wider ramifications. (*The Cambridge Phenomenon: The Growth of High Technology Industry in a University Town*. Segal Quince and Wicksteed, February 1985.) This is due in part to the worldwide cachet of the name 'Cambridge' and of its indissoluble link with one of the world's oldest and most prestigious universities. But there are more profound reasons too, and in order to understand the thrust of this paper it is necessary briefly to discuss two of them that apply in many, if not most, industrial countries: the change to a harsher environment within which universities now have to create; and the promotion by central and local government of small firms as part of the overall effort to stimulate economic growth.

The British higher education sector, that only twenty-five years ago was confidently embarking on an unparalleled phase of public-sector financed expansion, is today in an altogether less favourable position and less buoyant mood. As in other Western European countries, this is a consequence of the general restraint now being exercised on public expenditure and of an accident of demography that is causing a prolonged even if temporary decline in the population of student age. In Britain it is also the result of a questioning by the government of the strategic management and administrative competence of universities, and to some extent even of their traditional role in society.

The university sector is thus in a process of change, and in some respects one could reasonably say of crisis. There are chronic shortages of public-sector monies for research; faculty pay scales are increasingly unfavourable and career opportunities restricted; there is growing evidence of a renewal of the 'brain drain' of previous decades, principally to the USA; the competition for student places is increasingly severe (this in a country where the proportion of young people in higher education is already very low), though ironically, if not unexpectedly, this is leading to an impressive rise in the scholastic qualifications of those who are now accepted as students.

The responses of the educational institutions to this changed and uncomfortable environment are many and varied, reflecting all manner of differences in the internal and external circumstances of individual universities. But there are common features too, and two of them are relevant to this paper: the drive to find new sources of income and, partly related, the drive to foster stronger links with industry. The question to be addressed here is how the growth of high-technology industry in Cambridge illuminates these two issues.

The second reason for the wide interest in the Cambridge phenomenon is to do with the set of beliefs, widespread among industrialized countries, that their future economic strength lies in development and exploitation of new technologies and that small firms (and universities) have special roles to play in this process. Again, what can be adduced from the Cambridge experience on these matters? In order to explore these questions it is clearly necessary to describe and analyse the phenomenon briefly.

What is the Cambridge phenomenon?

The phenomenon does not lend itself to a simple and concise definition. It is essentially a process, resulting from a fascinating amalgam of long-term and preconditioning factors, the involvement of people of outstanding quality and a multiplicity of particular events and decisions. Moreover, it is a process that is continuously evolving in the sense of becoming larger, more varied and more complex, and not without its 'downs' as well as its 'ups'.

Nevertheless, a number of aspects of the phenomenon stand out clearly as representing its defining characteristics and making it so distinctive a development in Britain and indeed in Europe. In highly compressed form these features are as follows. There is now a large number of high-technology businesses in and around Cambridge. There were some 350 by the end of 1984, and currently the net annual increase is probably of the order of thirty to forty.

These firms are mostly in computing hardware and software, scientific instruments, electronics and telecommunications, scientific consultancy and r&d, and increasingly, the life sciences. They are principally engaged in research – design – development or in low-volume, high-value production. Such large-scale production as there is is typically subcontracted elsewhere. They are small. For instance, in 1984, 75 per cent of all firms had fewer than thirty employees, and the mean and median size of the firms established since 1979 were sixteen and eight respectively. The firms are chiefly (some 75 per cent) indigenous and independent and are mostly young (well over 200 were set up in the decade 1975–84) though the two oldest date back to the last century (Cambridge Instruments was formed in 1881 by a son of Charles Darwin who was a member of Trinity College, and WG Pye was established in 1896 by the former chief mechanic of the Cavendish laboratory). They have a high birth rate as well as a low death rate. We calculate that the death rate over about the past decade has been approximately one-fifth of the national average for small firms generally. (Even the collapse this year of the microcomputer market and the well-publicized troubles of the two leading firms in that sector, Acorn and Sinclair, do not seem to have precipitated a deterioration in the failure rate.) Mostly they are set up by individuals (typically more than one in each case) spinning off from existing firms and other local organizations including the University.

National and international firms – not only in high-technology industry but also in financial and business services – are increasingly interested in locating subsidiary operations in the area. In total the firms account for some 17 per cent of employment in the area; even those established in the past ten years account for some 5 per cent of jobs. The firms are playing an important role in stimulating further development in the local industrial and commercial sectors and are adding a new and dynamic element to what has for long been a stable and prosperous but 'unexciting' local economy. Finally, the university has exercised a profoundly important influence, directly but especially indirectly, on the emergence of the phenomenon.

These characteristics together add up to Cambridge's now being a high-technology location of growing significance in the UK. It is by no means large in its absolute scale – after all, the population of Cambridge itself is only about 100 000 and the total labour catchment area (as it has evolved to date) has a population of only some 250 000 which is about the size of a typical London borough. Nor is it the only location in Britain where high-technology industry is flourishing. Central Scotland and the M4 corridor running west from London to Bristol are two other highly successful areas, where broadly speaking the prime movers so far have been large companies and inward investment; and in the case of Scotland the public sector (notably the Scottish Development Agency) has played an important role too.

However, the distinctive features of the Cambridge phenomenon are that it is being 'driven' by small local enterprises and that other local resources – the University, banks, business community and so on – have been closely involved in the whole development process. It is only relatively recently, as the pace of development has quickened and the number of companies has increased sharply, that the phenomenon has attracted serious and substantial interest from the outside business, financial and real estate sectors.

The pattern of high-technology development that is emerging in Cambridge has, despite many differences in local circumstances, parallels with Silicon Valley in California and perhaps more closely with Route 128 in Boston. These world-famous developments are now very large in terms both of the numbers of companies and their turnover and employment. While it is unrealistic to expect that Cambridge could ever achieve such scale, the relevant comparison with the two US locations is not as they are now but rather as they were in the early years of their development, say some twenty years ago.

All in all, the Cambridge phenomenon makes an absorbing story. That the leading centre of high-technology industry should emerge in a mediaeval market town, which accommodates one of the world's famous universities, set in a somewhat bleak even if prosperous rural environment, in a location that is not particularly well served by strategic communications links and that historically was far from the main centres of industrial development, is not something that could easily have been foreseen.

Factors causing and shaping the phenomenon

It need hardly be said that a development of the kind happening in Cambridge –that has evolved over many years, albeit at an accelerating pace in the past decade, spanning many technologies and markets and also involving innumerable individuals and organizations – has multiple causes. Tempting as it is – because so many of them are individually interesting and instructive in their own right, and collectively make up a good story – I shall resist discussing them simply for reasons of space. Instead, I shall somewhat arbitrarily pick out three particular factors that bear upon the theme of this symposium, and then, at risk of presenting an unbalanced picture and of inflating its influence, I shall dwell rather more fully on the role of the University in the phenomenon.

The first factor concerns the vital role played by the local financial and business services firms. It may seem strange that this should be worthy of remark at all; but in local economic initiatives in Britain, typically designed and implemented by the public sector, such firms have often not been deeply involved.

The story in Cambridge is an absorbing one, regrettably too long to be told here. The essential element is that Barclays Bank took a strategic decision in the late 1970s to invest not just money, but more crucially, the time of one of its business advisory managers, in development and implementation of the business plans of first-time technological entrepreneurs. Not only did this help create a good number of lively and prospering businesses; it gave confidence to accountants, solicitors and others in the local business community that they should similarly get involved in supporting such enterprises; and it encouraged other forms of financial institutions operating nationally and internationally, as well as other local investors, to finance the local high-technology companies both at start-up and later rounds of financing.

This in turn led rapidly to a situation in which there are now located in Cambridge four of the big eight international accounting/managing consultancy practices, a major US bank, a provincial office of a City of London merchant bank and similarly of a patent agent, and offices of some of the big national real estate agents. There have recently also sprung up locally a number of venture management firms, typically financed by one or a combination of City of London institutions, Cambridge colleges and private individuals. Increasingly too, individuals from elsewhere in the country who have substantial industrial and business experience are being 'sucked into' Cambridge, whether through active recruitment on the part of the high-technology companies, or through a certain amount of fortune-seeking by the individuals themselves. All this is adding to the existing local capability in these and other professions, and is enhancing the ability of the young firms themselves to operate internationally and to deal with increasingly sophisticated problems.

So far, with a few notable exceptions, the venture capital industry – especially the new US-style 'hands-on' venture capital firms – has not been particularly active on the Cambridge scene. This contrasts strongly with the US experience and is due in part to the start-up method, type and size of many of the technology firms. But there is no doubt, given the continuing growth of the firms and the substantial capability that now exists locally and nationally in the venture capital industry, that the situation will change in the coming years. Interestingly, however, those Cambridge firms that have grown rapidly to any size, have done so either through internal growth, drawing on 'conventional' financial and other resources, or through being acquired by substantial international (foreign not national) firms offering both financial and the requisite management, marketing and financial resources. Such acquisitions have sometimes taken place out of a position of short-term weakness of the Cambridge firms – the recent example of Acorn Computers (taken over by Olivetti) springs readily to mind, as does that of Cambridge Consultants more than ten years ago (which now operates highly successfully as an essentially autonomous subsidiary of Arthur D. Little). But other cases have arisen out of a position of strength, such as Cambridge Interactive Systems being acquired by Computervision, and very recently, Applied Research of Cambridge by McDonnell Douglas.

The second factor highlighted is that of the impact on the phenomenon of Cambridge's short and modest industrial history and of the town's small size and its relative remoteness and compactness. This may seem an unlikely factor to mention in this forum, but it is useful to note the influence of history and structure on subsequent economic change (sometimes that is too easily forgotten at both local and national levels), and also to recognize that what might be expected to be disadvantageous can turn out to be fruitful and full of future possibilities.

Without going into all the salient facts, the essential elements of this impact are several. First, specialist market opportunities – generated originally by demand mostly from the University, now by already established larger local firms – have been readily identifiable locally and, in the absence of firms to whom know-how could readily be licensed, have been open to new firm penetration.

Second, the fact that there has never been heavy industry, or industries in which large plants and large unionized labour forces have been prominent, has helped create a labour market and a general attitude in which flexibility and individualism have never been suppressed. A history of low wages – due to the long dominance of the agricultural and low-level services sectors (the latter partly a result of employment patterns in the University and colleges), reinforced by the early industrial employers and a generally low penetration of trade unionism, have contributed to the effective functioning of the labour market.

Third, there is no question of the University's becoming engulfed and inconspicuous within a large metropolis. Similarly, it has been much easier than it would in a large city for a 'critical mass' of high-technology firms to be reached. There are numerous interlocking networks of talented, influential and accessible individuals, which make for informal, congenial and efficient business dealings. All these circumstances have allowed the firms to be noticed – in effect the phenomenon to be recognized – with the attendant benefits of practical support and generation of confidence among themselves and among the outside financial, business and academic community in the firms. In London or Manchester, say, these benefits are much harder to realize because what high-technology firms there are, and the higher educational institutions themselves, tend to be 'lost' or at least their collective impact minimized.

At the same time, given the fact of emergence of the phenomenon, there is no doubt that the small population in its labour catchment area, the limited development to date in its housing market, and other factors to do with the physical form and nature of the city and its links with the surrounding villages, are all actual or potential constraints on its longer-term growth. The future success of the phenomenon is dependent not only on the skills of the high-technology businesses involved but also on the physical planning policy and how the Cambridge sub-region develops, in the widest sense, as a place to live and work.

The third issue highlighted here concerns the provision of property for high-technology industry. The experience in Cambridge stands in interesting contrast to that elsewhere in Britain, on three main counts. First, in Cambridge supply has by and large followed rather than been ahead of demand – in most other areas purpose-built property is being used as an instrument to stimulate demand. Second, the private sector has dominated provision in Cambridge (and continues to do so), where elsewhere it is the public sector. And third, until quite recently, Cambridge property has generally been quite conventional with few or any special features in the buildings themselves; elsewhere there is a tendency to believe that high-technology firms, even those at start-up or very early stages of development, necessarily require premises that are themselves high technology in some way.

Any contemporary discussion of property for high-technology industry necessarily leads on to science parks (or technology parks, or innovation centres, or whatever the facility is called in the case concerned). There is no doubt that throughout Britain and much of the industrial world expectations of what a science park can realistically achieve by way of fostering new technology industry have become greatly inflated. As one of the oldest and unquestionably the most successful university science park so far in Europe, the Cambridge science park offers some interesting pointers, and a few general comments will be useful here.

To many people in Britain and abroad, Cambridge high-technology industry and the Cambridge science park are virtually synonymous. This is far from being the actual case: in terms simply of the numbers of companies, for instance, the science park accounts for a small proportion (between 10 per cent and 15 per cent) of the overall high-technology scene. Indeed, it is true to say that the science park is successful because of the phenomenon – the large numbers of high-technology companies have created strong demand for the quality of property and general environment that the science park offers – and has not been a cause of it. (Though it may be noted that the origins of the science park stem partly from a dispute about local planning policy, and it was through involvement in this that the University's thinking on links with industry underwent a material change in the 1960s – see further below.)

But the science park has come to play a critical role in sustaining and enhancing the phenomenon for several reasons, of which probably the most important derives from the fact that it has become a visible and prestigious symbol to the outside world that high-technology industry is flourishing in Cambridge. The fact of a high degree of international interest in the science park has given both confidence and a sense of status to the local high-technology sector, in the same way that it has come to constitute a no less significant symbol to the University of the success of Cambridge as a location for high-technology industry and of the easy compatibility of this industry with Cambridge as a university town.

More generally, the lesson from Cambridge, and indeed from every other situation that we know of, is that planned provision of property is not itself a sufficient factor (and sometimes not even a necessary factor) in stimulating development of high-technology industry. A science park can be helpful in playing particular roles at different stages of development and in helping change attitudes; there are cases too where it can be decisive in enabling a particular project to go ahead. But other, 'non-property', ingredients are needed too, and in their actual or prospective absence investment in the property would not be worthwhile. These arguments should never be lost sight of in any wider discussion especially because the property aspects can sometimes (even if wrongly) be regarded as 'easy'.

The role of the University

The University's role, even if mostly indirect, has been central to the phenomenon. In part this derives from the fact that there has been within the University a significant degree of specialization in certain disciplines that have ripened commercially over certain periods: electron optics in the 1950s–60s and computer aided design in the 1960s–70s are good examples of this. More fundamentally, it stems from the historically pervasive influence of the University on most aspects of life in Cambridge. It is, directly and indirectly, because of the University that sizeable numbers of research scientists live in the area, and that there is a continuing vitality about the local cultural and social scene. The university has set a tone and style of quality, individualism and confidence; and, especially because of the collegiate structure, it has created a unique environment for social and interdisciplinary contact within the entire academic and research community and, increasingly, now also extending to the local high-technology and business communities. The concept of networks, touched on earlier, goes a long way towards explaining how Cambridge has operated as a university and market town in the past, and now also as a high-technology business centre.

These and other aspects of Cambridge life are probably not so very different from those of many other university towns elsewhere in the world, even though only a few will be able to rival Cambridge in its combination of age, excellence, prestige and physical beauty. But there are two other particular aspects of the University that are distinctive compared to most other universities, at least in Britain, and that have exerted a powerful influence on the phenomenon.

The first aspect is to do with the terms of employment of staff. Most other UK universities have a uniform and highly specific structure for all employment contracts, with little if any margin for flexibility. (Even Oxford has strict and circumscribing rules about how much time faculty members can devote to non-academic activities.) Cambridge, by contrast, has a variety of loose contractual relationships which place rather more emphasis on academic staff living close to the city and seldom being absent during term than on formal job descriptions. The essence of the relationship is that academics are expected to devote themselves to advancement of their subject, to give instruction to students and to promote the interests of the University as a place of education and research. Beyond this – subject only to informal pressure exercised by their students and peers, perhaps reinforced by the head of department – the individual academic is free to decide how he wants to spend the rest of his time and whether and in what way he wants to engage in outside work. Indeed, in the applied sciences there is a natural presumption that staff, because of their quality, will be involved in consultancy or other such work.

The second distinctive feature of the University that impinges on the phenomenon has to do with the authorities' policy towards commercial exploitation of academics' know-how and towards links with industry generally. In essence the University has a benign and supportive posture towards faculty members' involvements of all kinds with industry. It is acceptable for individuals to engage in outside work on their own account if they wish to, and also acceptable if they do not. If they do so, the rewards are theirs but so are the risks. The University's financial interest is protected only to the extent that it insists that if its physical facilities and other resources are used in the course of private work, they should be commercially costed and paid for. (Though there is a tacit assumption, perhaps even an expectation, that an (ex)-academic who makes a great deal of money out of applying his know-how will share some of it with the University.)

This 'hands-off but positive' posture of the administration, that stands in marked contrast to most other universities which typically seek to become directly involved in all aspects of industrial linkage, is no accident. While in broad terms it is based on an accumulation of history and a realistic recognition of the sheer impossibility of imposing a centralized regime on such a large and fragmented collegiate university, there are more immediate and positively conscious reasons for the industrial linkage strategy.

Some twenty years ago a few key individuals in the University, influenced by what they saw happening around Stanford and MIT, perceived that the vitality and relevance, and increasingly also the funding, of the University's research would be dependent upon there being in the vicinity of the University a good number and diversity of science-based companies and of non-academic research establishments. They also saw that research students would increasingly have to find careers in industry not academe, which would be facilitated by the proximity of science-based industry. Most importantly, they saw that the way to achieve this was through reliance on excellence of research combined with liberal ground-rules governing exploitation of academics' know-how and not by means of formal regulations and institutional devices.

These strategic perceptions led to the formation of what has come to be known as the Mott committee and which, after much argument and lobbying, greatly influenced the relevant policies not only of the University but also of the local planning authorities. (It was this committee's thinking that contributed directly to the establishment of the science park.) They have also had two effects of great consequence in Cambridge. First, they have made it easy for faculty to enter into commercial activity while retaining their academic posts and salaries, with minimum risks to income and lifestyle if they want progressively to move fully into business life.

Second, they have helped create a relaxed and generous attitude on the part of individual faculty members and departments in their dealings with the outside business world. Where the businesses are small high-technology firms in Cambridge itself, this attitude – reinforced by the compactness of Cambridge as a community, the limited extent and particular form of previous industrial development, the abundance of social and business networks that so often originate and interconnect in the colleges, the informality of academic – industry dealings and the calibre of the people involved – has in turn allowed the individuals and departments concerned to play both a stimulating and a supportive role in the development of the young firms. And the role models played by already successful entrepreneurs, some of them originally academics, serve further to encourage faculty members to engage in outside work.

But despite the above paragraph it is important not to exaggerate the direct role of the University in the phenomenon. Rather one must appreciate that its impact is principally through creation of a 'culture of excellence and openness' and through its being a dominant element in the life of the town.

This genealogical analysis shows that only some forty-five of the high-technology businesses in the area have been set up by individuals coming straight from the University (or still remaining in it). However, the University (chiefly the physics, computer and engineering departments) has indirectly been the ultimate origin of virtually all of the other high-technology companies in the phenomenon. This is because first generation spinoffs from the University have themselves spawned new companies, and so on; and also, even where the parent companies (or other companies that have not yet become parents of spinoffs) have not come from the University, the latter has constituted a central reason for the organization concerned to be located in Cambridge in the first place.

Similarly, one must not exaggerate the farsightedness of the Mott committee in the sense of knowing or even planning exactly what the consequences would be of a liberal policy towards commercialization of the academics' know-how. Their thinking was broadly in terms of mobile science-based industrial projects and non-university research institutes setting up in Cambridge, and certainly not of development proceeding by way of spontaneous formation of local small enterprises. In this and in other respects the phenomenon has 'grown like Topsy' and, although emerging out of a multiplicity of diverse but mutually reinforcing decisions and events involving numerous individuals and organizations, has emphatically not been the product of careful across-the-board planning.

Issues raised by the Cambridge phenomenon

University–industry links
In a country so trapped in its declining industrial fortunes and so unused to success, and in which universities have mostly been so far removed from the real world of innovation and economic growth, the Cambridge phenomenon – small-scale and embryonic in many ways as it may be – stands out as an unusual and exciting development. That some of the country's leading companies in a variety of high-technology sectors – such as computer-aided design, certain scientific instruments, high-speed printing and microcomputer design – should have been set up in a university town, and that many of those principals have been very bright young people who historically would seldom have gone into industry or small business, is of more than passing or local interest.

It is important to make clear at once that we recognize that the Cambridge experience is peculiar to Cambridge and is not to be blindly applied elsewhere. Many diverse factors, the great majority of them specific to Cambridge and evolving over a long period of time, have come together to create a local business environment in which commercialization of technology has taken the particular form described fully in our report and briefly outlined above.

The fact that other places do not have the same combination of circumstances as Cambridge certainly does not mean that they cannot potentially have a phenomenon of their own. After all, there is, among others, in the US a Route 128 phenomenon and in Sweden an emerging Gothenburg (Chalmers Institute) phenomenon which, though broadly similar in origin and form, have major differences. In earlier times too, there were phenomena in places like Manchester and Glasgow which, if subjected to the same kind of detailed analysis as the case of Cambridge, would surely show a good number of common features in the interconnected growth of new local businesses. Clearly there is no necessary reason why in Britain in respect of university/industry/small high-technology company development there should be only one phenomenon, and that in Cambridge, or why the Cambridge case constitutes the only possible model for Britain.

Of course Cambridge (along with Oxford) occupies a special place in Britain, not only in higher education but also in the wider political, business and social life of the country. Of course, too, Cambridge is a well-resourced university (by UK standards) and has an exceptionally high concentration of academic research resources, pure and applied, in both the physical and life sciences. But Cambridge does not have a monopoly on excellence nor does it embrace every scientific discipline with commercial application. More important, all other universities (and some polytechnics) have their own substantial research groups and national or even international centres of excellence.

So why not yet elsewhere, even though many other universities have, compared with Cambridge, far more elaborate and structured arrangements for promoting technology transfer and commercialization of research? At the most general level the answer lies, firstly, in the combination of its size and form and the role of the University in its urban environment that makes Cambridge such a special place, and where the phenomenon in embryonic form could be recognized as such and a critical mass more readily achieved. Secondly, it lies in the realm of the University's policies towards commercial involvement on the part of its academics. Both of these factors were examined above.

Beyond these levels, there are many specific circumstances and influences one can adduce in the case of individual universities. In our study we discussed the particular case of Oxford and touched on other broad categories of university such as those formed with lofty ideals in the period of successful industrialization and urbanization in the nineteenth century, those that have grown out of contemporary technical institutes, or those that set up in the expansionary wave of the 1960s. There are both profound and subtle differences between these and other types of the university in their attitude and capability in respect of industrial links; and, although we attempted to do so, generalizations are usually difficult to make.

All these caveats and complexities having been expressed, however, the facts in Cambridge remain that:

1. an environment now exists in which technological entrepreneurship and new firm formation flourish;
2. the University's original and continuing motivation for forging stronger links with industry derives from its long-term commitment to excellence in research, teaching and scholarship, and emphatically not from short-term revenue-raising pressures. Moreover, the University has not so far been in any way deflected by the local growth of high-technology industry from what it sees as its true role as an academic institution, and indeed it believes that in this role it is benefiting appreciably from the phenomenon. (Interestingly, it seems that Cambridge has thus far been able to escape the fierce pressures for a more activist policy towards social involvement and responsibility, as opposed to the purer pursuit of academic freedom, that beset many of the leading US universities around the turn of the present decade);
3. the University's benign but laid-back, non-interventionist posture to industrial linkage and commercialization of research is very different from that of many other such bodies which, if they have not done so already, are seeking to exercise a direct, institutionalized and income-raising role in all the relevant dealings with the outside world;
4. the proliferation of small high-technology companies in Cambridge has taken place despite the lack of a business school and any systematic programme to support would-be and fledgeling entrepreneurs.

This is an awkward set of facts to deal with. They almost suggest that the harder and more deliberately a university tries to promote commercialization of its research, the more likely it is to embark on a structured approach that has an opposite and inhibiting influence. There is indeed empirical evidence for this view, both in Britain and the USA, and Cambridge University has been directly involved in some exercises that bear out the contention.

The logical conclusion is that all universities should adopt Cambridge's liberal approach to commercialization of academic know-how: giving a clear incentive to the individual to play the principal role himself, but placing the onus on him to protect himself and denying the responsibility of the university, and at the same time leaving it to the (local) private sector to provide the requisite financial and business support. It has the great merit of being a simple, comprehensible and workable approach which, though potentially vulnerable to abuse and legal pitfalls, has so far proved robust.

But few, if any, other universities feel they can pursue this strategy at least quite so overtly as Cambridge; or, even if persuaded of its long-term validity, feel that they can move swiftly towards its implementation. It would be simplistic too to expect that other universities, given the realities of their own history and their inherited institutional structures – not to mention the new technology transfer schemes, science parks and other devices that they have set up in the past few years – could suddenly change direction and/or gear in order to follow the Cambridge model.

It is important in this context to recognize that university spinoff companies and creation of a community of small high-technology firms in the vicinity of a university are together but one of many different ways in which academic – industry links can be affected. Cambridge happens to be a particular, and so far successful, example of this model. But there are other universities where different approaches may be appropriate, in which for instance the application of new technology to existing businesses is likely to be a more prominent element in the whole range of links with outside industry. (In the case of the old industrial areas of Britain there can be no doubt that technological upgrading of existing small and medium firms represents a quantitatively and qualitatively greater challenge than does formation of brand-new high-technology enterprises alone.)

Even here, however, a long-term view of the Cambridge model shows its prospectively beneficial influence on the use of new technology by ordinary firms. A variety of academic studies over the past decade have demonstrated that new technology is more swiftly and widely diffused in a local/regional economy where r&d and innovation are already taking place. In theory Cambridge thus constitutes an excellent environment for technology transfer to be effected among the full range of small firms; empirical observation and anecdotal evidence amply confirm that in practice this is the case too.

The above are complex and contentious issues and are beyond the scope of this paper to examine thoroughly. There are other issues too, such as whether and how the 'true' purpose of a university is influenced, adversely or beneficially, by its pursuit of industrial links and commercialization policies. Or again, where interventionist approaches are taken to industrial linkage and new structures established, are the costs outweighed by the benefits? There is anecdotal evidence on both sides. The precise form of institutional arrangement seems to matter rather less to the success of industrial linkage activity than does the history of the institution's relationship with industry and the authority's overall policy towards new relationships. Thus, those universities that have grown out of colleges of advanced technology or similar institutes, those that have all along specialized in applied sciences and engineering, or those that are embarked upon a multi-faceted programme of contacts with the outside world, tend to have a rich diversity of industrial links irrespective of how they structure their industrial liaison arrangements.

The Cambridge phenomenon study explored some of these matters in the spirit of providing food for thought, but we lacked hard and broadly derived evidence to reach any firm conclusions. The whole area of university–industry relationships is seriously underresearched and misunderstood in Britain, which regrettably impedes good decision-taking at a time when universities are slowly perceiving that their links with industry (widely defined) are not just a peripheral or occasional activity but are central to their whole strategic evolution.

New technology small firms

It would be easy to regard the Cambridge phenomenon as quantitatively trivial in its direct, aggregate impact on output and employment, and to lead on from there to dismiss the economic significance of new technology small firms. But it would be simplistic and unsatisfactory to reach such conclusions on three main counts.

First, and perhaps least importantly, any assessment of the quantitative impact must take account of the high local multiplier effects on a whole range of other industries. The experience of Massachusetts, and the growing evidence in Cambridge, is that these indirect effects greatly outweigh numerically jobs and incomes generated directly in the high-technology industries themselves.

Second, by virtue of their inherently greater flexibility and responsiveness than large firms, small firms have a special role to play in developing certain new technologies, in creating specialized products or processes and in moving into niche markets. These characteristics are increasingly well recognized by large firms (and central government) in the US, far more so than in the UK, and a mutually beneficial symbiotic relationship exists between large and small technology-based enterprises.

Third, new technology small firms – especially those that grow up on the edges of a university or research institution – are helping to encourage more positive attitudes among scientific researchers and among the academic community generally towards industry and towards being in business. This impact on a local culture may be the least tangible but, in a country such as Britain (probably not the United States where the prevailing culture is already more entrepreneurial), it is arguably the most important long-term consequence. Where there is a clustering of firms and associated growth of the sophisticated financial and business services community, this impact is all the greater and far-reaching.

Given this statement about the importance of the high-technology small firms sector, what can be said about its actual performance to date? The Cambridge phenomenon provides abundant evidence of the start-up and growth experience of high-technology firms. Interestingly (and very surprisingly for Britain) the availability of finance for start-up and the mechanics of start-up have not been major problems. There are several reasons for this, which need not be discussed here.

But growth of the firms, especially as they necessarily must become market rather than technology led and as they move above, say, fifty employees in size, is proving rather more difficult. It is noteworthy that those firms that have grown to any size (irrespective of how rapidly) have experienced considerable organizational and management problems; and it is disturbing from a national point of view that it has been mostly foreign rather than British firms that have been involved in take-overs.

It would be quite wrong, however, to present a gloomy picture of the management capability and the prospects of the firms. Where ten years ago virtually no such capability existed except in the long-established firms, now there is a wide and growing pool of management and of specialist business expertise in the Cambridge area. It is only a matter of time before the problem of growth is more readily solved.

It is interesting to see some of the ways by which the local management pool is being strengthened. These include normal processes such as the accumulation of on-the-job experience (learning by doing), 'recycling' of entrepreneurs from established and successful to new firms, head-hunting and the like, and, of course, acquisition by larger outside firms. In addition, one of the consequences of the severe difficulties experienced by the local microcomputer firms is that the refinancing package typically is accompanied by the introduction of professional managers to replace as principle executives the technologists who started up the enterprises. Painful as the process may be for the individuals concerned, there is no doubting the benefits to the firms themselves and in the wider sense to the business community as a whole.

Taking a long view, it is these questions of growth of the young companies that present the major challenge for the future. Very few of the Cambridge companies (and indeed of high-technology companies anywhere) are in markets where spectacular growth and very large scale are possible; but equally there is no doubt that they must grow if they are to survive and prosper. Yet it is here that the British record generally – not just Cambridge in particular – is greatly in need of improvement. The change in attitudes and business and financial infrastructure that has transformed the national start-up picture over the past decade has yet to find its equivalent in the task of growing firms, once established, into sizeable enterprises.

Conclusion

The Cambridge phenomenon is still, despite its long-standing origins, in an early stage of development. Whether and how it will prosper and grow are matters of much importance that go beyond the performance of the individual businesses themselves. There can be little doubt that universities, governments, local authorities and development agencies in many different countries will watch with interest how the phenomenon matures and will want to continue to learn from its evolving experience.

These are issues for the future. For the present, the significance of the phenomenon is that it has emerged at all. Universities and advanced technology small firms together make up a combination of institutions that only a decade or so ago would have seemed unlikely if not incomprehensible, but which today are regarded as constituting key actors on the economic stage of the future.

It is worth emphasizing that the Cambridge case is not a model to be slavishly followed in other locations; it is indeed food for thought, for helping set such a stage elsewhere. There are no unique ways of achieving this. Each teaching or research institution, each set of institutions in a regional or local economy, each of the concerned public and private sector interests involved, must find its own approach. But, for the moment, the Cambridge phenomenon stands as an important example of local economic development that has been triggered by academic–industry interaction and technological entrepreneurship, which can be fruitfully pondered by others seeking to create their own phenomena in their particular environment.

The university sector and technology transfer

William K. Bolton
University of Cambridge, UK
Cambridge Robotics Limited

The potential contribution of the university sector to economic growth, based upon high technology, is well recognized in most developed countries. The difficulty lies in achieving this potential. Within the UK a severe recession, which particularly hit the traditional industries, and the resulting high levels of unemployment has left many feeling that high tech is the only answer to economic prosperity in the twenty-first century. For this reason, the universities have come under increasing pressure from government, industry, and the general public, to be more cost effective and for their teaching and research to be more directed to national needs.

Although it appears from the outside that the response by the universities to these pressures is slow and inadequate, there are, in fact, a wide range of initiatives under way which should steadily improve the industrial and economic relevance of university research and undergraduate courses. Genuine technology transfer is taking place and the task now is to enhance and reinforce these initiatives as a matter of urgency.

Vitally important as they are, such national initiatives take time to have any real effect and it is noteworthy that a high technology sector has grown up in the Cambridge area almost totally independent of them. Instead, local parameters have been important. For example, the rural nature of the Cambridge area meant that there were no large established companies and no industrial infrastructure which had first to be changed. Also there was a local concentration of knowledge in one growing area of technology, namely computer aided design (CAD).

Technology transfer and the growth of a high-tech community in Cambridge was thus possible because of a sound technological base and because it was a matter of evolving the application of the technology rather than transferring it as a block to a pre-existing group. Now, of course, an infrastructure does exist, but as this is oriented towards the small high-tech company, transfer of ideas and people is rapid and straightforward.

In considering the role of the university sector in technology transfer, it is necessary to keep their research resources in perspective. The figures for the UK in terms of money spent, are that 60 per cent of its r&d related to science and technology is conducted in private industry and 22 per cent in Government research establishments; the figure for the university sector is only 9 per cent. Although this data relates to 1978[1], there is no reason to believe that these proportions have changed significantly. The influence and importance in the UK of the university sector in the research area is, of course, greater than 9 per cent but it still cannot be considered as large.

This chapter deals first with recent initiatives to open up the university sector to industry as a basis for more effective technology transfer. It then describes particular initiatives in Cambridge with which the writer has been associated.

National initiatives

At the undergraduate level in the universities there have been major revisions of courses in science and technology to reflect more closely the current state of technology and the needs of employers. Some totally new courses have been introduced particularly in the area of manufacturing engineering. Many of the changes have been in high technology where the demand from the students themselves for courses in electronics, computer, biotechnology and so on has been a further pressure for change upon the universities.

On the research side there have been important initiatives in the UK over the last three years to direct government spending on university research into strategic areas such as information technology and computer-aided manufacturing. Special national programmes have been formulated and criteria such as industrial support and future take-up by industry are used in assessing proposals. Within this approach a balance is sought between research for its own sake, and research that has obvious commercial implications.

In June 1983, the UK Government Advisory Council on Applied Research and Development published a report entitled 'Improving research links between higher education and industry'[2] This report concluded that whilst universities, industry and government were all involved, 'given the steps they are already taking, the initiative for forging new and productive links should lie mainly with the Higher Education Institutions'. To encourage this to happen, it was recommended that government money for basic research should be provided in proportion to the value of contract work done by the universities for industry. Government money should also be available to fund specific initiatives that 'contributed significantly to the infrastructure for academic – industrial cooperation'.

Of the six collaborative schemes, operated by the Government Science and Engineering Research Council (SERC), described in the above report,[3] the two largest have particular relevance to technology transfer. These are the Cooperative Award in Science and Technology (CASE) scheme, and the Teaching Company scheme. Both involve research work being carried out in an industrial research laboratory or operating company under academic supervision and by students funded through the university system. In this way, transfer of the technology to the user is taking place as the knowledge base is being built up.

The CASE scheme generally involves the student in study for a postgraduate degree and, in 1981, about 30 per cent of the awards made by the SERC for PhD studies were through these CASE programmes. The Teaching Company scheme is more concerned with the application of research and development than basic research, and so is not always associated with doctoral studies. The scheme takes its name from the Teaching Hospital of the medical student and the similarity is that it provides a vocational-based learning environment with some degree of academic supervision. These original objectives have now evolved to the point where the scheme is seen by industry as a very effective means for the transfer of technology from the university sector. The provision of an academically supervised and independent team of high-calibre people to implement, as well as advise on, new technology is particularly attractive to industry. It is also a significantly less-expensive option for the company than employing a team of professional consultants.

From 1980 to 1984, the writer was responsible for a Teaching Company programme between Cambridge University and the Plessey Electronics Group. It enabled one of the Plessey companies to take a major step towards true computer integrated manufacturing so that they are now able to provide unmanned production over several days, of a variety of mechanical parts down to a batch size of one. To continue with and expand the knowledge base so established, the company set up its own Advanced Manufacturing Group and offered positions in it to the Teaching Company research students on completion of their two-year contract with the University.

Throughout the UK there are now more than 140 Teaching Company programmes in operation, with plans by the government Department of Industry and the SERC to double this over the next five years. While transferring technology to the participating companies, the Teaching Company programmes have also produced a regular spinoff of ideas and products. The writer's own company, Cambridge Robotics Limited, was to a large extent a spinoff from the Cambridge/Plessey programme, and its first full-time employee was the Senior Research Associate who had headed the University research team at Plessey.

In addition to focusing research funding on key areas of technology and of providing schemes where universities develop the technology alongside industry, the long-established procedures for exploiting university inventions and ideas have been restructured. The British Technology Group (BTG) was formed in 1981 from the old National Enterprise Board and the National Research Development Council (NRDC). This brought research and business experience together and was an important move. Even so, it was not until this year that the obligation was lifted for a university researcher on government funding to give the BTG first refusal on any invention or product development. Although some important inventions have been successfully exploited, this restriction was on the whole unsatisfactory. The new freedom should encourage technology transfer and will mean that BTG has to compete with other commercializing and funding agencies on an equal footing.

The Cambridge scene

The growth of high-tech commercial activity in and around Cambridge, England, is an example of a multi-initiative approach to technology transfer. There have been many small initiatives by local entrepreneurs, the University and colleges, individual academics, local research groups, banks (notably Barclays) and so on. It is true that some of these initiatives have resulted in quite large enterprises but they all started small. The Cambridge science park, for example, grew at the rate of only one company per year for the first five years[4] yet now has fifty companies employing a total of 1500 people.

These initiatives were many and small because they were generally the result of two or three individuals, rather than their organizations, getting together and generating the initiative. It is this feature that gives the Cambridge phenomenon its strongly indigenous character.

The presence in the area of a strong technological base through the activities of the university departments and other research institutions was also clearly important. Even so, transfer would probably not have taken place at such a rate but for the many initiatives taken and the presence of triggers to force some of them into reality. However, now that an entrepreneurial climate has been created, these triggers are less important.

The initative for the Cambridge science park was taken by the Senior Bursar of Trinity College, Dr Bradfield, who felt that the derelict land, owned by the college on the edge of the City, could best be exploited in this way. The availability of this otherwise non-revenue earning land thus provided the opportunity for an important transfer mechanism to be established.

Triggers were unwittingly also provided by the slow decision-making processes of the funding authorities. This chiefly affected groups on government funding such as the CAD Centre and University research teams, and had the effect of causing high-tech spinoffs on a regular basis. In addition to these decision delays, there is a trigger built into the employment of SERC-funded research workers which limits their tenure to six years after which time they must find alternative employment.

Initiatives in the financial and management area were less evident but grew as the high-tech scene developed. Two people in the local Barclays Bank and one local accounting firm played an important part in providing financial support and advice.

Informal networks have become an important feature of what has grown up around Cambridge. These provide information and know-how which contribute to the transfer of technology and, often more important, the business opportunity represented by that transfer. The opportunity aspects of technology transfer can too easily be neglected and informal networks are an effective way of keeping these to the fore.

Specific local initiatives

With so many initiatives happening, it is difficult to give a balanced picture of the position. The following have been selected on the basis of the writer's direct knowledge and the important issues they raise for technology transfer mechanisms.

TopExpress Limited   This small company specializes in high-quality contract research. It is thus concerned with both the generation and transfer of technology. It was founded by Professor Ffowcs-Williams of the University Engineering Department, who was finding it increasingly difficult to recruit good postdoctoral people into the university system because of unattractive pay and employment conditions. By setting up his own private company, Professor Ffowcs-Williams has been able to set appropriate employment terms to allow first-rate research groups to be established.

This emergence of a company to conduct research in the shadow of a University such as Cambridge, has important implications for the future of research work in universities if terms and conditions of research staff cannot be improved. There is an obvious danger that university research will slip to a level of mediocrity that will be of little value to the high-tech industry of the future.

Cambridge Life Science Limited   This is one of a number of rapidly growing biotechnology companies in the Cambridge area. The company is noteworthy for the way in which it has structured itself around a particularly technology-transfer policy.

Although it is only a small company, it has been able to raise sufficient venture-capital funding to support research work in a number of universities. The research teams and areas are carefully selected by the company in line with their product strategy. The assumption in providing this 'up-front' money to the universities is that the lead time on the commercial exploitation of research in the biotechnology field is only two to three years. The technology is then transferred into the company and the product development completed.

Whilst this kind of arrangement may only work with biotechnology, the use of a small entrepreneurial company to sponsor research in larger establishments is a transfer mechanism worthy of wider consideration. It would ensure that research is market-led and bring an enthusiasm and reality to the research groups.

Undergraduate project   In 1979, the Cambridge University Engineering Department set up a new four-year course in manufacturing engineering. Within the third year of that course, the writer has developed a 'New Business Proposal' project to integrate the engineering subjects with those of a financial and management nature. Reality is added to the project by simulating a true-to-life entrepreneurial situation. The students are required to assume that they are in their mid-twenties with family and financial commitments. They assume that they are already employed in the Cambridge area but wish, as a group of four, to set up their own business. A product area is specified and the group must work through the marketing, design and manufacturing stages concluding with a business plan as a basis for raising venture funding and launching the company.

Over the past six years, the project has produced new business proposals covering nearly twenty products. At least four patents have been taken out by the students themselves, and one group won a National Design prize. Despite the obvious potential, the undergraduate nature of the project has made subsequent exploitation impractical.

Although the technology transfer element of this project has been limited, it has had the unexpected and important result of revealing the would-be entrepreneurs among the students. There are normally about 10 per cent of them in this category but the absence of any enabling mechanisms relating to product development and funding has meant that most take their ideas no further.

Despite this difficulty, three new companies have in fact been set up by these students. The first, Rhombus Systems Limited, works in the area of factory data collection systems and was founded in 1981: this company has recently located in the Cambridge science park. The second company, Light-work Limited, was founded in 1984 by two students who wanted to design and manufacture a new type of bicycle lamp. The students used the last of their fourth year project periods to prepare a business proposal, and were then able to obtain local bank funding. They also won an East Anglia Regional prize with their business plan. The third company, Montec Limited, was launched this year and was the first to be based upon the third-year student project. Their product is concerned with the remote condition monitoring of water pumping stations.

Though these developments are encouraging, much more could be done if the right technology and business transfer mechanisms were in place. One proposal under serious consideration is to set up a programme whereby the new graduates or research students can be given help in bringing their ideas to a stage where a viable business plan can be drawn up. Educational input would be provided as required, for example on the financial side. Such an entrepreneur school could help provide an important link in the transfer mechanism by providing support to those actually wishing to do the transfer.

St John's College, Cambridge   The links between the Cambridge high-tech industry and the University are indirect and difficult to quantify. However, an initiative by Dr C. Johnson, the Senior Bursar of St John's College, and the writer to provide direct and effective links is now under way. Within the College, the Fellowship provides links with all the science and technology departments in the University, and St John's has the largest number of students of any college.

Using this 'people and ideas' base, the College is planning a building to house student entrepreneurs who are at the embryo and fledgeling stages of their new businesses. Inspiration and help for this has come from the Utah Innovation Center and it is hoped that some formal link will be possible. Temporary accommodation has already been provided by the College and the company Montec Limited, referred to above, is now housed there. The main building was planned for completion in late 1986 to be located close to the site of the Cambridge science park. This innovation or enterprise centre will be the focus for a range of satellite buildings into which the small companies can move on leaving the centre. The idea is to develop an innovation park in which the centre plays a central and supportive role throughout. As companies grow, they will move through the facilities offered by the centre and the park and move into permanent premises elsewhere. This will not be a rapid process but it is important to have a steady flow of enterprises if the dynamism of the park is to be sustained.

Wolfson Industrial Liaison Unit   This unit was established some time ago with funding from the Wolfson Trust. In 1983 Mr Stephen Bragg, who was previously a research director in industry and a university Vice-Chancellor, was appointed its director. He has been behind a number of initiatives to help industry identify the exact location in the University of the area of expertise they require. With such a large number of specialists, this has been no easy task but it is an essential part of any university technology transfer programme. Mr Bragg was also behind a seminar run for research students on how they should go about setting up and running a business. The good response to this seminar was another indication of the considerable potential that still remains to be exploited.

Experience in the UK with university/industry liaison groups has been mixed. The enabling role that they can play in helping academics relate to the outside world and providing the connections needed by industry is considered to be crucial.

Conclusion

This paper has described some of the approaches in the UK to technology transfer from the universities. The government and industry-linked initiatives are seen as important but necessarily long-term. The initiatives involved in the Cambridge high-tech scene have, on the other hand, been local and very effective on a relatively short timescale. This argues for control funding, controls which enable things to happen and flexibility to allow local initiatives to flourish. A multitude of small initiatives is to be encouraged since the winners can emerge and a network develop.

As to the future, it is to be hoped that the national initiatives are followed through with urgency and that industry as a whole sees and seizes the opportunity that technology transfer can provide. The high-tech community in Cambridge is poised for a second stage of growth. A number of the international accountancy companies has recently moved into the area and some of the more successful CAD companies have been bought by larger firms, generally from the USA. In addition, Cambridge is now part of the circuit for venture fund companies and some have or are about to set up a permanent base there. Major business parks are being planned and some large companies are hoping to move into the area.

All these activities point to a second stage of growth which will be larger than the first, but of a different nature. It is likely to be less indigenous, though this will still be an important element. Larger groups will emerge and the quality of management will steadily improve with a maturing of the high-tech business community. It will be important to retain the dynamism and enthusiasm of the last few years and this will depend to a large extent on whether the informal networks continue to operate.

The exploitation of the university as a source of ideas and people has still to be achieved and this could be one of the really important elements of the second stage of growth. This gives a strategic importance to some of the local initiatives outlined above and in particular, that by St John's College.

References

1 *Economic Trends* 1981 August. HMSO, London.
2 ACARD 1983 *Improving research links between higher education and industry*. ACARD Report June. HMSO, London.
3 Bolton W. K. 1985 Recent university–industry initiatives in the United Kingdom *European Journal of Engineering Education* 10 (2): 97–101.
4 Bolton W. K. 1982. The Cambridge Science Park. SEFI Conference on the Education of the Engineer for Innovation and Entrepreneurial Activity, Delft, 87–95.

High-technology companies that are university spinoffs

Everett M. Rogers
Anneburg School of Communications, University of Southern California

The purpose of this paper is to summarize what is known about the process that leads to the spinoff of private firms from research universities. The focus is upon the United States, and upon high-technology firms in the microelectronics industry, a sector in which a high rate of technological innovation is occurring and which represents the main arena for close university–industry relations in the 1980s.

The information society

In recent years, the United States, Japan, and most Western European nations have passed through an important transition in the make-up of their workforce, the basis of their economy, and in the very nature of their society. Information has become the vital element in the new society that has emerged, and so these nations are called 'information societies'.

An information society is a nation in which a majority of the labour force is composed of information workers, and in which information is the most important element (Rogers, in press 1986). Thus, the information society represents a sharp change from the industrial society in which a majority of the workforce was employed in manufacturing occupations, such as auto-assembly and steel-production, and where the key element was energy. In contrast, information workers are individuals whose main activity is producing, processing, or distributing information, and producing information technology. Typical information-worker occupations are teachers, scientists, newspaper reporters, computer programmers, consultants, secretaries, and managers. These individuals write, teach, sell advice, give orders, and otherwise deal in information. Their main activity is not to raise food, put together nuts and bolts, or to deal with physical objects.

Information is patterned matter-energy that affects the probabilities available to an individual making a decision (Rogers and Kincaid, 1981). Information lacks a physical existence of its own; it can only be expressed in a material form (such as ink on paper) or in an energy form (like electrical impulses). Information can often be substituted for other resources, such as money and/or energy. Information behaves somewhat oddly as an economic resource in the sense that one can sell it (or give it away) and still have it.

Applications of the steam engine to manufacturing and transportation,

Figure 13 The USA became an industrial society in about 1900, and an information society in about 1950

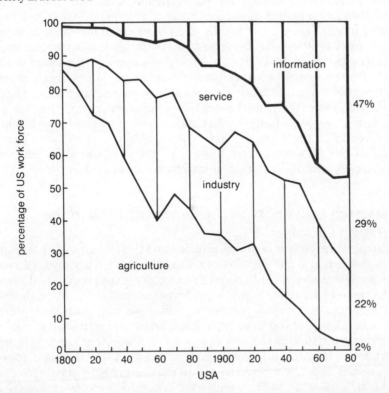

Table 13 Comparison of the agricultural society, industrial society, and the information society

Key characteristics	Agricultural society	Industrial society	Information society
1. Time period	10 000 years (and continues today in most Third World countries)	200 years (began in about 1750 in England)	? years (began in about 1955 in the US)
2. Key element/basic resource	Food	Energy	Information
3. Main type of worker	Farmers	Factory workers	Information workers
4. Key social institutions	Farms	Steel factory	Research university
5. Basic technology	Manual labour	Steam engine	Computer and electronics
6. Nature of mass-communication	One-way print media	One-way electronic media (radio, film, TV)	Interactive media that are demasified in nature

beginning around 1750 in England, set off the Industrial Revolution that began the transition from an agricultural society to an industrial society. The agricultural society has been dominant for about 10 000 years until this point, and most Third World nations are still agricultural societies today. The Industrial Revolution spread throughout most of Europe, to North America, and later to Japan. Figure 13 shows that the US began to industrialize in the mid 1880s; from 1900 to 1955, the largest part of the workforce was employed in industrial jobs. Then, in 1955, an historical discontinuity happened in the US when industrial employment began to decrease and information workers became most numerous. Today they are a majority, representing about 55 per cent of the workforce. While the United States led other nations in becoming an information society, Canada, England, Sweden, France, and other European countries are not far behind.

Certain of the important characteristics of the agricultural society, the industrial society, and the information society, are compared in Table 13.

The research university as the key institution in the information society

Fundamental to the growth of the information society is the rise of knowledge industries that produce and distribute information, rather than material products, or goods and services. The research university firstly produces information as the result of the research that it conducts, especially basic research, and secondly produces information-producers (individuals with graduate degrees, who are trained to conduct research). This information-producing role is particularly characteristic of the fifty or so leading research universities in the United States. A research university is an institution of higher learning whose main function is to perform research and to provide graduate training.

The research university fulfills a role in the information society analogous to that of the factory in the industrial society. It is the key institution around which growth occurs, and it determines the direction of that growth. Each of the several major high-technology regions in the United States is centred around a research university: Silicon Valley and Stanford University; Route 128 and MIT; and Research Triangle and the three main North Carolina universities (Duke, North Carolina State, and the University of North Carolina). The research university is especially important to its nearby high-technology firms when they are relatively new.

A high-technology industry is one in which the basic technology underlying the industry changes very rapidly. A high-tech industry is characterized by: highly educated employees, many of whom are scientists and engineers; a rapid rate of technological innovation; a high ratio of r&d expenditures to sales (typically about 1:10); and a worldwide market for its products (Rogers and Larsen, 1984). The main high-technology industries today are electronics, aerospace, pharmaceuticals, instrumentation, and biotechnology. Microelectronics, the sub-industry of electronics, centred on semiconductor chips and their applications (such as in computers), is usually considered the highest of high technology because the underlying technology is changing more rapidly than in other high-technology industries.

Microelectronics technology, applied in the form of computers (especially microcomputers) and telecommunications, are driving nations like the United States into becoming information societies. That is why the role of the research university is so important in understanding the emergence of the information society. Research universities today are helping to redraw the economic map of the United States, by creating clusters of high-technology industrial firms around certain university campuses.

The trend to closer university–industry relationships

What caused the trend in recent years to closer university–industry relationships, especially in the conduct of research? During the 1980s the US federal government cut back severely on its funding of university research (except for military research). Consequently, universities looked to private industry for research funds. The National Science Foundation (NSF) estimates that industrial funding of university research has increased fourfold in the past decade, to about $300 million. During the 1980s many state and local governments launched initiatives to encourage the development of high-technology industry, in order to create new jobs and to fuel economic growth. Fearful of Japanese competition, US microelectronics firms formed university–industry collaborative research centres, and invested considerable resources in funding these centres.

Largest of the new r&d centres is the Microelectronics and Computer Technology Corporation (MCC), which is located on the campus of the University of Texas at Austin in 1983. Fifty-six other cities in twenty-seven states competed with Austin for the MCC, with state and local governments offering a variety of incentives. Three hundred Texas leaders in state and local governments, universities, and private companies put together a multi-million dollar package to win the MCC.

Arizona Governor Bruce Babbitt, whose state was a finalist in the selection process, remarked (1984): 'Some 60 mayors and 27 governors complained about the unfair advantage of Texas oil money, and promised their constituents a better showing next time.' Certainly the 1983 MCC decision heightened awareness among states and local officials about the importance of high-technology development, and created a fuller realization of the role of research universities in attracting high-technology firms.

What did the University of Texas, the state of Texas, and the city of Austin get in return for their efforts to attract the MCC? The MCC is supported at $75 million per year by a consortium of twenty-one US firms that are the giants of the microelectronics industry, plus government research grants (mainly for the US Department of Defense). The MCC presently has a research staff of about four hundred. During its first year of operation, the MCC created a boom-town mentality in Austin. Fourteen high-technology firms moved all or part of their operations employing 6100 people to Austin during 1983, while in 1982 only four companies with 900 jobs moved to Austin. The average selling price of a new single-family home rose 20 per cent to $106 157 during 1983.

But the main benefits to Austin of getting the MCC will appear years from now, when a high-technology complex in microelectronics develops around the city. It is possible that this complex may eventually rival or surpass California's Silicon Valley as a centre for the production of information technology. In this sense, the MCC decision may have settled the location of the future capital of the information society.

The MCC is only one of several new university–industry research centres in microelectronics. Others include the following centres. The Center for Integrated Systems (CIS) at Stanford University was founded in 1981 and is supported by $15 million from twenty US microelectronics firms, and $15 million from the US Department of Defense. Arizona State University launched its Center for Solid-State Electronics Research as part of its Excellence in Engineering Program in 1981, to encourage the development of high-technology industry. Funding for the first five years consists of $20 million from the state of Arizona, $10 million from private firms, and $3 million from the federal government. The Microsystems Industrial Group at MIT is sponsored by about a dozen companies, many of them on Route 128. The Microelectronics Center of North Carolina (MCNC), a research and training facility in Research Triangle Park, was launched in 1980 with $24 million from the state legislature.

Today there are about twenty-five university–industry microelectronics research centres at US universities. Other such collaborative r&d centres have been founded for robotics, biotechnology, and other high-technology fields. In addition, many other technology transfer mechanisms are used by research universities such as research parks, like the Stanford Research Park (which was the first of its kind, and still is the most successful). Industrial liaison programmes by universities provide a means for private firms to get an early look at research results and to identify promising students to hire as future employees, in exchange for paying an annual membership fee to the university. Another useful mechanism is provided by faculty consulting by universities' professors. President Carl Taylor Compton of MIT in the 1930s not only allowed his faculty to consult for pay one day a week, but strongly encouraged them to do so. After World War II, the MIT faculty consulting policy spread to Stanford University, and, in recent years, to a number of other research universities that wish to foster technology transfer. Typically a university allows its professors to work for pay one day per week. Especially in recent years, professors have formed companies of their own, often launching their start-up around a technological idea that they bring with them from their university laboratory. In some cases, the faculty entrepreneur who founds a high-technology company then cuts off his/her academic ties.

What government initiatives promote high-technology industry?

Figure 14 shows how federal, state, and local governments directly encourage high-technology development, and how they indirectly seek this goal through facilitating the role of local research universities. Although state and local governments are far more active than the federal government in promoting high-technology development, a variety of federal policies and programmes encourage high-technology industry to cooperate with research universities. The Economic Recovery Tax Act of 1981 provides a 25 per cent tax credit for increased corporate r&d expenditures over a base year; up to 65 per cent of research contracted to universities and to certain other institutions is covered by this Act. Further, federal policy allows firms to deduct from their taxes as charitable contributions part of the cost of equipment donated to universities. Changes in federal tax policies in recent years also have aided the expansion of venture capital; as a result, it has been easier to obtain financing to launch start-up firms (Rogers and Larsen, 1984).

Figure 14 Federal, state and local government initiatives promote high-technology development through technology transfer exchanges between research universities and microelectronics firms

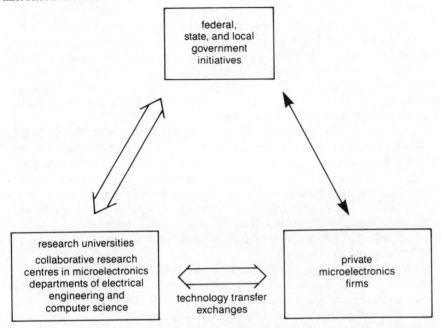

The recent easing by the federal government of antitrust restrictions on collaborative r&d activities has facilitated closer university–industry relationships. The MCC in Austin could not have been founded had it not been for a favourable opinion by the US Department of Justice on 28 December 1982. In 1984, federal legislation was passed to remove certain antitrust barriers to collaborative r&d.

State governments have initiated programmes to coordinate the activities of state and local governments, private industry, and universities to facilitate technology transfer between the research university and its surrounding high-technology firms. State and local laws are factors affecting technology transfer and the development of high-technology industry. For example, absence of a state income tax in Texas is cited by some firms as an important reason why they moved to Austin.

Benefits and costs of university–industry relationships

Clearly the university–industry collaborative research centres in microelectronics represent a new and important force on the university campus, and one that has already generated a great deal of policy controversy. 'Few subjects have received as much attention recently in university circles as the prospect of closer relations with American business' (Rosenzweig 1982). Some observers see this recent development in a very positive light. Governor Bruce Babbit (1984) of Arizona refers to 'a new awareness that the fruits of university research and development activity have little economic value unless they are systematically harvested in the marketplace'. The university obviously benefits from the research funds that it receives, and the professors may gain useful experience which they can incorporate in their courses for the benefit of their students.

In general, both the research universities and private industry are pleased with their new, closer relationships. Microelectronics companies feel that their membership fees paid to the collaborative university–industry research centres are one means of dealing with Japanese competition (for example, the MCC justifies its existence publicly as the US response to the Japanese Fifth-Generation Computer Project). In addition, semiconductor companies in Silicon Valley report they participate in the collaborative centres as a means to identify future employees and faculty consultants from among university students and professors (Larsen, 1984).

But there are also a variety of problems connected with the industry-sponsored research centres on university campuses. For instance, the priorities accorded by a university to certain disciplines and to certain research problems may be affected by the priorities of private firms that donate research funds, thus causing a feeling of relative deprivation on the part of departments and professors not so favoured. The growing emphasis on technology may come at the expense of arts and humanities. University scientists fear that the price of industry collaboration will be a shift from basic research to more product-oriented development.

Problems of inequality also can occur between universities, as well as within a university. When Stanford, Texas, Arizona State, and MIT create university–industry collaborative research centres in microelectronics, are other universities adversely affected? Hancock (1983) noted that in the new era of university–industry relationships, 'One trend is apparent; corporate money goes to the academic haves, not the have-nots.'

'Concern about the propriety of university–industry relations has been a central theme on the country's research campuses for the past couple of years' (Culliton, 1983). Perhaps one turning point in the recognition of this problem occurred in 1982 when the presidents of five universities met with eleven corporate leaders at Pajaro Dunes (California) to explore such questions as:

> How can universities preserve open communication and independence in the direction of basic research while also meeting obligations to industry? Is it acceptable for one corporation to dominate research in an entire [academic] department? Are there adverse consequences in terms of collaboration among faculty in various departments if one group must worry about protecting corporate right to licences? Will extensive corporate ties erode public confidence in university faculty as disinterested seekers of truth? (*Science*, 1982).

Three main points of potential conflict between the university and private firms exist in the present era of closer relationships: restrictions on the communication of research results, where company secrecy policies may conflict with the scientific desire for free communication; the relatively short-term research orientation of the private firms versus the longer-term orientation of university scientists toward basic research; and the agenda of priorities for university research may be affected by corporate sponsorship, with emphasis upon scientific fields with a direct potential for commercial pay-off. Clearly the new relationships between industry and the university, often fostered by government initiatives and intended to encourage high-technology development, mark a very important change in the role of the US university.

Lessons learned about promoting high-technology industry

The experience of recent years indicates that state and local governments often are engaging in a futile activity when they try to attract high-technology firms away from other locales in the United States. It is more effective for a state or city to grow its own high-technology industry, than to try to steal it from another city or state. One seed for starting local entrepreneurial activities is to invest in improving a nearby research university, especially in such academic departmments as electrical engineering, computer science, and molecular biology. Investment in improving a local university is likely to pay off, eventually, in technology transfer to private firms and, later, to generating an entrepreneurial head of steam in starting-up high-tech firms.

A considerable time lag is usually involved from the improvement of a research university, to the rise of a local high-technology industry. Evidence on this point is provided by the case of the Research Triangle in North Carolina. Governor Luther H. Hodges had the original vision of a North Carolina high-technology centre back in the 1950s. Hodges followed the Stanford University model of establishing a university research park in order to create a high-technology complex. Only after twenty years of concerted efforts did many high-tech firms begin to move to the Research Triangle, with the key turning point occurring in 1965 when IBM located an r&d unit there. Total employment in Research Triangle Park's forty firms is now over 20 000 with an annual payroll of $500 million (Rogers and Larsen, 1984, p 241). But there is not yet much entrepreneurial activity in starting up *new* firms. Several decades were also necessary for the rise of Silicon Valley in Northern California and for the beginnings of Route 128 around Boston. So high-technology industry does not usually get underway overnight. (On the other hand, the present Austin take-off is occurring very rapidly.)

The presence of an outstanding research university in a locale does not necessarily cause the development of a high-technology centre. Evidence of this point is provided by such excellent universities as Harvard, Columbia, Chicago, Berkeley, and Cal Tech, none of whom have played an important role in technology transfer to local firms. Obviously, other factors than just the presence of a local research university are involved in launching a high-technology centre: a high quality-of-life, models of the entrepreneurial spirit, and the presence of venture capital. Even when a research university is present, it must have policies that encourage faculty to assist local firms, or else not much technology transfer will occur. Such favourable policies exist at Stanford, MIT, Texas, Arizona State, the North Carolina universities, and at other universities.

Throughout this chapter it has been implied that the research university and private firms each have an important role to play in the rise of a high-technology community. 'Universities are not good incubators because they are too far removed from the marketplace' (Miller and Coté, 1985). Obviously then, the increasing degree of collaboration between industry and the research university augers well for high-tech spinoffs. However, not much technology is transferred from the university to industry (or vice versa) through the mechanism of a formal agreement such as a collaborative r&d centre, unless the firms are immediate neighbours to the university. 'Physical proximity facilitates the absorption of new technologies. Technological diffusion is still a geographical phenomenon' (Miller and Coté, 1985).

Striking evidence for the importance of spatial nearness in university
–industry technology transfer is provided by Eveland's (1985) communication-
network analysis of nine collaborative r&d centres that were assisted by the
National Science Foundation. Figure 15 shows the communication networks
among the forty-seven industry representatives of fourteen private firms belonging to one of the university-based r&d centres, plus the five university
administrators, fourteen faculty, and twenty-two students affiliated with this
centre. Very little communication occurs between university personnel and
their industry counterparts, at least on a weekly or monthly basis (once-a-year
contracts are not shown here, because not much technology-exchange could
happen on such a limited basis). Eveland's (1985, p 46) network analysis shows
that the professors are fairly interconnected, and that students constitute the
next layer of the onion, with each student communicating mainly to his/her
professor. The next layer out in the sociogram (Figure 15) consist of industry
representatives; about 70 per cent are isolates and only six of the forty-seven
communicate with the university people on a monthly basis.

Figure 15   Network Analysis of Research Project-Related Communication among 88
individuals in a Collaborative Industry–University Research Center.

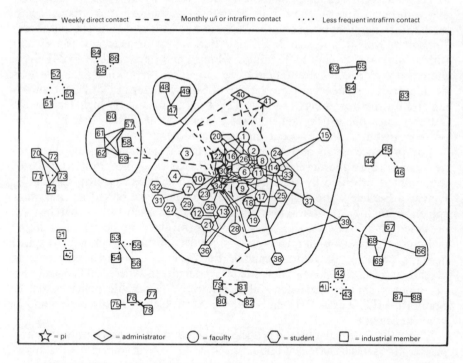

Source: Eveland (1985, p 46).

The r&d centre depicted in Figure 15 conducts basic research in a very
traditional scientific discipline, and this mission may be one reason for the lack
of much industry–university communication. Also, the network data was
gathered in the second year of the r&d centre's operation, and perhaps
effective industry–university communication requires longer to begin.
Nevertheless, Eveland's network data conveys an important cautionary lesson

for those who think that industry–university technology-exchange will occur readily and directly as a result of forming a collaborative r&d centre.

The research university in the United States is changing its role from that of mainly conducting basic research to also taking a more active role in transferring technology to private firms. The most advanced case of this trend is happening in microelectronics, the engineering/scientific field that is driving the information society. Whether the trend to closer university–industry relationships will result in greater benefits than costs to the participants and to society remains to be seen.

References

Babbitt B. 1984 The states and the reindustrialization of America *Issues in Science and Technology* (1): 84–93.

Culliton J. 1983 Academe and industry debate partnership *Science* (219): 150–151.

Eveland J. D. 1985 *Communication Networks in University–Industry Cooperative Research Centers* National Technological Innovation, Productivity Improvement Section, Report, Washington, D.C.

Hancock E. 1983 Academe meets industry: charting the bottom line *Alumni Magazine Consortium* (7): 1–9.

Larsen J. K. 1984 *Policy alternatives and the semiconductor industry*. Cognos Associates, Los Altos, California. Report to the National Science Foundation.

Miller R. and Coté M. 1985 Growing the next Silicon Valley *Harvard Business Review* (63): 114–23.

Rogers M. 1983 *Diffusion of innovations*. Free Press, New York.

Rogers, M. (in press 1986) *Communication Technology*. Free Press, New York.

Rogers M. and Kincaid D. L. 1981 *Communication networks: toward a new paradigm for research*, Free Press, New York.

Rogers M. and Larsen J. K. 1984 *Silicon Valley fever: growth of high-technology culture*. Basic Books, New York.

Rosenzweig R. M. 1982 *The research universities and their patrons*, University of California Press, Berkeley, California.

Science 1982 The academic-industry complex *Science* (216): 960–1

Technology transfer: a focus on university/industry interactions

Robert M. Colton
National Science Foundation

Generic model for technology transfer (industrial innovation)

The generic model is called the Industrial Innovation model and is shown in Figure 16. Its driving force is based on the presumption that mechanisms can be put in place that effectively utilize research and development results. For commercial markets the industrial innovation model is based upon technology transfer occurring in one or more of three modes: direct, interactive, and third party.

Direct

In the direct form of technology transfer the researcher and user are part of the same general organization. They are either in industry or government where transfer usually is accomplished across divisional lines. A typical example in industry would be the General Motors Technical Centre and GM's manufacturing divisions, and, in government, The Waterviet Arsenal where the research development and manufacture of weapons systems are fully integrated. The direct form represents the major transfer technique in the United States and, of the approximately $110 billion of research funds expended in the US in 1985, over 80 per cent is attributed to this direct form, about $60 billion from industry and $30.0 billion from government.

The direct form is probably the most effective way of transferring technology and represents the methodology by which most industrial innovation takes place.

Interactive

In the interactive form the researcher and user are in entirely different organizations but have direct contact in a specific research area. In this case the transfer is normally through direct personal contact between the researcher and user. More often than not the researcher is funded by the user, as is the case with contracted research between a company and a university, research institute or government laboratory. It is also the mode of cooperative research centres where a group of companies jointly fund a university in a basic or applied research area, such as biotechnology or interactive computer graphics. The interactive form represents the lowest level of funding, certainly less than $1.0 billion per year, or less than 1 per cent of the nation's r&d funding level. It represents an effective technology transfer mode and in many

Figure 16 Industrial innovation model

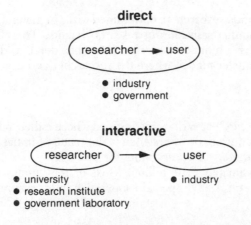

driving force: effective utilization of
research and development results

direct

researcher → user

- industry
- government

interactive

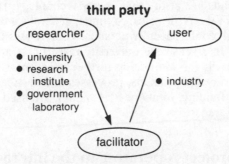

researcher → user

- university
- research institute
- government laboratory

- industry

third party

researcher   user

- university
- research
  institute
- government
  laboratory

- industry

facilitator

- technical information services
- publications
- libraries
- technology transfer agents/licensing agents
- conferences/seminars
- personnel exchanges/visits

cases rivals the direct mode described above in promoting industrial innovation.

Third party
In the third-party form of technology transfer, the researcher and user are in entirely different organizations and transfer of the knowledge is normally through a third party. Most commonly, the third party takes the form of a publication, technical information service, technology transfer agent, conference or personnel visit.

The third-party form is probably the least effective from the standpoint of utilization and industrial innovation, but represents a large expenditure of r&d funds, almost 10 per cent of the total available, or about $10.0 billion in 1985.

National Science Foundation (NSF) programmes as related to the technology transfer (industrial model)

Direct
NSF primarily funds research at universities with, in general, no specific ties to industry or commercialization of research results. Therefore none of the $1.5 billion of NSF's funded research can be considered as direct in terms of the technology transfer model, where the researcher and user are in the same organization.

Interactive
NSF sponsors research at various institutions where either industry/university interactions are required, or where such is the result of initial NSF funding of the research institution. This accounts for less than 7 per cent of the NSF budget, or approximately $0.1 billion. Most of this money goes directly to various types of centres or to special cooperative industry/university projects.

Third party
Most of NSF's funds are of the third-party technology transfer type. In this case the recipient of the NSF research funds, generally a university, produces a report, or through conferences or personal visits relates the research results to potential users. In a sense the university researchers are also users of the research, but primarily for stimulating further necessary research rather than for developing marketable products, processes and services. As such over 90 per cent of NSF's funding, or about $1.4 billion, are used for the third-party type of technology transfer.

NSF Centre projects operating in the interactive mode
This section will deal primarily with detailing three NSF programmes that are of the interactive mode, where direct contact is maintained between the researcher and user over an extended period of time. The three programmes are: engineering research centres (ERC), cooperative research projects (CRP) and cooperative research centres (CRC).

Engineering research centres
The goal of the centre's programme is to develop fundamental knowledge in engineering fields that will enhance the international competitiveness of US industry and prepare engineers to contribute through better engineering practice. Engineering education and research are key elements in improving US industrial productivity, and they must be firmly linked in the centres. The centres are supported to meet a need for providing fundamental knowledge which can contribute to the solution of important national problems, and for preparing engineering graduates with the diversity and quality of education needed by US industry.

While the centres differ from one another, they all share four defining characteristics: first, they provide for working relations between students and faculty on the one hand, and practising engineers and scientists on the other. Second, their programmes emphasize the synthesis of engineering knowledge: they seek to integrate different disciplines in order to bring together the requisite knowledge, methodologies, and tools to solve issues important to engineering practitioners. Third, the programmes contribute to the increased effectiveness of all levels of engineering education. Fourth, the centres have a strong commitment from industry (money, equipment, and people) to assure its involvement in the research and educational aspects of the centres.

The centres are located at academic research institutions where they are expected to promote strong links between research and education. Cooperation between one or more schools in a region is encouraged where the combined activity will enhance the centre and the engineering education and research activities of the region. Each centre focuses on a particular area of both industrial and national importance, where development of fundamental engineering knowledge will enhance international competitiveness and is a major technological concern.

The centres possess the following features. They provide research opportunities to develop fundamental engineering knowledge in areas critical to US competitiveness where team efforts of individuals from various backgrounds, possessing different engineering and scientific skills, will contribute more to the research and goals of the centre than would occur with individual research grants. The nature of the centre's research should be cross-disciplinary.

The centres emphasize the systems aspects of engineering to help educate and train students in synthesizing, integrating, and managing engineering systems. They provide experimental capabilities not available to individual investigators because of large instrumentation acquisition costs, requirements for a large number of skilled technicians, or other maintenance and operating requirements. The centre is included in participation with engineers and scientists from industrial organizations in order to focus the activities on current and projected industry needs, and enhance the education of students in the systems aspects of engineering. State and local agencies or government laboratories involved in engineering practice may also be participants.

A signficant education component is included involving both undergraduate and graduate students in the centre research activities, since such participation would expose future engineers to aspects of many engineering fields and better prepare them for the systems nature of engineering practice. New methods are developed for the timely and successful transfer of knowledge to industrial users. Modification of new knowledge generated at the centre and continuing education of practising engineers may be another component.

The centres strive to involve a significant number of its home institution's graduate engineering students at both the master's and doctoral levels. The centre's programme should also have a substantial impact on undergraduate engineering students. A minimum faculty commitment of three full-time equivalent (FTE) positions is probably essential. It is anticipated that faculty staffing will be supplemented by engineers provided by industry.

In 1985 six centres were selected for awards and are described as follows: The University of California at Santa Barbara will receive up to $14 million over a five-year period. The first award of approximately $1.17 million will be used to establish a Center for Robotics Systems in Microelectronics. The centre's principal objective will be to create new technology in flexible automation for semiconductor-device fabrication, and to educate engineers for skills in the implementation of robotic systems.

Columbia University, in New York City, will receive up to $20 million over five years. The initial award will be approximately $2.2 million to be used to set up an Engineering Research Center for Telecommuncations. The main thrust of research will focus on the integration, within a telecommunications network, of data, facsimile, graphics, voice, and video transmissions. The centre will implement a highly flexible network testbed to explore various aspects of integration.

The University of Delaware, Newark, will receive approximately $750 000 of a five-year award, that will total up to $7.5 million, for the establishment of a Center for Composites Manufacturing Science and Engineering. There will be an affiliate programme in ceramics at Rutgers University, New Brunswick, New Jersey. This centre will extend the scope of an existing smaller Center for Composite Materials to focus on cross-disciplinary engineering research and training on composite manufacturing. The new centre will focus on fundamental research issues which are barriers to the growth of the composites industry. Five research programmes are planned: manufacturing and processing science; mechanics and design science; computation, software and information transfer; materials design, and materials durability.

The University of Maryland, in collaboration with Harvard University, will establish a Center on Systems Research at the College Park Campus. Additional research, including that in robotics, will be carried out in Cambridge, Massachusetts. Maryland will receive up to $16 million over five years with approximately $1.5 million to be received in the first year. The research theme at this centre will be basic research in the implications and applications of Very Large Integrated Circuits, computer-aided engineering and artificial intelligence in the design of interactive automatic control and communcation systems. The participation of Harvard will add to the theoretical and applied systems engineering aspects of the centre and bring a wider range of industrial firms into the effort.

Massachusetts Institute of Technology, Cambridge, will be awarded up to $20 million, with approximately $2.2 million coming the first year, to establish a Center on Biotechnology Process Engineering. In addition to NSF support, the National Institutes of Health indicated it will cofund the centre with an initial grant of $100 000. The objectives of the centre are to foster cross-disciplinary research to enhance the country's competitiveness in biotechnology. Four generic areas will be stressed: genetics and molecular biology; bioreactor design and operations; product isolation and purification; and biochemical process systems engineering.

Purdue University, West Lafayette, Indiana, will establish a Center of Intelligent Manufacturing Systems, with initial funding of approximately $1.6 million and up to $17 million over the five-year period. The centre will focus on automation for batch manufacturing of discrete products. The central concept will be to develop an 'intelligent' manufacturing system which is capable of at least semiautonomous reasoning to reduce the cost, time and errors involved in batch manufacturing.

Cooperative research projects

The objective of the cooperative research programmes is to advance science and engineering knowledge, which is relevant to technological innovation, through the means of research cooperation between industries and universities. The management of the programme is decentralized, with technical review and project selection located in the research divisions of NSF. It was designed in this mode from its inception in 1978, and has developed procedures for working with the rest of NSF to emphasize industrially relevant research, while still maintaining NSF focus upon cutting edge, frontier science. In this decentralized mode, the functions of the IUCR programme are first to provide oversight on the projects to ensure strong research cooperation and technological relevance.

The programme provides uniform NSF policies for cooperative research. For example, NSF policy requires that industry must pay for at least 50 per cent of their own costs in the cooperative project; or at least 10 per cent for a small business. The purpose of this cost-sharing requirement is to select, from all the basic research in which industrial researchers are capable of participating, those particular projects of interest to management. Accordingly NSF cooperative projects advance science while accomplishing the desirable technological transfer of basic information into useful industrial applications.

The programme budget provides an internal incentive to encourage the NSF research divisions to fund cooperative projects. In about half of the cooperative projects, some funds must be provided to industry, in addition to the normal academic support. Through the matching funds from the IUCR budget, the discipline programmes are encouraged to focus upon the research quality and excitement and not upon who gets the funds. On average, about three-quarters of the funds have gone to universities and one quarter to industry.

The IUCR budget provides an external incentive to the research community by visibily reassuring them that a significant level of cooperative research will be funded by NSF. Cooperative proposals take more effort to create than regular academic proposals. Two research groups from two very different sectors must agree about the research topic, tasks, and schedules. Approval from two different administrations must be obtained, a much more difficult procedure for the industrial than for the academic researcher. In an evaluation study conducted by the National Science Foundation, about three-quarters of the cooperative researchers said that their research collaboration would not have occurred except for the programme.

Cooperative research projects occur most frequently in the science and engineering areas which are directly in contact with industrial technology: chemistry, physics, computer sciences, electrical, computer, and systems engineering, chemical and process engineering, mechanical engineering and applied mechanics, civil and environmental engineering and physiology, cellular and molecular biology.

Projects are both fundamental in advancing scientific frontiers and technologically important in deepening and expanding the knowledge base upon which to build new technology. The industrial problems provide university researchers with challenging fundamental problems; while the academic perspective encourages industry to try more fundamental approaches than industry is accustomed to use.

Cooperative projects in the science areas investigate basic phenomena underlying technological devices, processes, and materials. In the engineering areas, projects investigate the basic principles in design or operation of generic industrial devices, processes, and materials. In addition, there is creation of technological feasibility for new genera of technological devices, processes and materials and the creation of new scientific instrumentation. The IUCR budget for 1984 was $7 million, which indicates that at least $14 million will be spent by participating firms on their own research participation, providing a significant movement of federal research funds. Cooperative research encourages university scientists to deepen and renew their appreciation of significant problems in society, toward which scientific advances can provide new knowledge bases. At the same time, industrial researchers are encouraged to join with their academic colleagues in defining the fundamental problems and in providing the complementary facilities and skills to advance science and basic engineering.

Cooperative research centres

The Industry/University Cooperative Research Centers Program, initiated by the National Science Foundation in 1973, stimulates industrial support of university research. This is accomplished through the establishment of centres that create long-term collaboration between the university and industry research programmes, with cofunding from groups of industrial firms that are compatible with university research objectives and also responsive to industry's research needs. NSF and industry's joint support in initiating a centre provide for a broad-based research programme that is large enough to be of interest to industry. Research programmes of the centres generally correspond to the university's scientific and engineering areas of expertise, and generally have participants that are or have been principal investigators of other NSF research grants. Most centres have or develop interdisciplinary research programmes to meet industry's research needs. All centres are expected to increase the industrial support covering both direct funding and equipment for their research programme, as NSF support is phased out, within a period of five years as shown in Figure 17. A centre is considered a success when its research funding is at its original level or higher and NSF no longer provides support. Most centres level off at the $500 000–$1 000 000 annual level in non-federal support.

The programme usually starts out with a planning grant to study possible alternatives for both structure and content of the research, and the management plan to be pursued, and to evaluate industry's interest in a potential centre. Successful planning can be followed by an operations grant leading to

Figure 17   Typical five year funding projection for centre

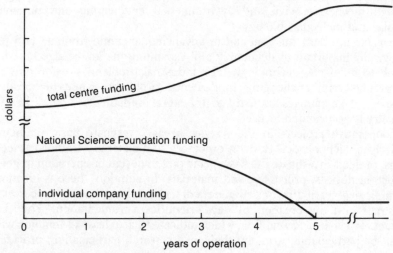

self-sufficiency within five years. Since the programme emphasizes local autonomy and separate development, each centre develops along its independent path determined by the principal investigator, the university policy and objectives and the industry requirement.

Currently there are about thirty centres in either the operations phase (majority of funding from non-federal sources) or the planning phase (primary funding from NSF to develop research agendas, structure and non-federal support). The funding history for the Centers Program is shown in Figure 18. This indicates continual increases in support from 1978 until 1984 as provided by NSF industry and state governments. During 1985 total funding from these three sources was expected to be in excess of $25 million. NSF's current investment is $3 million, thus leveraging non-federal funds by about 8 to 1. Industrial support of the centres has not only grown in dollar amount, but the number of companies committing funds has increased to well over 150 in 1985.

Figure 18   University/industry cooperative research funding history fiscal years 1978–84

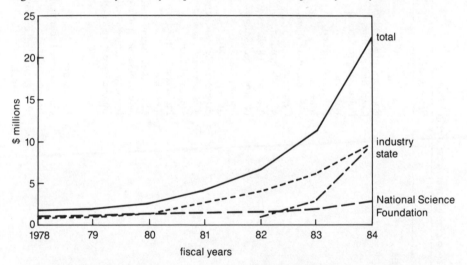

A listing of all centres, both existing and at the planning stage, is shown in Table 14 indicating areas of research and date initiated. Between three and five new centres per year are expected for planning purposes during the next few years. A model for centre development is shown in Table 15. In the model, four distinct phases are identified and the actions associated with each phase are detailed.

Conclusions

Technology transfer takes many forms and can be associated with any or all stages of the innovation process – the long and complicated route that moves an idea or scientific theory to the market place. This chapter depicts a model that in part characterizes the process of technology transfer from researcher to user and details some of the programmes sponsored by the National Science Foundation that have successfully accelerated this transfer for the purpose of stimulating industrial innovation.

Table 14 National Science Foundation cooperative research centres in 1985.

Location	Science area	Year initiated*
Current operational centres/evaluations		
Massachusetts Institute of Technology	Polymers (processing)	1973 E
Rensselaer Polytechnic Institute	Computer graphics	1979 E
University of Massachusetts	Polymers (properties)	1980 S
Ohio State University	Welding	1980 E
Case Western Reserve University	Polymers (applied)	1981 E
University of Rhode Island	Robotics	1982 E
North Carolina State University	Telecommunications	1982 E
Rutgers University	Ceramics	1982 S
Georgia Institute of Technology	Materials handling	1983 E
Worcester Polytechnic Institute	Automation technology	1983 B
Texas A&M University	Hydrogen technology	1983 E/S
Pennsylvania State University	Dielectrics	1983 E/S
Colorado School of Mines	Steel processing	1984 E
University of Washington	Process analytical chemistry	1984 S
New Jersey Institute of Technology	Toxic/hazardous waste management	1984 E
University of Arizona	Optical circuitry	1984 S
West Virginia University	Fluidized bed research	1984 E
Northeastern University	Tribology	1984 E
University of North Carolina	Monoclonal lymphocyte technology	1984 S
University of Arizona	Microcontamination control	1984 E
Westat Incorporated	Innovation centre's evaluation	1984
Utah Innovation Center	Innovation centre's evaluation	1985
Current planning centres, operational		
Dartmouth University	Ice research	1985 E
Washington University, St Louis	Computerized chemical engineering	1985 E
University of Texas, San Antonio	Biomolecular	1985 S
Iowa State University	Non-destructive evaluation	1985 S
Carnegie Mellon University	Steel making	1985 E

Northeastern University	Electromagnetics	1985 E
University of Minnesota	Biological process technology	1985 S
Purdue University/North Carolina State University	Plant molecular biology	1985 S
Lehigh University	Innovation and research management	1985 B
University of California, Santa Barbara	High speed image processing	1985 E
Direct operational centres		
Lehigh University	Process modelling	1985 E
University of Massachusetts, Amherst	Process design	1985 E
University of Tennessee	Management of control engineering	1985 E
Oklahoma State University	Flexible material handling	1985 E

*E, engineering; S, sciences, B, business.

Table 15   Industry–university cooperative research centres evolution model

Goals	Conduct high quality research and achieve self sufficiency; Increase r&d funding and use of university research by industry	
Process	Expertise identification	
	Centre product(s) designation	
	User/supporter identification (industry/government groups)	
	Marketing of centre (long term industrial/public sector financial support)	

Stage	Preplanning (No NSF Funding) (3–6 months)	Planning (NSF Funding) ($25–$50K over 6–12 months)	Operations (NSF Funding $250–500K over 5 years plus industry/state funding)	Maturation (No NSF Funding – industry/state funding) (6th year on)
Event	Expertise identified	Issues examined	Issues resolved – Confidence developed	Industrial relevancy achieved
	University	University	University	University
Action	Expertise identification	Leadership consolidation	Achieves self-sufficiency within 5 years (primarily industrial support)	Self-sufficient at annual budget of $500–$2000K;
	Leadership designation	Centre structure/functions/organization	Resolves issues	10–40 memberships;
	University backing/support	Centre committees	Continuous output of research results to achieve objectives	10–40 graduate students/centre
	Preliminary meetings with (potential) industrial supporters (single/multi)	Technical/administration functions	Major graduate student/lesser undergraduate student activity	Marketing complete – centre fully successful in achieving funding/research objectives for long term viability
	Preliminary research agenda development	Issues examined	Holds 2–4 meetings per year (technical/business)	
	Potential industrial support/interest determinations	patents/proprietary information	Membership, annual budget and student increases to maturation levels	
		publications		
		membership criteria (companies/federal agencies)		
		membership levels/fees/terms		
		foreign membership		
		frequency/types of meetings		
		dissemination of information		

Action	Industry	Industry	Industry	Industry
Awareness of industry need for university expertise	Justifies support of centre long term basis	Develops mechanism to transfer centre results to company activities	Supports centre's concept on a long term basis	
Preliminary justification for industry support	Identifies industry personnel for centre interactions		Integrates centre results into company r&d activities	
	Group of companies interacting and supporting university research	Companies continue to interact with each other and university	Uses centres for higher risk/cutting edge research to complement internal activities	

state support
project type (one on one versus multi-company support)
University support
facilities
equipment
overhead/faculty release
faculty rewards
Industry Commitment
50% first year based on:
breakthroughs
leverage
recruitment
Evaluation
indicators of progress towards centre's goals continue through operations and maturation stages.

References

Portions of this article were excerpted from the following National Science Foundation documents:

Program Report, February 1984 Industrial Science and Technological Innovation.
Program Announcement, Fiscal year 1986 Engineering Research Centers.

The Shannon Innovation Centre

Thomas Carroll
Ireland Innovation Centre

The Shannon Innovation Centre was formed in 1980 by Shannon Develop-ment, which is an economic development agency of the Irish government. Since the late 1950s Ireland's industrial policy has placed heavy reliance on foreign investment. This policy brought great benefits to Ireland through the 1960s and the 1970s. For example, there are three hundred American sub-sidiaries in Ireland employing 40 000 people; total manufacturing employment in the economy is 200 000 people. In 1978 Shannon Development was direc-ted by the government to undertake a pilot programme for the intensive development of indigenous enterprise. Shannon Development spearheaded a number of new approaches, one of which was the Innovation Centre.

The role of the Innovation Centre

The Innovation Centre is in the business of starting businesses; businesses that are Irish-owned, innovative, and export-based. The following illustration (Table 16) puts the role of the centre in context. The typical Irish-owned company would fit the category shown in the left-hand column. The task of the centre is to help grow the 'new breed' ventures shown in the right-hand column.

Table 16   Traditional and 'new breed' industries in Ireland

'Traditional' indigenous	'New Breed' indigenous
Production-oriented	Venture team
Craftsman entrepreneur non-differentiated ('Me too') products	High added-value knowledge-intensive products
Products sold to localized markets	Products sold to special niches in international markets
'Closed-frontier' company	'Open-frontier' company
One-man-show entrepreneurship	'Organization-building' entrepreneurship

People who have ideas for new or improved products (Figure 19) can have those ideas evaluated and progressed in the centre from the idea stage right through the marketplace (Figure 20).

The Innovation Centre does this by providing four services. Each client of the centre has a Business Development Adviser who is trained and experi-enced in the management of innovation. The Business Development Adviser

Figure 19

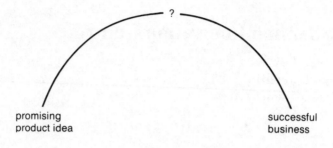

Figure 20

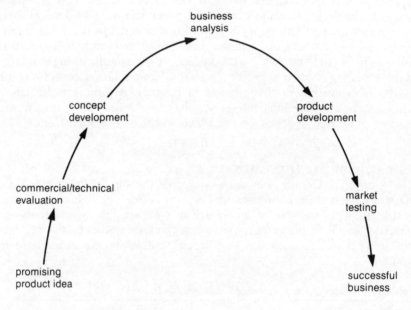

provides practical and intensive help over a period of one to two years, eg: the sourcing of commercial and technical information; the development of a business plan; the construction of a prototype in the centre's machine shop; and the sourcing of grants and venture capital. An organizational chart is given in Figure 21.

The Innovation Centre is located at Enterprise House – a special building for the centre constructed by Shannon Development Company – located on the Plassey Technological Park at Limerick City. Enterprise House includes forty workshops. Clients of the centre may rent a workshop while a product idea is being developed.

The centre has an Innovation Fund. Each year, investments are made out of the fund in a small number of highly innovative projects. The centre's pay-back on these investments is by means of a royalty on sales. Ancillary services include: a machine shop to build and test prototypes; a computerized financial modelling system for the preparation of business plans; access to specialists eg, patent agents, financial advisors, suppliers of venture capital; and secretarial services.

Figure 21 Shannon Innovation Centre

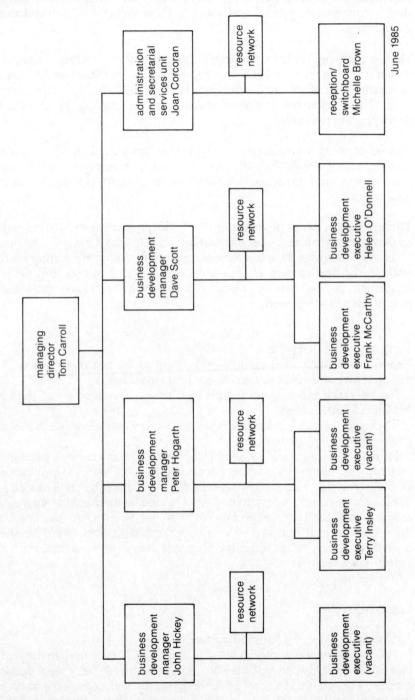

June 1985

The centre has taken a number of initiatives, or cooperated with other agencies, to stimulate the supply of people who are capable of, and committed to, establishing their own innovative, export-based business. Three examples of such initiatives are the following.

High-technology entrepreneurship programmes   Three of these six-month programmes have been provided to date by the Shannon Development Company. Each of the programmes was led by a successful American entrepreneur. The programme comprises training and counselling in all aspects of developing a business plan.

Idea-generating workshops   The centre has trained all of its staff in an idea-generating methodology known as Synectics. This expertise is now 'packaged' as a two-day workshop and sold to people who are trying to crystallize an innovative business idea.

Young entrepreneurs programme   In this programme the centre has drawn on the resources of higher education institutions in Ireland. University staff identify ideas which appear to have commercial application. Young engineering graduates work on the development of their ideas over a period of one year. One such programme is now nearing completion; the results are encouraging and the programme will be repeated.

Finance and outputs

Capital expenditure by Shannon Development to the end of 1984 was $1.933 million. This included the construction of Enterprise House.

Net operating expenditure, funded by Shannon Development to the end of 1984, was $1.501 million.

The centre charges fees for its services. In 1985, income was about 20 per cent of gross operating expenditure.

From its inception in 1980, until December 1984, the centre's net output of projects was twenty-six. These twenty-six projects were in production in December 1984. The sectors represented by these projects included electronics engineering, computer software, food, mechanical engineering, robotics, and health care. Five of these twenty-six projects have been backed by the venture capital industry – the aggregate valuation was $4 672 000. The centre's medium- term target is an annual output of about ten innovative, export-based ventures.

Case histories

Ashling Microsystems Limited, Limerick

In 1982, three years after their graduation in electronics systems from the National Institute of High Education, Limerick, Gerry Stockil and Gerry Joyce decided to team up. The venture idea involved the design and manufacture of microprocessor development systems (MDS) – a new concept in microprocessor applications. Such systems are used mainly by small-to-medium electronics and engineering industries as a cost-effective means of applying microelectronics in new products or production processes. According to Gerry Joyce:

The Innovation Centre provided crucial help and advice in those very difficult early days. It gave us first-class workshop facilities; access to various services such as meeting rooms, secretarial services, telephone and telex, funding under a special Innovation Fund, and extensive management advice on matters ranging from finance to marketing.

Recognizing the need to strengthen their business start-up expertise, Joyce and Stockil decided to participate in an 'entrepreneurship and high-technology' training programme provided by Shannon Development Company at the Innovation Centre from January to June of 1983. This training programme was the catalyst for the formation of a well-rounded management team.

The new company, Ashling Microsystems Limited, then participated in the first Venture Market organized by the Innovation Centre in November of 1983. Venture Market is a mechanism which brings together ventures seeking venture capital and suppliers of venture capital. Valuable exposure to the Irish venture capital industry is offered to new companies through the medium of Venture Market. In the case of Ashling, a total of 0.5 million pounds sterling of venture capital was provided by Development Capital Corporation, and Alta-Berkeley (UK).

Ashling has now penetrated several West European markets. It has also set up a subsidiary company in Silicon Valley. Ashling was to move in 1986 to a new factory on the Plassey Technological Park. Meanwhile, the company is in production at the Innovation Centre. Twenty-six people are now employed; project employment is fifty. Innovation Centre inputs were: innovation management; innovation fund; workshops; venture market; and ancillary services.

Golfstar Corporation Limited, Dublin
Golfstar is the brain-child of P. J. O'Connor, an entrepreneur, who decided that existing golf-swing analysers are lacking in presentation and performance. He came up with the concept of an integrated teaching machine, and visited the Innovation Centre for assistance.

The Innovation Centre assisted him to build a team of young engineers to pursue the project, initially through an Irish Development Agency (IDA) feasibility study, and later by means of financial assistance from the centre's Innovation Fund.

Golfstar has now developed two working prototypes which have a system of interactive video to enable a golfer to analyse the swing in hitting a ball and then be coached on a VDU by a professional golfer.

A great deal of interest has been shown in the machine by a world renowned professional golfer who wishes to market the system for America. Final negotiations are now in progress and production was expected to start in 1986. Innovation Centre inputs were: innovation management; innovation fund; and venture market.

Intepro Limited, Limerick
Intepro was established by two former lecturers at NIHE Limerick, Denis and Eoin Sugrue, to design and manufacture power supply test equipment. The project had an input of twenty man-years by the time it left the Innovation centre workshops in 1983. It had also received awards from the Bank of Ireland 'Start Your Own Business' Competition and from the NBST.

Intepro had a venture capital requirement of £300 000 sterling and this was supplied by Development Capital Corporation and Alta-Berkeley (the European associate of a US venture capital firm).

The company continues to innovate both in terms of product and market. The average price of a power supply test system sold by Intepro is almost £50 000 sterling, and they are European market leaders in this specialized market segment.

Innovation centre inputs were: innovation management; workshops; and ancillary services.

Oglesby & Butler Limited, Carlow
The three promoters were employees of a foreign-owned firm in Carlow. Their patented product is a gas-powered soldering iron.

The Innovation Centre provided: money from the centre's Innovation Fund; innovation management, especially the development of a business plan; introductions to the Irish venture capital industry through the medium of Venture Market. The venture was aided by the IDA's Enterprise Development Programme. Venutre capital was provided by the Hill Samuel Designated Investment Fund, and a mix of private individuals under the Business Development Scheme (a personal tax incentive scheme introduced in the 1984 Finance Act).

The product has been introduced to markets in Ireland, UK and the USA. Related products are being developed and the venture is expected to create twenty jobs.

Innovation Centre inputs were: innovation fund; innovation management; and Venture Market.

Omnicorp Technology Limited, Limerick
Software has become a sector of phenomenal growth over the last ten years, fuelled by rapid advances in microcomputer hardware. The modern 16-bit micro is now capable of handling the data and text-processing needs of a wide variety of small- and medium-sized firms. A network system can often offer even larger firms the power and flexibility they need.

Omnicorp Technology began in late 1982 to develop a suite of programmes geared to small- and medium-sized manufacturing firms, broadly called Materials Requirements Planning.

Peter MacGregor and Kevin McBride pooled their knowledge of multinational mainframe MRP systems and, with the programming expertise of Brian Hurley and Dympna Ryan, developed a suite of programmes which has won enthusiastic support from firms, consultants and investors. An integrated account suite will soon be added to allow total data production and financial management in one system. The programmes are now being marketed in the UK and Ireland.

Equity for the project has been provided by the National Enterprise Agency, a state initiative established to invest in new and existing manufacturing and service activities of key importance to the economy.

Innovation centre inputs were: innovation management; workshops; Venture Market; and ancillary services.

Waterford Automation Limited, Waterford
Robots have captured the imagination of both industry and the public at large. However, the cost of converting fragmented production systems to the auto-

mated factory is often prohibitive. Manufacturers frequently require customized equipment and certainly need a local source of advice, expertise and design capability.

Waterford Automation is a combination of two experienced senior engineers, Noel Newman and John Lyons. Noel Newman had extensive engineering experience at managing-director level and received Innovation Centre funding to pursue his research into automation and robotics. Simultaneously, John Lyons, from his position of promoter and managing director of his successful firm, Hitol Ltd (Waterford), was pursuing similar research through CTT. The merging of interests resulted in Waterford Automation Limited, with immediate capabilities in both design and custom manufacture of production automation tools.

The IDA Enterprise Development Programme assisted the new firm with a package of grants, and equity investment was provided by the Equitas Business Development Fund. Equitas Business Development Fund was established following the 1984 Finance Act, as a fund manager for individual investors taking advantage of the generous income tax incentives contained in the Act.

Current employment is ten, projected employment twenty. Innovation Centre inputs were: innovation management; innovation fund; and Venture Market.

The role of innovation centres for economic development: the German experience

Jurgen Allesch
Berlin Centre for Innovation and New Enterprise

When the Berlin Centre for Innovation and New Enterprise (BIG), the first institute of its kind in Germany, opened its doors in November 1983, there was no thought about the popularity which the concept of science parks and innovation and technology centres would gain in the Federal Republic of Germany. To date about twenty-five establishments have been started and about forty more are in different planning stages. Experts take a critical attitude towards this explosive development. The expectations and hopes that go along with the establishment of science parks and innovation centres are manifold and often exaggerated. Considering and anlaysing international experience of these schemes, many of these hopes will hardly be fulfilled.

From the outset it is clear that there are two tasks that these establishments will certainly not be able to do on a short-term basis: they will not create as many new jobs as are currently being lost in other sectors of industry; and, they will not turn less-developed regions into prosperous industrial centres within a couple of years. The main focus of this paper is not, however, to reduce high expectations, but to discuss the optimal framework and the adequate instruments that might help science parks and innovation centres on their way to success.

It is well-known that the rapid development in science parks and innovation centres that has taken place at such a high speed in Germany and in other European countries, is rooted in developments in the United States. Silicon Valley in California, and the Route 128 area around Boston, are the examples on which most of the science park initiatives in Great Britain, the Netherlands and Sweden have been based and whose success they were aiming at when they developed their own schemes. But the European initiatives can hardly be measured against these American prototypes.

One reason for this is the fact that the European schemes are based upon different concepts. The conglomeration of technolgoy-oriented enterprises south of San Francisco began some decades ago. This area, known today after the worldwide diffusion of microelectronics, as Silicon Valley, was never a science park in the sense Europeans associate with the term. Although the first enterprises settled in the area of Stanford University and the first entrepreneurs were scientists, the symbiosis between university and enterprises and also the symbiosis among the enterprises themselves, took a long time to grow. It developed almost incidentally.

But the framework that led to the success of Silicon Valley was not of incidental, but of a more fundamental nature – a nature that Europeans tend to neglect. One essential factor in the USA that led to a traditionally much more positive climate for young technology-oriented enterprises than in Europe, lay in the confidence that public institutions had in the innovative capabilities of young entrepreneurs. During and after World War II, the American Department of Defense (DOD) collaborated effectively with a large number of small-and medium-sized enterprises, especially in fields of military interest such as broadcasting, radar and microwave technology. The positive experience of the DOD resulted in manifold cooperations between other ministries and small technology-oriented firms, which thereby had the chance to develop and prosper. Another factor that should not be underestimated is the fact that the American industry often uses young technology-oriented enterprises as a 'window in technology': large, well-established firms support spinoff enterprises formed by former employees, thereby gaining the chance to follow new paths of technological development without any susbstantial risks to themselves.

Another factor is to be found in sociocultural conditions, and has to do with the American appreciation of entrepreneurial spirit. In American society, traditionally more open towards entrepreneurial thinking, bankruptcy is not such a stigma as in Europe. Even people, who have several times failed with business ideas, are not considered to be failures. It is the serious attempt and the engagement that counts in the American value system, not just the commercial success. There is no question but that these factors are rather underdeveloped in Europe, and will have to play a more important role in the future.

At this point one can differentiate between two basic concepts of German initiatives: some schemes concentrate on young firms or enterprises that are undergoing formation and try to help them to survive this critical initial phase; others try to assist already established firms or departments of existing companies. This chapter will concentrate on the prerequisities of the latter kind, which are called 'innovation centres'.

A typical German innovation centre consists of an old or new factory building that is subdivided into small units to create space for twenty to forty young enterprises. The centre has a central management and provides services for the enterprises, eg conference facilities, cafeteria, secretarial services and consulting. The positive effect of innovation centres and their services on the economic development of the young enterprises are manifold. The possibility of using cost-intensive facilities on a joint basis is complemented by easy access to information, the possibility of establishing informal contacts, and assistance in public relations and marketing. The first German innovation centre, the Berlin Centre for Innovation and New Enterprises (BIG) has become a model for similar institutions that have been established in Germany.

The Berlin Centre for Innovation and New Enterprises (BIG)

The Berlin Centre for Innovation and New Enterprises was opened in November 1983 as a result of cooperation between the Technical University of Berlin and the Senator for Economics and Labour. In 5.250 square metres in an old, refurnished factory building previously belonging to the Allgemeine Elektrizitäts Gesellschaft (AEG), twenty-four companies with about a hundred employees are in operation. The proximity to research institutes active in the fields of measuring and control technology offers manifold opportunities for cooperation and for the utilization of academic infrastructures and equipment.

The target group of BIG are young, technology-oriented entrepreneurs with scientific or comparable qualifications. The common features of all companies involved are as follows. The companies are supposed to have started from within research institutions and universities, with scientists and graduates as entrepreneurs. The date of establishment should not go back more than two years. There is an outspoken interest in the use of laboratories and workshops, and willingness to cooperate with other enterprises in the BIG. The design of the company should demonstrate its potential to create qualified jobs. Of course, not all of these criteria have to be fulfilled in every case.

The majority of the twenty-four firms are operating in the field of microelectronics and soft- and hard-ware. Their activities include controlling, measurement, data processing, communication technology, electronic components and medical equipment. Besides the companies operating in electronics, there is a chemical company, a manufacturer of industrial robots, and an engineering office.

Promotion during the start-up phase

During the start-up phase the centre offers a variety of supportive measures aiming at consulting, training and motivation: negotiation of contracts to consultants, chambers of industry and commerce, and public authorities; seminars and working parties focusing on motivation and information for scientists and graduates interested in the formation of a high-technology based new firm (HTBNF); organization of regular informal meetings that should help the young entrepreneurs to get to know each other in a relaxed atmosphere and to exchange experiences. Moreover, production space and a functioning infrastructure are offered during the start-up phase at fees that depend on the real-time of utilization. To keep the cost of administration and representation at a low level, a shared office and conference centre has been established. This centre offers secretarial services (telephone service, administration, etc) to all companies. Operational functions such as bookkeeping and cost accounting can be taken on as well.

Usually HTBNFs are typical 'soft companies'. The 'soft company' is a type of enterprise whose market entry is based on contract works and developments. Typical products of a soft company, for instance, are measuring, developments, prototype design, expertise, etc. These tasks are carried out on a contractual basis within a limited period of time for a single client (public institutions, larger companies). In the course of time, most soft companies tend to reduce the development expenditures of specific customized orders and introduce standardized procedures. After a time, some companies offer standardized products and processes to a larger group of clients. This development can be seen as a process of 'hardening' (see below).

A young entrepreneur with an academic background is usually well-acquainted with the way soft companies operate, because they normally deal with single projects of research and development. But, the acquisition of management functions and commercial ways of acting and thinking, require active support not only during the planning phase, but also during the phase of consolidation and growth. The promotion during this period has to focus on marketing. Only products and services that are actually sold help the young entrepreneur. This argument was the main reason that, on 4000 square metre extra space available in the BIG, an industral fair for new technology has been established under the name 'BIG-TECH'. BIG-TECH is a technology fair especially designed for the needs of small technology-oriented enterprises. BIG represents the ideal place for presentation and contacts. From the very beginning, BIG-TECH was a success. In 1984 there were seventy-four exhibitors from Berlin, the Federal Republic of Germany and abroad, and more than 1500 visitors. The fair was accompanied by thirty workshops, the international workshop 'Management of Science Parks and Innovation Centres' alone having a hundred participants. In 1985, more than 150 exhibitors were expected to come to Berlin.

This marketing concept is accomplished by an up-to-date enterprise catalogue. In the *Innovation Market Berlin*, published for the first time in 1984, eighty-nine technology-oriented enterprises from Berlin introduced themselves and their products, which ranged from exhaust gas measuring systems to cell cultures. The booklet aims at the provision of easier market access for young high-tech enterprises, at the more efficient utilization of the regional potential in applicable new technologies, and it tries to provide established companies with a window on technology.

The success of BIG has encouraged the scheme to expand. Since January 1985 the Technology and Innovation Park, Berlin (TIP) has been under construction on the site of a former AEG factory. When completed, the TIP will house application-oriented research institutes of the Technical University of Berlin, private research institutions and innovative small-and medium-sized firms. Moreover, the TIP offers plenty of space for the expansion of BIG-enterprises and HTBNFs. The usable floor space amounts to 80 000 square metres. 50 000 square metres are reserved for enterprises and 30 000 square metres for research institutions. By the end of 1985 the TIP will house seven companies with 330 employees on a floor space of 17 000 square metres.

Emphasis will be put on the following technological fields:

civil engineering technology and new materials
automotive engineering and transportation technology
gene technology, microbiology and food technology
energy and environmental technology
microelectronics and software technology
medical technology

This list does not cover the TIP's potential technological fields of activity completely. It is meant to give an impression of the potential for development that can be seen today.

The following institutions, organizations and companies are planning to move into the TIP.

Research institutes of the Technical University of Berlin   These are the Institute for Ferro-Concrete Engineering, the Institute for Automotive Engineering, and the Institute for Microbiology.

High-tech companies   Industry has shown strong interest in moving into the TIP. There are concrete negotations with firms from Germany and abroad operating in the following branches: construction and testing technology;

computer and measuring technology; testing techniques for electronic components; and power technology and other fields.

Expansion of the BIG within the TIP   For the expansion of the Berlin Centre for Innovation and New Enterprises within the TIP, technology-oriented enterprises and start-up companies from the following fields have applied: measuring techniques/electronics; technical analysis in medicine; operation data processing; and software technology/microcomputer applications.

Within the establishment of the TIP the growth potentials of promising new technologies are utilized and made accessible. Already in the planning phase, the attraction of the TIP has become clear. In direct proximity to the TIP, NIXDORF AG has begun to erect a new industrial plant (130 000 square metres floor space) in which computer systems, monitors, electronic components etc will be manufactured. In addition, private research institutions will be among the first tenants of the TIP.

Prerequisites of success

To a certain extent, the success of the Berlin Centre of Innovation and New Enterprises is the result of a careful analysis of the factors relevant for innovation centres and science parks.

One factor that is of essential importance for the success of these institutions is the analysis of the specific process of the formation of enterprises and of the factors relevant to the success of this process. In an examination of young enterprises around Boston, the British economist, Matthew Bullock, categorizes the types of newly formed companies. Essentially, he distinguishes four kinds of start-ups: soft companies, hard companies, garage companies and spinoff.

The soft company is a widespread type of company that is also to be found in the Federal Republic of Germany. Its access to the market strongly depends on contract research and development activities. Typical products are testimonials, measurements, contract development, design of prototypes, and so on. These tasks are typically carried out for specific clients (public institutions, larger companies), within a limited timeframe and on a contractual basis. After a certain period of time, most of the soft companies tend to reduce developments for specific contracts and introduce standard procedures. After a certain time, some enterprises offer standard products and processes to a larger group of clients. This development can be named 'hardening process'.

The so-called hard companies offer a well-defined, standardized spectrum of products to a large group of clients. In contrast to the soft companies, these enterprises work predominantly product-oriented rather than contract-oriented.

According to Bullock, garage companies are companies that start to develop a specific innovative product, process or service. During the first phase, research and development is financed on a personal basis, as are the manufacturing costs of the first series. Garage companies, such as Apple Computers Ltd are typical hard companies which after their foundation are highly suitable for venture capital operations.

Spinoff companies are enterprises whose initiators have worked immediately prior to formation in a larger company of the same branch, in which the largest part of the research and development required for the new product has already been achieved. Therefore, most of the spinoff companies are hard companies right from the start, and focus on a specific product or spectrum of products which they offer to a wider market.

For innovation centres, such considerations are of particular interest, since they want to create an optimal climate and a creative environment for start-up companies. The needs of these companies vary according to type and level of development and they, therefore, require highly flexible organizational structures and service offers from the innovation centres. Even more essential is that in the conceptional and planning stage, current and future supporters of innovation centres consider the factors that guarantee a positive innovation climate and a creative environment.

An innovation network that integrates these factors has a variety of positive effects on the development of young technology-oriented enterprises.

Proximity to high-class universities and other research institutions

For many young technology-oriented enterprises, whose founders were often themselves academic scientists, the proximity to research is of essential importance, not only in the sense of the supportive services that, eg, German universitites are starting to develop, or have already developed, but also in the sense of possibilities for the establishment of fertile informal contacts that can lead to problem solutions. Moreover, research institutions represent important potential clients of young technology-oriented enterprises.

A relatively well-developed industrial structure

Young enterprises need the cooperation of larger, established companies. Established companies represent an important market for the products, processes, and services of young enterprises. They can, as depicted in the American example shown above, explicitly support the formation of new companies in order to follow new technological paths of development more comprehensively.

Sufficient availability of qualified personnel

Young technology-oriented enterprises depend on the easy acquisition of qualified personnel that on the one hand can be supplied by a developed regional system of higher education, but on the other hand are available in sufficient quantity in a developed industrial environment. For the availability of qualified personnel the following factor is not to be underestimated.

An attractive cultural infrastructure and a good quality of life

In the United States, the importance of this infrastructure has been recognized. Increasingly, regional and local authorities try to promote the settlement of companies by means of advertising the cultural advantages of the region: high-class institutions of higher education, attractive geographical environment, theatres, museums and so on, factors that facilitate the recruitment of highly qualified employees.

Availability of venture capital

The importance of venture capital for start-up companies is quite clear. Although in the past the general shortage of venture capital was responsible for the poor entrepreneurial climate, this no longer holds true. But even today, in regions with a well-developed industrial structure the availability of venture capital is much better than in less-developed regions.

A dense network of institutions of regional industrial development

Innovation centres can hardly be successful without any government subsidies. Although a comprehensive system of government subsidies should not be propagated, it has to be emphasized that, in their critical phase, young enterprises have to be able to acquire financial support from the state. Support from the state does not necessarily have to take the form of voluminous supportive schemes (the importance of which will not be disputed here). A strategy of giving more orders to young technology-oriented enterprises, for example by the Federal Post Administration, could give important impulses for regional development and for the creation of a positive climate for start-up companies.

However, of crucial importance is that the factors mentioned above do not stand isolated from each other, but are interrelated within the framework of a dense informal network. A dedicated innovative regional policy should therefore have as its main priority supporting the creation, expansion, and consolidation of informal and formal networks. These networks should eventually integrate all the people, organizations and institutions that are pertinent to the formation and the growth of technology-oriented enterprises: venture capitalists, bankers, academic scientists, established high-tech entrepreneurs, key individuals of regional and local business administrations as well as industrial associations.

To a high degree the long-standing American experience corresponds to the more recent one in Europe as far as a directed public and private promotion of high-tech company start-ups is concerned. Nevertheless, it is necessary to develop patience and steadiness in order to find a specific European way to more autonomy and entrepreneurship. Overdone economic and political expectations will only delay this process rather than accelerate it. It is, therefore, most important for universities to stay in close contact with innovation centres and science parks, as they guarantee a continuous and lasting regional development.

The Dutch Inventors Centre

Ralph van Hessen
Dutch Innovation Centre

Creativity

In every one of us there is an inventor! It does not matter if you are a professor, a senator, or an entrepreneur, every one of us would like to invent something during their lives. Inventing does not necessarily have to mean that you must come up with something new. Discovering also means 'dis-covering', the opposite of 'covering-up'. Creativity has been covered-up for years, so it is time to 'discover': innovation, creativity and perseverance. These are the terms especially needed in an economic crisis; they give us strength to go on, and it is these qualities that every inventor has. And that is why it is good to stimulate the development of new products, and stimulating does not mean just writing out reports.

We have to aim for that stadium in which creativity and imaginative developments are rewarded. These developments will have to take place at school. Teaching can play a big part in creative developments. So teaching has to be modernized; no more lectures about theories, but make students work together so they can actually develop practical creativity for themselves. By making them work together, they will stimulate each other, and this is essential to our welfare. Institutes like universities, industry and even the government would get better results by working as one team, both nationally as well as internationally.

What is so special about handling things in a creative way? In what sense does it differ from handling things without that special touch called creativity? The answers will be the essence of this chapter.

So many different management systems have been promoted during the last years: strategic management, management by methods, entrepreneurial management, no-nonsense management and, back-to-basics management. All these methods were profitable for those who invented them, but what does it mean in reality? In fact the entrepreneur has to be a specialist in every field in order to fulfill his duties within the company in every possible situation.

Some time ago, during an interview, I was asked, 'What is the most important characteristic of a dynamic leader?' Well, one of the most important characteristics is not to wear blinkers! Established ideas and principles can waver, and creativity can make them waver. To run a company in a proper way one needs a fisheye lens. You will have to prevent yourself from being one day imprisoned in your own company; and you will have to know what the wishes are of your customers and your suppliers.

You will also have to know what is going on down at the assembly line and make your employees understand what your policy is, and why. It is the combination of being a manager and being an entrepreneur. You will have to be constantly making your staff work in a creative way by stimulating and supporting creativity. Success is like a snowball, once it is there, it gets bigger and bigger. Once you are successful in a certain field, you are bound to be successful in other fields too. And this success has already been experienced by the Dutch Inventors Centre.

The Dutch Inventors Centre

New discoveries on the market
Since the establishment of the Dutch Inventors Centre Foundation, dozens of enterprises have been able to embark on innovative activities, thanks to the inventions of Dutchmen. The Inventors Centre has thus realized one of its objectives; to stimulate innovation in The Netherlands. There are numerous examples: a folding trailer, a hydraulic steering system, a skate-sailor, a folding hairbrush, a filing system, etc. The Inventors Centre has brought the discoveries of inventive Dutchmen to the attention of trade and industry, and the business world has in turn made grateful use of these inventions. The Inventors Centre has thereby developed into what it aims to be: a focal point of innovation; a place where people with inventions can come for advice, and where at the same time the economic feasibility for the business world can be examined.

Some 2000 inventions per year are submitted to the Inventors Centre; big and small, good and not so good. To separate the wheat from the chaff, the Inventors Centre has a professional staff, backed by a number of institutions and experts. Their job is to determine whether a discovery is really new, whether it could be economically remunerative and whether it could be put into production. At the Inventors Centre every invention is examined for its legal, technical and, above all, commercial value. If it has been irrefutably shown that there is a chance of success, then the discovery is presented to the world of trade and industry. Entrepreneurs, both large and small, who want to introduce new ideas, can widen their product range and are not averse to innovation. In the Dutch Inventors Centre, ideas are ready and waiting for the entrepreneurs. Tomorrow's innovation is on view there today.

The way the centre works
It is no small matter to make an invention ready to launch on the market. It calls for commercial insight and skillful negotiation of contracts. Moreover, there must be a thorough examination as to whether elsewhere in the world a similar invention exists that is protected by a patent: the invention has to be technically assessed and the possibilities of production subsidies investigated. In these activities the Dutch Inventors Centre receives support from various institutions including: the Order of Chartered Patent Attorneys, whose members can regularly be consulted at the centre; the Government Industrial Service, to which requests can be submitted for preliminary investigation into the newness of an invention; more than fifty experts, including professors of technical universities throughout The Netherlands; some ten specialist firms, which can give advice on the market feasibility of specific ideas for products; numerous institutions whose advice or subsidy helps to put the product in the market sooner than would otherwise occur; and the International Inventors Centre.

Those who really want their ideas to be taken into account, whether it be an inventor or the director of a firm, need this support. To put innovative products on the market calls for sound professionalism and keen business insight. Thanks to the backing of so many experts, the Dutch Inventors Centre is in a position to provide just that. That is why it has developed in the course of a few years into a focal point of innovation, able to encourage new ideas in the business world and to stimulate inventors.

The centre's head office is in Rotterdam, with branch offices in Zwolle (IJssel Delta Region) and Helmond. In this way the centre aims to be accessible to as many progressive enterprises and creative people as possible. The Inventors Centre offers both the inventor and the enterprise a number of possibilities, which are important for both of them.

The centre and the inventor

Any inventor who has an idea for an innovative product can rely on support from the centre, provided his idea has a certain degree of inventiveness. Further conditions are that the invention must be commercially feasible, and that it is quite clear how the new product works (no 'black box'). The procedure is generally as follows. The inventor describes the idea on a form (obtainable from the centre). He explains the background and the effect. If necessary the inventor can visit the centre to elaborate on his idea in person. After a week at the latest, the inventor receives confirmation of the receipt of his idea and/or model. The centre aims to provide, within two months, a critical assessment of: the innovative value, the technical feasibility and the commercial possibilities. The inventor receives a written report of the assessment. If the invention appears feasible, then it can be submitted to interested enterprises and the centre can act as an intermediary between the inventor and the enterprise. Depending on the stage of development for the idea, and the amount of work called for from the centre, the inventor is asked to pay a commission, which amounts to between 10–40 per cent of his income from the invention. If there are no results, no expenses are incurred: no-cure, no-pay. In order to speed matters up, no written progress reports are produced. The inventor can get information by phone as to the stage reached by the idea/product and whether there are interested enterprises.

The development of prototypes and the protection of property are in principle for the inventor's account. Arrangements can be made concerning these issues in consultation with the Inventors Centre.

The centre and the enterprises

Any enterprise can call on the services of the Inventors Centre. This may be with specific questions, but also in order to gain insight into inventions which are available at that time. The latter aspect in particular has produced some unexpected results in the past.

In general the procedure is as follows. After discussion, a range of product ideas can be presented, which are attuned to the scope of the enterprise. If a particular invention interests the firm, then the centre acts as the intermediary between the firm and the inventor. If a basis has been established for further contact over the invention, then the centre puts a proposal both to the inventor and to the firm setting out the legal and commercial consequences of putting the invention into operation. If the centre has no suitable invention on its books when a particular firm makes an inquiry, then the firm can ask for a specific idea to be developed. In cooperation with technical and commercial members of the centre's staff, the assignment is described and development specifications drawn up. The Inventors Centre asks one or more inventors from its pool of creative minds to work on the assignment. The centre keeps in constant touch, so that both parties know the course the idea is taking and the speed of development. The costs of such an assignment consist of a set amount, and a no-cure, no-pay share. A quotation for this is drawn up beforehand.

A focal point of innovation
It will be evident that the Inventors Centre may justly be called a focal point. It is a place where the inventor can have his invention tested, and where he can find out from the centre's list of enterprises whether there is a firm or institution with whom he can do business. It is a place where entrepreneurs can not only at all times examine the inventions which the centre has in stock, but can also give a specific assignment and call on the wealth of ideas of the inventors registered at the centre.

The Inventors Centre may be regarded as a continuous National Inventors Fair, which also provides legal, technical and commercial advice and looks beyond Dutch frontiers. This is the place where contact between the entrepreneurs and the inventors is 'short circuited'. That is why the Ministry of Economic Affairs and the Municipality of Rotterdam have seen fit to give this focal point a subsidy. The importance is proved by the inventions which are now in the course of production.

New products service
During each year, thousands of inventors frequent the centre bringing new product proposals, and hundreds of companies come to look for new ideas. However, the ideas of inventors and the needs of companies often do not match. So the Inventors Centre started looking for ways by which the creativity of the inventors could be used more effectively.

The result of this search is the New Products Service (NPS). With this service the normal route is reversed: the starting point is the need of the company. It functions as follows. If a company shows interest in the NPS, representatives of the Inventors Centre visit the company to get a clear idea of what they are looking for and to explain the procedure. The company pays a low entrance fee. The Inventors Centre formulates instructions and selects from its files a number of inventors whom they expect to be able to come up with solutions. The problems dealt with range from very specific problems to the request for new product ideas that fit in with the existing range of products of the company.

The inventors are asked to return their solutions within a month after receipt of their instructions. No worked-out solutions, complete with technical drawings are expected, but merely principles that show creativity and orginality. For that reason no emphasis is laid on the professional background of the inventors: often the solutions originating from other disciplines are the most refreshing.

After reception of the solutions, the Inventors Centre makes a presentation to the company. If one or more solutions are accepted by the company, licence fees will be paid to the inventor.

It is still too early for an evaluation of the New Product Service. However, the inventors are encouraged, because now they know someone is waiting for their solutions. And the demand from companies for the NPS is so high, that the first bottleneck will be that the inventors cannot work at too many problems at the same time.

Hospital innovation project

Since 1983 the Dutch Inventors Centre has been confronting Dutch manufacturers and purchasers of hospital equipment with the possibility of not importing medical products, but producing them in Holland. On the initiative of the Dutch Inventors Centre, which was leading the project, I tried to analyse what kind of disposables were being used in hospitals and which of them would be interesting from the point of innovation.

The main partners of this ambitious project are: purchasers of hospital equipment, inventors and manufacturers. The tactics followed can be compared with a rugby game. You cannot say 'I run here, now you take it over.' Just like rugby, every member of the team has to run the whole track. The hospital purchasers invented improvements to their own product-lines, and, in making these improvements they were guided by the inventors, who were in turn guided by different hospitals. These excursions were essential for the invention process. Following this, the inventors made technical drawings of the new, selected products. Subsequently the manufacturers, who were members of the project team, were able to produce an experimental series of the product and to commercialize initial product idea.

So, the advantages of this special rugby strategy are: saving time with the development, greater flexibility, and intensive spread and transfer of know-how.

One of the main interests of the excercise was to bridge the gap existing between hospitals and industry and the gap between inventors and industry. Many manufacturers and inventors had never been in a hospital before. It was surprising that hospitals did not realize that their buying strategy contributed very little to the Dutch economy. The major activity of this project was the inventing and making of new products in an active way.

Before something could really be done, there was much that needed to be discussed. First, the actual possibilties of this project were determined. This was done on the basis of the results of the visits paid to the hospitals. It was decided to concentrate on the cheaper utensils, but every low-tech product could not be taken into account.

As soon as the hospitals had listed all the utensils they purchased, something new was done. Previously utensils were selected which, at first sight, looked as if they could be improved. Up to that moment (mid 1984), the purchasers had by far the most important role in this project. Now the inventor has taken over. The products selected were divided between inventors. Most inventors worked on their own, but some inventors worked on a product in pairs.

Around each product a group was formed, in which the purchasers, the inventors and the producers were represented. Each of these so-called working groups had its own topic and held brainstorm sessions during which an exchange of ideas took place in a very unstructured way. The guideline that was followed during these sessions was determined by the reports on the use of a specific product compiled by the inventors. During the discussions of the working groups, the multidisciplinary nature of each team proved its usefulness, which will be illustrated by means of the following statements. A businessman about inventors:

> At first I only thought of these inventors as weirdos (real weird people). Until we reached a certain stage in this project, I thought I knew everything about my products, but these guys had a very refreshing way of looking at my products that surprised me in a pleasant way.

An inventor about purchasers:

> The purchasers were the ones that were very vital to this project. Certainly in the beginning. They know all the problems and bottlenecks we spotted in the hospitals. And more than that, they feel a very strong responsibility for the products they select and purchase. They are very eager to purchase better and/ or cheaper products.

An inventor/medical doctor about producers: 'They were so important because they always remained realistic. While we were thinking and inventing, they were keeping an eye on the feasibility.'

By the beginning of 1985 the work was completed. The project had given birth to ten product ideas. Several manufacturers were attracted by these ideas and were willing to turn them into real products.

Results

About forty new products will appear on the market this year with the help and support of the Inventors Centre. A turnover of $30 million at the consumer level is involved. The strength of this centre is that with a small staff, several working relationships have come about and have caused surprising results.

The Netherlands has a number of advantages over other countries: geographical distances are small; industry is well organized; inventors are well protected by law; industry is innovation-minded; and the government is stimulating innovation.

In a period of five years the Dutch Inventors Centre has grown from a low-tech initiative into a high-tech stadium. The Dutch nation is now aware of the benefits of innovation and that the centre is a good instrument to cultivate the mentality or cultural techniques appropriate to entrepreneurship. Because The Netherlands is a country favourable to inventors and to innovation, the centre (as a part of the industry) would like to make more international contacts. The institute is a perfect partner for foreign inventors and commercial institutes who would like to obtain a licensee in Europe. The Dutch Inventors Centre is a stepping stone forward to a more affluent society.

Locally grown high-technology business development: the Utah experience

Wayne S. Brown
University of Utah

Economic policymakers throughout the developed countries of the world are increasingly turning to technology-related businesses to encourage economic growth. These countries typically spend large sums of money on basic research in both the public and private sectors, with the usual objectives of providing new services or products useful to mankind, improving their national defence posture, or gaining economic advantages. These r&d expenditures have resulted in an explosion of new useful technology with great economic potential. However, translating this technology into viable commercial products and services is invariably a frustrating and difficult task. In the USA, new technology firms, created by technical entrepreneurs, have led the way in commercializing such technology.

Evidence abounds in the United States that small firms vastly out-perform large firms in creating jobs, bringing innovations to the market place, and effectively utilizing research and development funds. In addition, small firms, particularly those originating as high-tech spinoffs from research in university, government or even large corporate laboratories, have established an enviable record for transferring technology from the laboratory to the market. Indeed, these firms have demonstrated that the most effective way to transfer technology is to transfer the technologist who understands that particular technology. Start-up companies provide an unusual opportunity for engineers and scientists to which they own substantial equity. America has produced a significant number of wealthy individuals who have created their wealth by forming a new corporation based on technology into which they have a special insight. The potential for attaining wealth is one of the strong driving factors that encourages the creation of new business ventures. It is apparent that the entrepreneurial spirit provides an important incentive in technology transfer.

As community leaders seek out means to stimulate their economies these days, they often consider technology-related businesses as a way to create a clean environment, attract an educated work force, and expand the tax base, as has been done so successfully in the Boston area, Research Triangle, and Silicon Valley. As a result a number of communities have established incentive programmes to encourage such business development.

The Utah scene
Recent activities in Utah are somewhat typical of many communities attempting to establish a high-tech business culture. This is a logical goal for Utah. The state has a small, but highly educated population noted for its strong work ethic.

Geographically, Utah is far from major markets, which imposes costly transportation penalties on heavy manufacturing, but insignificant penalties on high-value-added products. The state's traditional mineral resources industry has suffered badly with the intense competition from foreign steel and copper. Agriculture has always been limited in the state by lack of a reliable source of water. Tourism has expanded greatly in the state, primarily due to the skiing industry, but Utah needs diversification to provide challenging jobs for its youth.

Utah has three major research-oriented universities: University of Utah at Salt Lake City, Utah State University at Logan, both state supported, and Brigham Young University at Provo, operated by the Church of Jesus Christ of Latter Day Saints. Each of these universities is heavily involved in research and each has an engineering school as well as strong programmes in the physical and biological sciences, and business administration. The universities provide a good technology base and an ample supply of well-trained people to operate technology- related business ventures. However, prior to the mid-1950s virtually no such businesses existed in the state.

Creating a high-technology culture from near zero is difficult because the infrastructure of support personnel and industry is not generally present. A community faces the task of creating its own infrastructure or importing it from the outside. In Utah both paths have been successfully followed. High technology in Utah began with the influx of aerospace firms in the late 1950s, including the Sperry Corporation, Morton Thiokol Corporation, and Hercules Incorporated. In addition, the United States Air Force greatly expanded its aerospace activities in Utah at Hill Air Force Base. These actions resulted in the creation of many engineering jobs in the state and numerous support firms to service this industry.

Home grown high-tech firms in Utah

It was from one of these small support firms, Utah Research and Development Company, that the author and a colleague, Kenneth A. Richins, spun out Kenway Engineering Inc (now known as the Eaton Kenway Division of the Eaton Corporation) in 1964. Utah Research and Development Inc, illustrates an interesting phenomena in creating new technology-based companies. This firm began in 1958, when two men engaged in contract research at the University of Utah, Drs William S. Partridge and Emerson T. Cannon, created this company to expand their university research activities into the commercial arena.

Capitalizing on well-established reputations in the narrowly defined speciality area of hypervelocity impact, they spun out of the university and built their company on contract research, initially from the Department of Defense and later from NASA, two government agencies vitally concerned with developments in this field. Their technical expertise, coupled with well-honed skills of proposal writing and acquiring government contracts developed over many years at the university, enabled them to attract sufficient contract volume to expand their workforce to approximately a hundred employees. The company was acquired by Interstate Engineering Inc, of Anaheim, California in 1959, which provided the expansion capital required for growth. Building on its base of government r&d contracts, the company branched out into manufacturing specialty hardware, testing components and solid propellants for the space programme, and designing and fabricating aerospace test facilities.

It was from this latter activity that Brown and Richins spun out Kenway Engineering Inc. The initial impetus for the formation of this new company came from the desire of the parent company of Utah Research to transfer Brown and his division of the company to a location near the corporate headquarters in California. Rather than make that move Brown elected to start a new company and remain in Salt Lake City. In its early history Kenway specialized in the design, fabrication, and installation of sophisticated aerospace testing facilities. Eventually, the firm concentrated its entire efforts in automated materials-handling systems, applying advanced engineering talents developed in the aeorspace industry. The company grew rapidly under the imaginative leadership of Kenneth Richins to become a national leader in supplying automated warehouse systems. It was acquired by the Eaton Corporation in 1978, and currently employs approximately 850 people located in an attractive high-rise office building in downtown Salt Lake City and with modern manufacturing facilities in Bountiful, Utah. Kenway is an excellent example of a locally organized high-tech company that has grown up in the community to become a significant contributor to the economy.

In 1969 the author, who at this time was chairman of the Mechanical Engineering Department at the University of Utah, started Terra Tek Inc, as an outgrowth of his research activities in rock mechanics. Sidney J. Green was recruited as president of the company, and under his leadership Terra Tek developed a superb technical staff and excellent research facilities for studying the properties or rocks under high pressure. This capability soon became widely used by the oil industry as knowledge of underground space became more appreciated during the oil embargo of 1973. Terra Tek enjoyed rapid growth and was recognized as a successful university spinoff, providing an interesting role model for other spinoff companies. Terra Tek now employs approximately two hundred engineers, scientists, and support personnel in three buildings located in the University of Utah research park.

In addition to its regular business activities Terra Tek developed a business philosophy of expanding its influence by spinning off viable groups as separate new companies with the management, Terra Tek and investors sharing the equity. Managers, trained in Terra Tek, became successful executives of their own company with extensive help and support from the parent. This technique provided an opportunity for relatively inexperienced managers to develop their own talents and have the opportunity to achieve early success knowing full well they had the support and backing of the well-seasoned Terra Tek senior management team.

This simple technique for expanding the company's business by spinning out companies and maintaining an equity position, while providing ample financial reward for the new company management team, worked well for Terra Tek. However, as simple as this operating philosophy appears it should be recognized that it is contrary to well-accepted management practice in large US companies where management insists on complete ownership of subsidiaries, leaving little opportunity for exceptional financial reward for subsidiary managers. Large coporations could likely benefit from applying this operating technique to their own subsidiaries.

In 1977 Terra Tek acquired control of a very small plant biotechnology company, NPI. Terra Tek transferred its chief financial officer, Peter D.

Meldrum, to NPI as chief executive officer, arranged for a bank line-of-credit, provided space in one of its new buildings, and in general provided a supportive environment in a prestigious location. NPI developed a new aggressive self-image and recruited outstanding technical and management staff. It undertook joint research and development projects with major companies around the world, many of whom also made equity investments in NPI. With multinational corporations as partners, NPI developed facilities in Singapore and Brazil to supply agricultural materials for foreign markets. The company now has approximately five hundred employees, including forty PhD-level scientists, and occupies its own 80 000 square foot building in the university research park, as well as extensive production facilities in several western states.

In 1969, Drs David C. Evans and Ivan Sutherland incorporated Evans and Sutherland Computer Company, as a direct outgrowth of their research programme at the University of Utah in computer graphics. The company attracted venture capital and after struggling for several years quickly became the world's premier supplier of high-resolution computer graphics systems. Continued expansion capital was provided by a very successful public offering. The company grew rapidly and now employs approximately 650 people in several large buildings in the university research park.

Cericor Inc, a CAD–CAM company, was created by engineers from I-Omega Corporation, and Evans and Sutherland. This company developed exciting technology and was recently purchased by Hewlett Packard, which finally established a long-sought-after presence in Utah.

Kolff Medical Inc, now known as Simbion Inc was formed in the 1970s to commercialize products from a world-renowned research programme in artificial organs at the University of Utah College of Medicine. The company has received extensive publicity for its best-known product, the Jarvik Seven artificial heart, named after the company President Dr Robert Jarvik, but it has other equally exciting products such as its artificial ear. A public offering has provided ample operating capital to carry the company through the extensive testing programes required to obtain the necessary government certification to enable the products to be marketed widely. This company has high visibility and is closely watched by other aspiring medical technology entrepreneurs.

Two medical products companies, both engaged in disposable supplies for hospital use, exhibited very rapid growth and significant success in the Salt Lake City area. Deseret Pharmaceutical Inc (subsequently acquired by Warner Lambert) and Sorenson Research (bought by Abbott Laboratories) achieved large market shares in the disposable medical products market. Neither of these companies had substantial interaction with the university and their products are closer to medium technology than to high technology, but they played an important role in demonstrating the viability of building a company based on medical products. In addition, both companies attracted a cadre of capable managers to the area.

The companies described above are but a small sample of recently created high-technology companies which have sprung up in the state, primarily near its three major universities. These companies were included in this paper since they represent the diversity of high-tech firms in the region not only in their product lines, but also in their method of origin. The success of these companies has played an important role in convincing community leaders that high-tech firms can create jobs, and attract and retain the talented workforce required to make the companies successful in expanding to new markets. They have also served as important role models for others.

Support organizations

A number of events occurred which had significant impact on the early success of Utah's efforts. The University of Utah created its research park in 1968 on 350 acres of prime land adjacent to the campus and overlooking the Salt Lake valley. The research park provided a focal point for development of high-tech business and was successful in attracting such firms as Terra Tek and Evans and Sutherland, providing an environment in which both of these firms could grow and develop. The research park continues to be the most prestigious location for high-tech companies in the region largely due to its prime location and the ready access to the university facilities. The University of Utah has exhibited a friendly, open posture with companies in the park, further enhancing its ambience. Utah State University has recently begun development of its own research and technology park in Logan to provide similar services in northern Utah.

The Utah Innovation Center was created in 1979 at the University of Utah with Professors Stephen C. Jacobsen and Wayne S. Brown as principal investigators under a grant from the National Science Foundation (NSF). It became a private corporation in 1981. The primary goal of the centre is to provide an environment which can assist the formation and growth of high-tech firms. As a successful private outgrowth from the NSF Innovation Center Experiment it attracted considerable national and international attention.

The centre takes an equity position in its client companies, and provides them management, technical, legal, secretarial and general business management services. In some cases the centre provides limited seed investment funds. Typically, one or more centre officials take a seat on the board of directors. Every effort is made to make the centre an integral part of the business and a full business partner, while still leaving the day-to-day management of the company with the original entrepreneur or personnel who have been recruited with the aid of the centre.

An attractive mini-campus has been developed for the centre, its affiliate companies and other appropriate firms in the University of Utah research park. This facility includes three attractive buildings containing a total of 160 000 square feet of office and laboratory space. This complex is the headquarters for a dozen firms, most of which have direct ties with the centre. It also houses some support services and other companies which were attracted to the location due to its central role in the Utah high-tech business scene.

The Utah Innovation Foundation was created in 1982 to provide education programmes, forums, and conferences oriented toward technical entrepreneurship. It is governed by a board of prominent Utah citizens. Forums conducted by the foundation are an interesting way of bringing local people interested in high-tech business enterprise together. Speakers are invited to discuss a wide variety of topics such as marketing strategy, financing the company, how to establish effective banking relations, success stories, etc. Conferences have been held on a number of specialized themes and one venture capital fair organized by the foundation attracted outside venture capital to several local companies. The First International Technical Innovation and Entrepreneurship Symposium, which attracted nearly three hundred representatives of industry, government, and academia from around the world was the foundation's largest undertaking to date.

In 1983 the Utah Technology Finance Foundation (UTFC) was created by the State Legislature to provide seed financing to small technology-related firms, in recognition of the difficulty in obtaining such capital for small companies. Funded by the State Legislature as a separate nonprofit corporation, and managed by an outstanding board of trustees appointed by the governor, UTFC has become a significant force in the local high-tech community. UTFC has committed $1 million to a local venture-capital fund leveraged on the basis that the fund would invest an additional $4 million in Utah. It has created its own Small Business Innovation Research Program and funded four small companies to date. It also supports the Utah Innovation Foundation. UTFC is providing imaginative leadership in establishing a variety of innovative programmes which will contribute to the Utah economy. This organization has demonstrated that it is possible to recruit capable, committed, non-paid volunteers to assist the state in its economic development objectives. Terra Tek's president, Sidney J. Green, has been the most prestigious volunteer and its most effective leader in establishing UTFC as a viable and respected state-funded nonprofit corporation.

In 1985 a group of community-minded Salt Lake City businessmen organized the Utah Venture Capital Fund to provide private financing to promising young companies. Utah firms have had excellent success in attracting outside venture capital and have reciprocated by providing an excellent return on the capital invested, but it is difficult to attract the relatively small amounts of capital required by a start-up company. Recognizing the need for such investment capital and the potentially high rewards for successful investments in start-ups, this fund is being created to establish one more important element in the diversity of ingredients necessary to establish a high-tech, innovative, entrepreneurial culture in Utah. An additional venture capital fund with strong ties to Silicon Valley has recently been announced.

Collectively the organizations above, together with others unmentioned, have established a high-tech culture in Utah. Much remains to be done, but the state is gaining increased recognition for its numerous activities related to this important economic and cultural achievement.

Conclusion

In summary, it appears that communities that have the strong desire and commitment, plus several key important ingredients including one or more research-oriented universities, can create a high-tech business environment. In recent years Utah has had its greatest success by creating its own home-grown companies. Several supporting organizations have played key roles in stimulating this process. One hallmark of the maturity of a high-tech business environment is for new companies to spin-out of the existing ones. People employed in successful small companies are prone to starting their own firms. Fortunately, this trend has become quite apparent in Utah in the last several years. Utah appears to be on the threshold of extensive high-tech expansion.

The Aston Science Park experience: technology transfer policies

Harry A. Nicholls
Aston Science Park

The City of Birmingham, the second largest British city, was for over two hundred years, the prosperous centre of manufacturing industry in the United Kingdom. Home of the Industrial Revolution, Boulton and Watt once provided the world's supply of steam engines and Birmingham itself was the engine powering the nation's economic growth. The city of a thousand trades has been par excellence the area of a multitude of successful small companies.

In the late 1970s, city politicians and officials recognized its economic decline as structural rather than purely cyclical. In the manufacturing sector alone, which provided a third of local jobs, Birmingham has lost over 167 000 jobs and suffered a net loss of 25 000 jobs in the service sector. The loss of jobs, persistent high unemployment and the disappearance of many household name companies, made it essential for there to be a new initiative. It had to go further than the range of almost palliative local projects, seen by many to offer too little, too late and concentrating on preserving jobs in traditional industries. The structural decline had, in part, been brought about by successive governments' regional policy directing industrial growth to other depressed areas; and in part by the independently minded pragmatism of the city's entrepreneurs – once a strength which built prosperity but now a weakness bringing in a period of decline.

In 1976, the city invested £48 million to develop Britain's largest and most successful exhibition centre – the National Exhibition Centre – which has proved London-based sceptics wrong by achieving profitable operation by 1985. This development has generated some 8000 jobs in the service sector and similar scale initiatives were felt to be needed in order to revitalize the city's manufacturing base.

Science parks on the States-side model had been considered in depth by the local authorities in 1978, but were shelved at that time. There were no suitable sites for green-field low-density developments in the vicinity of the universities and the particular funding requirements of companies in new technology fields was a seemingly intractable problem for local authorities to tackle. Above all, the institutional style of UK higher education establishment offered little prospect of success for the encouragement of high-growth technology industries supported by academic and intellectual resources from the universities.

In late 1980, the new Vice-Chancellor of Aston University, Professor F. W. Crawford, circulated a paper on the establishment of a science park at Aston, based on his personal experience of twenty-one years at Stanford University.

The Vice-Chancellor was committed to changing the way the university viewed the entrepreneurial development of new ideas and called for the establishment of a local facility to draw together the entrepreneur and the university's resources.

Aston University, founded about a century ago by local industrialists, had by 1980 developed a well-established reputation as a sound technological university. However, the new Vice-Chancellor adopted new objectives and a strategy for the development of the university to become the finest of its kind in the UK. Drawing upon Stanford experience, his strategy was uncompromising concentration on the achievement of academic excellence within the university itself and the enhancement of interaction with local industry and the local community through the establishment of a science park and a related technology transfer centre.

Experience of successful science parks at Stanford and Boston in the US and Cambridge in the UK, suggested that successful science park developments had a gestation period of anything up to fifteen years. Evaluation of the success criteria for science parks suggested that all were present in Birmingham, but that the process needed to be pro-actively managed in order to ensure success and, if possible, shortened time scale. To do this, a commercially orientated independent managing company, Birmingham Technology Limited (BTL), was established by the city and the university.

An essential element required for success in the Birmingham context was felt to be the provision of venture capital under the control of the operating company. Thus, Lloyds Bank Plc, one of the four major clearing banks in the UK, was brought in as the third partner in the venture.

Using a former metal forging works, the first phase of Aston Science Park was established in early 1983, run by its own management team, tapping into university resources, and backed by its own venture capital investment fund. Having provided the initial building, and putting up £1 million of the £2 million venture capital fund created with Lloyds Bank Plc, Birmingham City Council also committed itself to extending the science park to its proposed twenty-two acres, backed by compulsory purchase action.

Aston science park – the package

Objectives

The mission of the science park is to encourage and facilitate rapid growth of knowledge-based companies through the provision of business, management and technological support, venture funding and the provision of flexible accommodation and leases to meet changing requirements.

Tenant companies are required to be engaged in activities to which the skills of the university can make a positive contribution. The aim is to develop the creative community with the university concentrating on the creation of knowledge through research, and the science park on the creation of wealth through the application of that knowledge and through interactions not only between companies and the university, but, importantly, between the companies themselves.

Aston Science Park is run by Birmingham Technology Limited (BTL), a private company limited by guarantee with no share capital. The board consists of members from the city, university and Lloyds Bank. To date, city membership has included the Leader and Shadow Leader of the Council, the Chairman and Shadow Chairman of the city's Economic Development Committee, and the Chief Executive; the city appoints the company chairman. The university members include the Vice-Chancellor and two Pro-Vice-Chancellors, with Lloyd's membership being represented by their regional director. The management team consists of the chief executive, the director of finance, the director of business development, a second bank manager from Lloyds Bank, two business development managers, a property development manager, two accountants and seven secretarial/administrative staff. The chief executive was previously Dean and Head of the Management Centre at Aston, the remainder of the executive team all have wide industrial experience at senior levels.

Liaison with the university is carried out at a formal level by a business development manager working with the University Science Park Liaison Committee. At a less formal level, liaison is carried out by all staff members through day-to-day contact with university personnel, through the assessment process outlined below, and through the individual involvement of university personnel with individual tenant companies.

Finance

The majority of BTL's income is generated from its investments in tenant companies. Investments to date total some £1.25 million in the form of straightforward loans, equity investments or whatever particular form of financing is considered most appropriate to a company's requirements. Clearly this reliance on investment income cannot provide short-term funding for the company and for the time being BTL relies for its deficit funding on the grant aid from the City Council under Section 137 of the Local Government Act.

The £2 million venture capital fund contributed by the city and Lloyds Bank is administered by BTL and investment decisions are taken by the board rather than the city or the bank independently. Contacts are being established with private funding institutions with a view to broadening the base of funding support beyond that provided by the city and Lloyds Bank. Currently, the operating budget for BTL is approximately £500 000 per annum and it is intended that a break-even point will be reached in three years time.

To date it would appear that more inquiries for tenancies are stimulated by the availability of finance than the other elements in the package. Consequently, a major element in the assessment of potential tenants consists of a financial appraisal, involving liaison with their private sector funding sources. It would be most exceptional for BTL to be the only source of funding for a tenant.

Business support

The Phase I development consists of accommodation geared to the needs of new companies. One of the founding philosophies of BTL is that through business support in the early stages of a company's development, the links with the university and the availability of additional funding from BTL will enable a company's idea to be brought to the market place far quicker than would otherwise be the case. The intention is to guide companies rather than run them, and the primary source of business support is through BTL's nominee working directly with the company concerned. BTL monitors that company's performance through regular financial reporting, which enables involvement to be very finely tuned to company requirements as they change. BTL is also able to call upon specialist resources within the university where there are gaps in the availability of expertise within BTL itself. At a more basic level, the science park offers newly formed companies a range of facilities which they would not otherwise be able to support in the early stages of development. These include conference room facilities for demonstration purposes and seminars, reception facilities, telex, photocopying, secretarial services, financial accounting on the BTL computer, on-site catering and rest-room facilities.

Accommodation

The basic refurbishment which forms the Phase I development, can be adapted to meet a wide range of individual company needs, whether size of unit, physical servicing or lease arrangement. The development itself is on a head lease from the City Council and BTL sublets this accommodation on terms derived from requirements seen in the context of the business plan prepared with each tenant company. The maximum length of lease is three years, although much shorter terms are available under licence arrangements. The objective is to provide a flexible arrangement which will enable the company to expand its accommodation requirements. Realistically, it also enables the company to withdraw from the science park if the venture is not successful, without ongoing lease commitments for that company. Where a lease is entered into with a tenant company, a court order under the Landlord and Tenant Act is jointly sought to exclude the provisions of the act relating to the creation of rights of tenure. BTL carried out the basic fitting-out of accommodation to tenants' requirements with grant aid from the city council and this stage of work can also include specialist tenant requirements at their own cost, ie, specialist services, environmental control, etc.

Technical support

Part of the assessment of incoming tenants is carried out by appropriate university personnel, selected according to the potential tenant's area of technology. This forms an immediate link between tenant and the university and, if the tenant comes to the park, this link develops into an ongoing dialogue. Through the regular reporting procedures, the quality of dialogue can be monitored and additional expertise drawn in from the university as required. Where a tenant uses university facilities, these are charged on an interdepartmental basis rather than at full cost. It should be noted that the initial assessment by the university is not charged for. Ongoing involvement by university personnel can be on a straight-forward consultancy basis or, as has happened in many cases, by the academic forming part of the management team of the tenant company, perhaps becoming a company director.

Development

The Phase I development was funded by the inner-city partnership programme at a cost of approximately £1.6 million with acquisition costs of approximately £400 000. The development consists of 45 000 square feet of rentable space and the rental is £3.90 per square foot per annum with a service charge in the region of £3.50 per square foot per annum. The service charge includes rates, insurance, heating, cleaning, security, reception, maintenance, parking, common services and, in the case of some of the office units, electricity.

In 1983, a development study was commissioned from the Weedon Partnership which established that the twenty-two-acre site adjacent to the university campus could support approximately 100 000 square feet of specialist research and development accommodation, with generous levels of car parking in a first rate 'campus style' environment. The development study also advocated the creation of an amenity core within the science park to ensure that a total working environment is created. The amenity core would include residential accommodation, some commercial units and restaurant facilities to supplement facilities already available locally. The entire science park area is currently the subject of compulsory purchase action, affecting nine existing businesses, all of which are negotiating with the city for alternative accommodations.

Largely through the inner-city partnership programme, the city is embarking on a canal enhancement project which includes the clearance and preparation of development sites as they become available. In addition to the Phase I development, the city council currently owns approximately five acres of sites capable of development. Subject to the compulsory purchase orders, the remainder of the science park is expected to be developed over something like a ten-year timescale.

Phase II of the science park consists of a development of 45 000 square feet of venture units designed to provide independent accommodations for 'graduates' from the Phase I building and the r&d arms of established companies. Each unit is of 5000 square feet on two floors, although units have been designed with a view to combining to form larger multiples. The units form quality office type accommodations and 25 000 square feet of the development has been designed to cater to light engineering uses on the ground floor. Work started in September 1984 and was completed in September 1985. Rents are between £4 and £4.50 per square foot depending on the type of accommodation let.

Aston Science Park – practice
Although in existence for a relatively short time, it is possible to comment on practice at the science park in terms of lessons learned to date.

Marketing
Initially the science park was marketed on the 'scatter-gun' principle which generated over 1000 inquiries. Given that there are currently twenty-six tenant companies, this was clearly an inefficient form of marketing, tying up scarce resources in unfruitful tenant assessments. It was also initially proposed to engage in overseas marketing to stimulate inward investment company interest, but it was decided at an early date to concentrate resources on more local marketing. Currently, marketing is being targeted on those industries and areas of technology to which the university is most able to make a contribution. In addition to confining marketing to these areas, the net is being widened beyond the initial target of the individual entrepreneur/innovator. This includes contact with major industrial companies and research establishments with a view to offering research and development facilities on site to carry forward projects which might not otherwise be pursued by these organizations.

Management
Rather than increase BTL's budget requirement by taking on additional full-time staff, the emphasis is increasingly on utilizing seconded staff from other

organizations or contracting out specific tasks. BTL is also able to draw upon available postgraduate resources within the university for this.

Finance and business support

The availability of financial support to companies has proved to be fundamental to the Aston Science Park package. To date Aston Science Park is the only UK science park with its own venture capital fund. The long term pay-back nature of investments has highlighted the extent of speculative risk entered into by the city and Lloyds Bank in the initiative.

Business support has emerged as an extremely time-consuming activity; however, it remains a major plank in the science park philosophy.

Technical support

Even given the Vice-Chancellor's personal commitment to the science park, there has been a need to pro-actively manage the interface between Aston Science Park and the university to maximize the involvement of academics in the affairs of science park companies. Through the active promotion of an open door policy, relations with the university are continuing to improve through the medium of regular departmental visits, informal seminars, etc. All the existing tenants have a useful relationship with the university, a better record than most other parks.

Development funding

Given the scale of development proposed and the timescale envisaged, the science park cannot rely solely on public-sector development funding. Although private-sector institutional funding is in principle available, the type of tenant companies, the high-risk areas of their activities and the core policy of flexible leases, clearly acts as a major disincentive to the institutions. At this stage developments are being funded by the city's main programme with some support from European regional development fund aid. The object is to demonstrate a demand for the accommodation being constructed and to pioneer developments to attract funding for the more forward-looking in-stitutions.

Some achievements to date

Twenty-six tenants selected from 1500 applications;
twenty-two new start-up companies established;
twelve BTL investments completed;
ten CEOs from university or BTL;
five other CEOs are Aston graduates;
first spinoff from established British corporation attracted to the park;
first company from US established on park;
first starter company moved from incubator space to venture unit;
first second-round financing, adding over £500 000 to an investee company's capital, attracted from London venture capital organizations.

Review of the Stanford Research Park phenomenon

Frank A. Morrow
Stanford University

The author is a real estate developer and consultant, formerly the Director of Real Estate for Stanford University. The topic of this chapter is the Stanford Research Park and the insights on the process which a university or similar foundation might consider in the development of their real estate for commercial purposes.

The presentation will fall into three parts: an overview of Stanford's real estate holdings; a short history and description of the Stanford Research Park and the rise of Silicon Valley; and a review of some of the elements that universities and foundations are faced with when considering commercial development.

Stanford real estate

In 1885 Leland Stanford endowed Stanford University with $21 million and 8800 acres of his Palo Alto Farm. (About 620 acres have been lost over the years to condemnations.) Of the remaining 8200 acres, approximately 1800 are currently used for academic purposes, 1000 are in a biological preserve, and 3500 are in an academic reserve. About 2000 acres are designed for interim development. About half of this has been developed: the industrial park (650 acres), shopping centre (100 acres), and housing and professional offices (200 acres).

Although this chapter will focus on the Stanford Research Park, that is only one element of Stanford's commercial real estate activities. The university owns a large regional shopping centre, it has developed several hundred housing units, it manages its academic reserve lands and it is an investor in real estate as part of the portfolio management of its endowment. For a point of reference, Stanford real estate is in many ways comparable to the Irvin Company, Bishop Estates, or Grosvenor Estates of the United Kingdom. One of the interesting footnotes to Californian history is that the Palo Alto area right of way for Southern Pacific Railway is owned by Stanford.

The Stanford Research Park consists of over 6 million square feet of office and research/development space. The tenants include some of the major US *Fortune* 500 companies. Some observers consider the research park the cradle of high technology.

Stanford research park: a brief history

By 1946 Stanford's endowment had grown by only $10 million to the not-so-imposing total of $31 million. The main campus used less than 500 acres and Stanford was a sleepy little school, fifty miles south of San Francisco, surrounded by orchards. Because of its desire and need to expand, the university found itself in need of money: money for classrooms, professors, student services, etc. As with any university both then and now, it seems the business of education has an insatiable appetite for money.

One alternative to raise the necessary funds was the designation of a small portion of Stanford's lands for commercial development. Included in these plans were: the Stanford Industrial Park on the southern extremity of the university's lands, an office park near what would become the Stanford medical centre, and the Stanford shopping centre. There were few historical models for an industrial park. Were it not for the terms of the original grant from Senator Stanford that precluded selling any piece of the land endowment, perhaps the park concept, with central control over use and architecture, might never have occurred. The administration was forced into the position of strictly controlling land use, knowing that if not in their lifetime, sometime in the life of the school, the lands would or could revert to academic/research use. Moreover, the tenants of the park would always have a visual and economic relationship to the university.

When the park began in 1951 it was open to all types of 'clean industry', not just electronic companies. Early tenants included book publishing, photo-processing, manufacturing, and medical research. However, electronics were to play the dominant role.

It is important to recall that the history of the electronics industry in the United States more or less began in Palo Alto. In 1909 David Starr Jordan, Stanford's President, invested $500 in a new company founded by one of his students. Federal Telegraph became the spawning ground for the early development of the electronics industry. The first milestone was Lee de Forest's perfection of the vacuum tube as a sound amplifier in 1912. Shortly thereafter two Federal Telegraph engineers founded the forerunner of Magnovox, and Charles Litton left to form Litton Industries. In the 1920s the flowering continued. The first successful all-electronic transmission of televised pictures was achieved in 1927 in San Francisco. Heintz and Kaufman Limited built advanced shortwave radio transmitters, including those used by Admiral Byrd. However, it took years to create the critical mass that started the chain reaction of new company formations and the unprecedented growth of the 1960s and 1970s.

In 1937 Fred Terman, a professor of engineering at Stanford, took a major step to end the exodus of his graduate students to the East Coast. With Terman's counsel, Bill Hewlett designed and built an audio-oscillator. Terman felt this invention had great commercial possibilities and enticed another former student, David Packard, to return to Palo Alto from his General Electric job in Schenectady, and join Hewlett. Hewlett and Packard's part-time endeavour in Packard's garage became Hewlett/Packard Corporation. At the same time, Stanford professor William Hansen, teamed with Sigurd and Russell Varian to develop the klystron tube, the foundation of radar and microwave communications. Stanford invested $100 for supplies and provided free use of the physics laboratories. Unfortunately, further development required more substantial backing and the Varians moved to Long Island with Sperry Gyroscope.

When World War II broke out Terman went East and headed an electronic counter-measures project at Harvard. This put him in the mainstream of electronic research. After the war Terman returned as Dean of the School of

Engineering. He set out to meet and benefit from the challenges and opportunities of the rapidly expanding technology. He fostered close cooperation between the school and industry. Eventually he opened regular graduate courses to industry engineers and later used television to bring courses into company classrooms.

The Varian brothers returned in 1947 and formed their own company in Menlo Park. But with their strong ties to the university they wished to locate somewhere on or very close to the campus. Hewlett and Packard had outgrown their garage and like the Varians wished to locate close to the university. Seizing on the opportunity, Terman worked closely with Alf Brandon, Stanford's Vice-President of Business and overseer of the park, first to encourage, and eventually in the 1960s and 1970s to restrict park use to tenants engaged in research and development.

This was when the park was first started, and still today, its administration was and is almost devoid of academic programme input. The strong university/industry times came about in the late 1950s and early 1960s. It was then that Fred Terman saw in the park a resource that could be used to attract both top faculty and students. But contrary to much that has been written, the initial impetus for the development was predominantly monetary. The park was the creation of the business office. The marriage of university academic programmes and commercial research and development came later.

In the 1950s the park was slow to fill. It took nearly ten to fifteen years to achieve significant growth, and twenty-five years to reach capacity. Some of the factors that inhibited early growth included: the requirement that land could only be leased; lease requirements for the reversion of the improvements to the university at the end of the lease term; uncertainty as to whom one's neighbour in the park might be; imposition of strict design and use guidelines; and doubt that the university could or would impose on future tenants the same controls that the early tenants had to deal wtih (in fact as the park grew the controls became tighter, the conditions of the leases stronger and the lease terms shorter). For years Stanford's policy had been to sell pre-paid leasehold interests to developers or users. The original leases were for ninety-nine years. More recently they were fifty-one year leases. Currently, Stanford has moved from a passive role to that of an active participant in the real-estate transaction activities of the park. This new role includes repurchasing existing prepaid leases and subsequently releasing them for redevelopment. The new leases are written to ensure direct university participation in the economic success of the park.

By the late 1950s and 1960s Terman was helping to create a place where his faculty and students could reach their full potential. Hewlett, Packard and Varian's experience was being repeated and was growing. Stanford's school of electrical engineering was awarding more PhDs than any other school in the country. After graduation many went to work for local companies and then moved on to form their own. Terman, then provost, enticed William Johnson and Carl Djerassi to join the Chemistry Department. This attracted many outstanding chemists to the university and Syntex's research arm to the park. Djerassi with Alex Zaffaroni spun-off four companies from Syntex: Syva, a joint venture with Varian; Zoecon; Alza; and Dynapol. Some trace the beginning of the new wave of bio-engineering to these ventures.

In 1957 William Shockley, the coinventor of the transistor, set up Shockley Transistor Corporation. Bob Noyce, one of Shockley's proteges, founded

Fairchild Semiconductor and later Intel. No fewer than fifty companies can trace their origins to Fairchild. At the same time the area became the centre for laser production. Some Varian alumnae formed Spectra Physics. Two engineers left Spectra and formed Coherent Radiation; and so it went on and so it continues.

The Stanford development decision process

With that history as background let us more closely inspect the philosophical context in which the commercial development of academic land takes place. Recognizing that its land is both its endowment and its legacy, Stanford continually addresses the issue of development. Two factors that are elements of the decision to develop or redevelop property are academic programme needs and economic return. Stanford attempts to balance the trade-offs of the employment of its resources: land, people, and capital with expected returns; returns as a function of both academics and economics. The trick is that benefits or returns may be direct or indirect, ie, development of a specific parcel of land could generate money that in turn funds an academic programme. However, the land resource now in commercial use is lost to near-term academic or research expansion. Obviously, the decision to use resources to serve academic programme needs directly, or in the alternative provide economic return to fund other programmes, can create tension between constituencies competing for these finite resources.

For all the publicity of Stanford's commercial use of its lands, only 10 per cent are in such use. The 3500 acres of Farmlands are dedicated to programme expansion rather than current economic return. Rather than exploit their full commercial potential, their use is restricted to relatively non-intrusive, non-permanent activities, primarily agricultural. The decision has been to minimize carrying costs but maximize availability for academic research foregoing near-term economic gain. One of the more noteworthy examples of the benefit of such a policy is the Stanford linear accelerator. When the national search for a site was on, Stanford had land, available not only for the initial installation, but for growth of the facility.

That is not to say that the development of the research park has not had a profound effect on the university. Furthermore, the benefits of that development go beyond dollars and cents. Among other things, in providing job opportunities to Stanford faculty and students, the park has been a conduit for the transfer of new technology to the market place. As has been amply documented, that conduit allows a flow of technology and dollars in both directions.

There has, however, been a downside to the university's developments. Some complain that Stanford focuses too much on the financial and academic benefits of developments to the university, and not enough on the impact on nearby communities. In addition to the pollution attendant to the phenomenal population growth, there is a deeper worry that our clean industries are not so clean. The management of the toxic residue of these new industries is at the bottom of the learning curve. A great deal of unseen but potentially extremely hazardous waste and residue has been created. Control and management of this waste will be one of the great challenges for the remaining years of this century. Planning for toxic waste management in new parks will be one of the considerable front end development costs. Also, by creating 23 000 jobs in the business park, Stanford is said to be a major culprit in Silicon Valley's jobs–housing imbalance or the inadequacy of new housing units in relation to new jobs. The debate rages as to the proper balance between the inevitable trade-off between quality of life and economic prosperity. This is a question that could easily be a major topic for another conference.

Everyone can learn from the Silicon Valley experience. Not everything has been done right. I mourn the loss of the orchards and the onslaught of congestion. However, the creativity that brought economic success to the area may also redress the degradation in environmental quality.

Given the interest in this conference and other symposiums, it is obvious that many would like to explore ways to duplicate the Stanford/Silicon Valley experience. First, it is extremely important but very difficult for university administrations, boards of governors, and trustees, to come to a consensus on the use of their real estate assets. However, without this consensus and a thorough 'buying into' the decision, any policy is doomed to failure. Worse than failure will be an embarkation on a path that continually changes grade and direction.

In the use of the university's resources for commercial development, one must try to enhance the current position of the institution while preserving its resources for the future. To a university whose useful life should be forever, internal rate of return is not always the correct measure for decision making. (Developers who wish to deal with these institutions would do well to remember this.) Therefore, the university at the higest level must make a clear statement as to its overall goals and objectives. Within that context the role which real estate is to play in achieving them must be determined.

If the university elects more actively to employ its land resources, such a programme should be constituted so that the long-term economic and educational benefits to the university are optimized, and also fit appropriately within the economic and social arenas of the university and the community.

Any such programme should take advantage of the university's diversified scientific and technological resources, be accomplished while remaining sensitive to and compatible with the local environment, and have long-term economic benefit to the neighbouring communities as well as the university. In order to implement a realistic real estate programme one should develop clear statements on general policy and objectives with market analysis of specific lands and sites. A specific policy statement should be developed that includes priorities for use of current inventory and priorities for the acquisition of new properties.

The potential commercial or quasi-commercial use of the lands within the context of the academic support needs of the institution should be reviewed. Examples of these uses are: joint-use research and development technology incubators; general office and light-research facilities for university and associated affiliates; faculty, staff and student housing; medical centre housing; and special university/industry humanitarian endeavours.

The relevant legal and regulatory position needs to be considered. A clear understanding of the constraints and degrees of freedom of the real estate function should be developed. Guidelines and statements on how participation in the development of the property is to proceed should be developed along with an organization capable of administering the programme consistent with the general goals and objectives.

No real estate programme can operate in a vacuum. One must be prepared for close and well-publicized scrutiny. This suggests a need for a strong coordinated community relations effort. Open lines of communication should be developed with those jurisdictions most closely affected by university land-use policies. The economic impact of university land decisions on these entities must be considered. Ways to implement appropriate mitigations for adverse economic and/or environmental impacts need to be anticipated and the potential for joint industrial/economic developments explored.

To repeat, 'The university at the highest level must make a clear statement as to its goal and objectives and what role real estate is to play in achieving them.' The 'why' of real estate must be set in a context of the overall mission of the university. Most of the leading universities in the country would probably define themselves first as comprehensive research institutions. They would more than likely place in their list of priorities: quality of research, quality of instruction, strength of student body, health care, community service, and perhaps most important preservation of the institution.

The role of real estate

Historically most colleges and universities have taken their real estate assets for granted. Most universities have spent considerably more time on the issues of faculty, staff, students, and physical plant rather than the disposition of their real estate. For these institutions, effort expended on the appropriate utilization of land resources has a great potential for impact relative to effort.

It can be argued that it is irresponsible not to plan properly for the future employment of one's land assets. Land is a finite commodity. The employment or holding of land for future academic programmes must be carefully considered. With only an ad hoc land policy, an institution is not able to make sensible or responsible decisions on the disposition of any one parcel.

The university is at its heart a conservator. Although most prefer a reactive mode when dealing with real estate, this may well be a luxury the institution can no longer afford. A reactive posture limits one to responding to the pressures of the moment.

It is incumbent on the university to preserve its land in perpetuity to accommodate unknown academic needs while attempting to meet near-term programme requirements and community expectations. This view to the extreme long-term, and the need to respond tomorrow to what was unknown today, is in immediate conflict with city and county planning processes that typically focus on the next ten to twenty years, and the political process where the horizon is not much beyond the next election.

The university, although a conservator of the past, is also an agent for change. It is this role as change agent that often results in conflict with surrounding communities. If the university is to become an active participant in the local real estate markets, participating in the development of property either for immediate profit or academic benefit, or investing in opportunities as they arise, it must be prepared and organized to deal in a highly visible, volatile, transaction-oriented endeavour. During all the commotion and hub-bub that accompanies real estate development, it is essential to keep in the forefront the overall goals of the institution and continue to test why this particular endeavour was important in the context of those goals.

Conclusion

The employment of real estate, whether to obtain near-term economic benefits or longer-term programming benefits, will affect all of the university's constituencies in differing and often conflicting ways. These constituencies, university administration, university faculty, trustees, students, the local communities, elected officials, and their staffs, have a particular view. Each is touched in a unique way by the disposition of a particular land parcel, and each has a separate avenue to pursue their cause. If the university is to become active in its local real estate market, it must be aware of these forces, be willing to assume the burden of the landowner/developer (even if it does not actually develop for its own account), and create a framework of institutional policies and organizations that allows it to maintain a more or less constant course in the midst of powerful, countervailing forces.

The Stanford/Palo Alto/Santa Clara Valley experience is one model, but certainly not the only one. Much of the development of the Valley was serendipitous. Fred Terman set out to create a community of technical scholars. Alf Brandon needed to raise money to keep the place going. Their endeavours were strongly assisted by the fact that the Santa Clara Valley is an extremely nice place to live. Another blessing was distance from Washington. Although Terman, Varian, and others did considerable defence work, much of the defence contracting went to Boston. This forced the Valley firms into a strong consumer orientation and helped them to survive the vagaries of defence and aerospace spending. The key to success lies in developing an environment where creativity can flourish. This would argue against rigid planning. What is required is the accumulation of that critical mass that allows the process to gain and sustain its own life. As noted earlier, there was a long history of electronic entrepreneurism in the area. This created a business climate that encouraged the formation of new companies. Many successful engineers and entrepreneurs became the venture capitalists that provided seed money for the next new company. The other fundamental element was a university, a place of learning, that could provide visible rewards, both intellectual and monetary, to faculty and staff. This flow of learning, knowledge and money keeps the pot boiling.

Research and technology parks: the Canadian experience

Glenn Mitchell
Edmonton R&D Park Authority

The Canadian environment

A little background on the Canadian reality may contribute to a better understanding of the progress and direction of research parks in Canada. Perhaps the most dominant of these realities is that Canada is a very large country with a very small population that is unevenly distributed. While the land area of Canada exceeds that of the United States, China, or Brazil, and is exceeded only by that of the Soviet Union, Canada is inhabited by approximately 25 million citizens, 90 per cent of whom live within two hundred miles of the Canada–USA border. Imagine a United States with a total population equal to that of the state of California or New York, scattered north of a line between Seattle and New York City, and you will have a better appreciation of Canadian demography. In addition, the Canadian population is heavily urbanized (75 per cent), with nearly half of the total population concentrated in southern Ontario and southwestern Quebec. This particular reality has made Canadians both aware of and sensitive to most events and trends taking place in the USA, including the development of research and technology parks.

A second major Canadian reality is best expressed by the word 'regionalism', which may be understood as a combination of government structure, population distribution, and regional economic differences. Canada is a federal state in which each of the ten provinces (roughly comparable to the states of Australia or the United States of America) has considerable powers and sources of revenue under the Canadian constitution. For example, provinces retain ownership of all mineral resources within their borders, a considerable source of revenue for those provinces with major reserves of petroleum and minerals. A second contributor to regionalism is the substantial differences in the economic basis of each provincial economy, which has often led to conflict, particularly between resource-producing provinces and those provinces which desire access to cheap resources for their dominant manufacturing industries. A third factor is the highly uneven distribution of the Canadian population, which has placed much political control at the national level in the hands of two provinces with the largest share of the Canadian population, Ontario and Quebec. For all these reasons, Canada has developed distinct regional identities, which in turn has led to those regions pursuing their economic destinies in different ways. Where research parks are concerned, their greater popularity in western Canada may be attributable to several factors, including closer north–south, ie, USA–Canada, economic and personal ties, a drive to make the dominant resource industries of agriculture, oil and gas, mining and forestry more competitive through research and development, and a desire to broaden the western Canadian economic base through the development of innovative, research-based manufacturing industries capable of competing on a world scale.

Another reality in Canada is that the universities are not as well positioned to play the leading role in the development of research and technology parks as American universities. Universities in Canada are publicly funded by the provinces and the federal government. There are no major private universities in Canada, nor have the public universities had access to large reserves of land adjacent to their campuses, which they could develop using their own resources. As a result, Canadian universities lack the three major ingredients necessary to lead in the development of research parks: money (no major private endowments), land, and freedom of action.

A final Canadian reality which directly affects Canadian research parks is the relatively poor research and development record of Canadian industry. Gross expenditures on research and development as a percentage of gross domestic product (GDP) range between 2–3 per cent for the last decade, in spite of generally perceived favourable tax treatment for the conduct of research and development. This performance is usually attributed to three factors: a historical colonial legacy in which Britain found it useful to maintain Canada as a source of raw materials and a market for its manufactured goods; a twentieth-century reliance on the extraction of natural resources to maintain and indeed increase the Canadian standard of living; and an economy dominated by foreign investment in general, and American investment in particular, that does, quite understandably, prefer to maintain its research and development activity in its own country. As a consequence, there are very few major industrial r&d performers in Canada whose research and laboratory establishments could form the cornerstone of a successful research park.

Canadian parks: a brief history

There are six cities in Canada where research parks are located. It is interesting to note that the two research parks located in eastern Canada (specifically southern Ontario) represent the oldest and youngest parks on the Canadian scene. Sheridan Park in Toronto was opened in 1964, while Research Technology Park in Waterloo is not yet officially open, pending university approval and financing. The four remaining parks are in western Canada, located respectively in Saskatoon (Innovation Place), Edmonton (Edmonton Research and Development Park), Calgary (Calgary Research Park), and the greater Vancouver area (Discovery Parks, located adjacent to three separate educational institutions). While there are one or two other initiatives under discussion in other cities, none has proceeded to the stage where their inclusion in this presentation is considered warranted.

Sheridan Park in Toronto is the oldest of the Canadian parks. Whereas the other parks are actively engaged in their communities' advanced technology economic development efforts, including university technology transfer, seed capital funding, incubator planning and development, etc, Sheridan Park is fundamentally a provincial land assembly that has gradually been sold outright to the research divisions of major national and international companies headquartered in Toronto. The affairs of Sheridan Park, including decisions concerning the sale of remaining property, are made by a board of directors dominated by the existing companies in the park. These companies, which include such well-known firms as Dunlop, Duracell, Gulf, and Inco, fund an association that governs their common interests in the park, including technical seminars, libraries and recreation.

Moving from east to west, we come to Research Technology Park, a planned 120 acre (49 hectare) research park located adjacent to the University of Waterloo. A proposed park, which has not yet officially opened its doors or leased any land, it is the single Canadian example of a research park to be developed, marketed and operated by a university. The University of Waterloo is Canada's largest technological university (along the lines of MIT or RPI), with major programmes in engineering, computing science and mathematics, an orientation which has made them particularly active in the technology transfer arena, and has resulted in the formation of a number of data processing enterprises in the Waterloo area.

Innovation Place in Saskatoon, Saskatchewan, is financed and operated by the Saskatchewan Economic Development Corporation (SEDCO) and is located adjacent to the University of Saskatchewan. Innovation Place has successfully attracted several federal government laboratories, including the Veterinary Infectious Disease Organization (VIDO), and the Animal Pathology Laboratory of Agriculture Canada. In addition to capitalizing on the university's strengths to attract federal laboratories, the Province of Saskatchewan has also located a number of its research-based institutions at Innovation Place. To date, the park has not been particularly successful in attracting private industrial research, in part because Saskatoon is a small city (150 000) in a small province with a limited industrial base, and, over the selection of tenants, has been reluctant to accept organizations engaged in manufacturing, regardless of the onsite r&d investment of those organizations. Innovation Place has assumed a much lower profile in the last two years, perhaps feeling that its resources are better directed to consolidating their links with the university and local industry than attracting non-resident industries.

The Calgary Research Park ajacent to the University of Calgary has been in operation since 1967. The tenants of the Calgary Research Park reflect the dominant industry in the city, in that most of the organizations are involved with oil and gas research and seismic technologies. The park is almost completely developed, a situation which has led to the designation of a major land assembly on the northwest edge of the city as a second research park. As a result of this temporary hiatus in research park development, the Calgary Research and Development Authority which has marketed (but not operated) the Calgary Research Park, has concentrated on a broader economic development role for the advanced technologies sector in Calgary. The authority recently opened an advanced technology incubator in leased facilities to assist the formation and growth of small advanced-technology companies in that city.

The Edmonton Research and Development Park was established in 1980 as a joint project of the city, the province, and the University of Alberta, with various private sector interests. The City of Edmonton has provided the land, capital financing and operating funds for the park, with land servicing loan assistance from the Government of Alberta. The Edmonton Research Park is developed, marketed and operated by a semi-autonomous authority directed by a board with representation from the public, university and private sectors. The first major industrial tenant of the Research Park was Bell-Northern Research, a division of Northern Telecom Limited and the largest industrial performer of research and development in Canada. The single largest organization located at the park is the Alberta Research Council, a provincially funded institution that carries out a number of industry-driven programmes in areas of strategic importance to the provincial economy, notably in the areas of oil sands, coal and conventional petroleum resources.

As part of its overall strategic plan to attract industries of varying size and maturity, the Edmonton Research Park opened a 40 000 square foot (3716 square metres) multi-tenant building in late 1983, to provide leased space for young companies requiring customized space in the range of 3000 to 15 000 square feet. This building is now 80 per cent leased and occupied by companies involved in data communications testing, close range photogrammetry, data logging systems, and high-pressure petroleum recovery research. The authority has planned, and will be constructing, a second facility in 1986, which is intended for lease to smaller advanced-technology companies. This facility will incorporate a number of common areas for tenants, including board rooms, libraries, lunchroom, etc, and may be operated as an incubator in which office, management and financial services are made available to tenants.

The authority, which has and continues to develop the Edmonton Research and Development Park, also takes an active leadership role in many of the city and provincial economic development activities related to advanced technology, including the formation of the Edmonton Council for Advanced Technology (ECAT), an industry group which provides a forum for the discussion of issues related to the development of advanced technology.

Discovery Parks, located in Vancouver, British Columbia, is arguably the most ambitious of the Canadian research park efforts. Discovery Parks is responsible for the development of three separate research parks at the University of British Columbia (UBC), Simon Fraser University (SFU), and the British Columbia Institute of Technology (BCIT), all located in the greater Vancouver area. Discovery Parks is part of a larger entity called Discovery Foundation, which is an arms-length creation of the Province of British Columbia intended to stimulate the development of advanced technology in the province. The foundation is managed by a board of directors and funded principally by the government of British Columbia. In addition to Discovery Parks, the foundation operates a consulting office to assist innovators successfully to commercialize their inovations (BC Innovation Office), a communications and technology awareness organization (Discovery Club) and a venture capital organization. While there are currently single, large tenants located at each of the parks adjacent to UBC and SFU, Discovery Parks is perhaps best noted for its 80 000 square foot (7432 square metre) multi-tenant research facility located in the research park adjacent to BCT. This award-winning structure which is close to capacity, is occupied by more than thirty-five small technology-intensive companies, as well as the offices of Discovery Parks.

Canadian parks: common themes
It should be obvious at this point that all Canadian research parks have been largely or entirely developed using public funds. In a country devoid of large

private universities and heavy concentrations of research-based industry that would make an entirely private development feasible, research parks could not have come into being without government funding. While Sheridan Park is theoretically a self-sustaining community run by the companies located there, the original attraction was low-cost, serviced land made available from the Province of Ontario, exclusively for research-based enterprises. Waterloo is a publicly funded university, and future developments in their park will presumably be funded from the annual budget of that university, which is approved by the Ontario Legislature. The land assemblies in Saskatoon, Calgary, and Vancouver are provincially financed. Edmonton is an exception, in that the City of Edmonton has been the principal financial supporter of both the land development activities and the operations of the authority.

A second theme of the parks is the semi-autonomous nature of their operations. While the four western parks, for example, must apply for and defend their annual budgets before city and/or provincial governments, they have considerable operating latitude, which they need in order to respond to opportunities. Typically, the parks are managed by a small professional group which reports to a board with representation from government, universities and private industry.

A third important theme in the development of Canadian parks has been the continuing involvement of the local research-oriented universities. With the possible exception of Sheridan Park, whose primary appeal has been to mature companies, the Canadian parks have strong university representation on their boards, and they work closely with university groups to encourage and support the development of spinoff companies from university laboratories. The parks in Waterloo, Saskatoon, Calgary and Vancouver are also located on property immediately adjacent to university campuses, which facilitates access to university services. In Edmonton, the University of Alberta has become increasingly involved with the creation of industry–university research institutes and university-spawned enterprises, which are potential tenants for the Edmonton Research Park.

A fourth theme of the Canadian parks, with the exception of the anomalous Sheridan Park, has been their willingness to accept light manufacturing and ancillary activities, so long as occupants have demonstrated a minimum research and development threshold, usually in terms of criteria that include laboratory space, research funding, and staff composition. Innovation Place in Saskatoon has precluded manufacturing in the past, but would appear to be moving towards a policy that would allow limited manufacturing within their park. The majority of Canadian parks could better be described as high-technology parks as opposed to science or research parks, using the scientific/industrial park continuum developed by Dr Charles W. Minshall of Batelle Laboratories.

One aspect of the mandate and operation of the four parks located in western Canada merits particular attention. In various ways, the boards and management of these parks have been aggressively pursuing the broader role of advanced technology economic development in their communities, including many initiatives which may effect only indirectly the progress of their respective research parks. It was discussed earlier how the Discovery Parks organization is part of a larger entity which is engaged in technology development in British Columbia. The Park Authorities in both Edmonton and Calgary have also taken an active role in many community developments that affect advanced technology, including the establishment of community technology councils, university technology transfer activities, etc. It is recognized that research parks alone are not sufficient to stimulate advanced technology development. Rather, the parks are one of the resources that communities possess to create a growing advanced-technology industry.

Finally, the management of Canadian research parks realize that they are frequently not in a position to compete head-on with many of the world's major advanced technology centres (eg, Boston, San Francisco) in high-stakes poker games to attract major international research facilities. The park authorities have limited resources with which to pursue a broad range of possible major research facility sitings, many of which are limited to locations in the USA. While there are a few situations in which a major Canadian company or the federal government plans a new laboratory, the site is frequently determined by the nature of the industry or the markets that it serves. As a consequence, Canadian parks have increasingly turned their energies towards providing an environment in their own communities where advanced-technology enterprise can rapidly form and grow successfuly. More and more resources are being directed towards 'growing our own', while still keeping one eye open for industries and laboratories that might wish to locate in Canadian communities for a unique advantage that may be offered there.

The future of Canadian research parks

Those of us involved in Canadian research park development have come to recognize that the parks themselves are only one of a number of factors which can contribute to advanced technology development in our respective regions and cities. We believe that we can contribute meaningfully to the development of advanced technology industry by engaging in a broad range of initiatives, and by continuing to forge strong linkages between all of the constituencies involved in the development of our communities, especially the major universities, the provincial and civic governments and their economic development groups, and the business community. We have in the past been heavily engrossed in the creation and early development stages of our respective research parks; we are now increasingly reaching out of our land development roles to work on a variety of fronts to develop our communities in a high technology way, and to use our limited means to promote the innovative technologies which are necessary to keep Canada competitive on a world scale.

Research parks: 'The times, they are a changin''

Mark Money
Texas A&M University System

Bob Dylan made a prophetic observation in his ballad of the early sixties, 'the Times, They Are a Changin''. It is not likely that he was thinking of research parks in the 1980s at that time, but in fact the ballad title would be a most appropriate theme for a study of research parks today. The times, they certainly are a changin'!

Encouraged primarily by the success of Stanford, a number of university-affiliated research parks were started in the 1960s. A report by the General Accounting Office noted that in a study prepared by Ohio State University in 1980, twenty-seven university-related research parks had been started since 1951, the year that Stanford park was opened. The report found that of the twenty-seven, six had clearly succeeded, sixteen had failed and five were 'in between'.[1] This indicates that the failure rate for these parks is quite high. Some never progressed past the announcement stage; others were announced and the land secured, but were unable to attract sufficient interest. Even now, some are languishing with two or three tenants while others have ceased operations. As is generally true with most real estate ventures, those that succeed are widely publicized and those which fail are quietly ignored.

There are some recent examples of university-affiliated research parks which are experiencing solid progress in their early years. A high degree of professional planning and effective management have produced favourable results at the Central Florida Research Park in Orlando; Arizona State University Research Park in Tempe; Rensselaer Technology Park in Troy, New York; and Forrestal Park in Princeton, New Jersey. Texas A&M University Research Park is an example of one which is just getting started with the installation of the infrastructure and construction of the first building.

Significant changes

A review of developments in the industry indicates there are some substantive changes occurring in the research park phenomenon. The more important changes which will continue to have an impact on all the research parks are as follows:

More research parks

Hardly a week goes by without news in national publications of another university, community, state, or industrial development agency announcing a new high-technology research park. Usually this will be accompanied by a quote from some official that this project will be the new Silicon Valley and will be the economic salvation of the area. In this world of uncertainty, one thing is certain: there are not enough high-tech companies starting, expanding or relocating to make all these new parks successful.

More competition

It is evident from the number of new developments which have been started that the competition for technology-related and science-oriented companies will be increasingly severe. In this era of more intense competition, those parks with momentum, a track record, and the publicity generated by attracting companies to them, obviously have an advantage.

More resources required

Unlike some of the earlier developments which could be started with modest expenditures, those now being started are committing substantial resources at the beginning of the project to develop a site which can be attractive and be a marketing and promotional tool in itself. Some examples are as follows. The Arizona State University Research Park is spending $15 million in placing the necessary roads, utilities, and landscaping on a 323-acre site in Tempe, Arizona. The Forrestal Center in Princeton, New Jersey committed $27 million to land acquisition and site improvements for this 1600-acre development started in 1975. The Chicago Technology Park, a joint venture of the University of Illinois and the Rush Presbyterian–St Luke's Medical Center, is being developed on a 56-acre site. Over $11 million has been committed for infrastructure and an incubator-type laboratory building now under construction. Texas A&M University has committed over $6 million to develop the first 122 acres of a 434-acre research park in College Station, Texas. The significant factor to be noted is the sizable commitment of resources without the guarantee of a return on investment in an extremely competitive environment.

Uses permitted

Those involved in the development of research parks have had to deal with the thorny issue of what uses should be permitted. The very title research park generally denotes heavy emphasis on research and science-oriented activities. Park covenants and restrictions generally describe what uses will be permitted in the development. Those which desired to emerge as 'true science parks' to be used exclusively for pure research, excluded manufacturing, assembly, administrative activity and support services related to tenant functions. Dr Charles W. Minshall of Battelle noted in his report on technology parks that, 'It is difficult, if not impossible, to identify successful true science parks. In most instances the covenants are so restrictive that few, if any tenants are attracted. Many of the failures of both university and private sector science parks have involved overly restrictive covenants with no demand to locate in these projects.'[2] Dr Minshall has also expressed the opinion that there has not been a science or research park devoted exclusively to research which has succeeded to date.

Most research parks which evolved during the 1970s generally stipulated that tenants locating in their project must be substantially research or technology-oriented and compatible with the research interests of the university. Professional or administrative activities that are an integral part or directly related to the research or technological operations of the tenants were permitted. In addressing the issue of whether or not manufacturing or assembly would be permitted, most of the projects stipulated that the manufacture or assembly operations would be limited to prototype development, or to the assembly of high-technology products which are clearly related to onsite research and development activities of the tenant. Most indicated that a tenant exclusively engaged in manufacturing or assembly without any research or engineering or development work taking place would not be permitted. Most covenants also required that tenants must be engaged in operations which are nuisance-free and clean with respect to smoke, noise, noxious gases, vibrations, odours, radiation, etc, and nearly all required careful attention to landscaping, parking, and other amenities to produce a 'quality' environment.

As these projects have developed, and it has been determined that a wider variety of uses could be permitted without causing deterioration in either the aesthetic quality of the park or the basic commitment to the desired interaction between the university and industry, the permitted uses have been liberalized. Research parks throughout the country are not homogeneous entities having the same objectives, structure, form, and other characteristics. Each is remarkably different from the others depending on the circumstances surrounding its establishment and the total environment in which it operates. Therefore, the decision on the permitted uses has to be made within the context of park objectives, community considerations and some commonsense. It is true that misunderstandings have developed over the distinctions created by the announcements, as to the objectives of the park in the early stages, and have prompted some observers to describe university research parks as disguised industrial parks set up by higher education to pursue their own objectives. It is probably true that in some instances financial concerns have caused some original research parks to change their primary orientation to manufacturing, administrative office space, and other uses. However, it is fair to say that these projects generally have not had direct university affiliations. John Griefen in an Arthur D. Little study has expressed the opinion that the label 'research park' was developed only because it had a certain snob appeal over 'industrial'.[3]

The Arizona State University Research Park now being developed is typical of a newer approach, allowing a broader range of uses within a quality development. The following principal activities are allowed: laboratories, offices and other facilities for basic and applied research; production or assembly or prototype products necessary for full investigation of the merits of a product; and pilot plants in which processes planned for use in production elsewhere can be tested and assembled.

In addition, the following are also permitted: corporate headquarters, professional services and retail uses in support of the uses previously cited such as conference/hotel centres, food services, banking facilities, venture capital corporations, personnel services, post office, mailing centres, or training institutes; incidental operations required to maintain or support any use permitted, such as maintenance shops, power plants, machine shops, waste water treatment facilities, and keeping of animals. Also designated as permitted uses are: day-care centres, recreational facilities, and any other uses reasonably related to the intended character of the research park.[4]

In summary, research parks are changing dramatically in the permitted uses, responding to the genuine needs of research-oriented tenants for support services, regardless of the basic nature of their operations.

Greater emphasis on university–industry relationships

One of the principal attractions of a university-affiliated research park for a company is the implied opportunity for interactions with the university's resources. This generally takes the form of utilizing the capabilities and expertise of the faculty, library resources, availability of graduates and graduate studies for employment and professional growth opportunities through seminars, conferences and continuing education leading to advanced degrees.

There are advantages for the university as well, such as opportunities for faculty and students to participate in the application of research skills and other expertise in the private sector, access to new types of research facilities and equipment, employment for spouses, and the possibility of utilizing company professionals as lecturers or adjunct professors. If these things do occur, there should be a positive contribution to the quality of education.

None of these potential benefits happen automatically. They must be structured and nurtured. The research park staff should provide the leadership in arranging introductions, informing company and university personnel of the opportunities available and clearing any bureaucratic roadblocks for use of appropriate facilities, which are usually made available on a cost-reimbursable basis. The importance of this was cited again by Charles Minshall in his observations:

> When one examines the complete range of attributes associated with the most successful high technology parks across the United States, probably eight out of 10 clearly have a structured and meaningful tie to local educational activities at both the university and technical school level.[5]

It can be predicted that in these times of intense competition for science-oriented companies, the more successful research park projects will be those which are able to identify the unique resources of the university, and match them with companies whose needs and interests are compatible with those resources. They will then, presumably, be able to attract those companies to avail themselves of the resources through a coordinated programme of university–company interaction.

More tangible assistance to embryonic companies

For those research parks which are attempting to encourage start-up companies, spinoffs from existing companies and companies resulting from technology transfer, there will be increased emphasis on providing assistance. This is appearing in several forms throughout the country.

Assisting firms to locate sources of capital   Leonard Goldman of the Rensselaer Technology Park staff indicates that a substantial part of his job is to seek out sources of capital for potential building tenants. A recent article in the *Wall Street Journal* described the unique approach of the community of North Greenbush, in which the Rensselaer park is located, where the town of 10 500 population used $750 000 of a federal economic development grant to invest in eight start-up companies.[6]

Incubator space   More research parks are providing 'incubator space' for start-up companies at low-cost or subsidized rates for a prescribed period of time. My early study showed that nearly 80 per cent of the companies surveyed considered the provision of incubator space an important factor in site selection. The newer research parks which are achieving the greatest success all have incubator or start-up space available. It is a high priority consideration, especially for emerging companies.

Innovation centres   The services of an 'innovation centre' sponsored by the park administration or provided by the private sector can be a positive influence in the growth of the park and the emerging companies. Briefly described, an innovation centre usually provides such things as moderate cost space, technical and legal assistance, financial planning and identifying sources of capital, shared secretarial services, conference rooms, printing or reproduction services, and other types of services which would be helpful to a new venture.

In a recent doctoral dissertation, Mike Franco described the positive influence the Utah Innovation Center has had on the University of Utah Research Park:

> The Park has enjoyed a relatively slow, but steady growth pattern, based primarily on the development of smaller, locally based high technology firms. A special commitment to providing entrepreneurial support (funded initially by the federal government and subsequently as a private venture [Utah Innovation Center]) has contributed significantly to this growth.[7]

Requisites for success

Even in these changing times, there are certain constants which are essential to the success of university related research parks. Based on my studies, observations of established research parks and consulting assignments with emerging developments, the following are requisites for success in this time of change.

A clear definition of goals and objectives

Before launching a research park or similar project, the sponsoring organization needs to ask the hard question, 'Why are we doing this?' It is not enough that 'others are doing it and we should be doing something'. Any such development requires the expenditure of substantial resources at the front end and a long-term commitment to sustain the project until revenues are sufficient to cover operating expenses.

The reasons for establishing a research park will vary depending upon the circumstances of the sponsoring organization. These may include fostering university–industry relationships, producing an economic return on under-utilized land, enhancing the prestige of the university, participating in economic development of the area, providing jobs for graduates, or any other goal which might be combined into a statement on the overall objectives.

The 'cast of characters' has a way of changing from time to time in universities, companies, and communities. The natural question most new leaders ask is, 'Why are we doing this?' A clear statement of purpose with broad support at the beginning of the project helps assure continuity when people and times change. While a certain amount of introspection is helpful at various stages of the development, an abrupt stopping for prolonged reappraisals can slow the momentum so necessary for success.

Location factors

From the regular list of factors considered by industry in location decisions, there are several where are given added emphasis by science and technology-related companies considering university-affiliated research parks. The ones most critical in contributing to the success of the project are as follows.

The site must be immediately available and capable of development with roads and utilities in place. It is an added advantage if moderate-cost inventory space with flexibility to expand is available. In the fast-moving world of high technology where the decision is made to expand or relocate, there is great pressure to do it quickly. Immediate availability is often a prime consideration.

The common rules of real estate development apply equally to any university-related development. High on the list of prospective tenants are community factors such as: good housing within reasonable commuting distance; quality elementary and secondary schools; shopping centres, cultural and recreational activities and other quality of life and cost of living factors.

A transportation network is vital. Location should be near an interstate highway and within an hour of a jet airport with major air service. If not near a jet airport, there must be several daily flights with an hour's flight time or less to the major airports on quality commuter airlines.

The existence of a support base of high-technology industries and services in the general area of the project is essential. Also, a favourable overall business climate, including tax structure, labour–management relations, and access to a skilled/educated labour force.

Management structure

Those research parks which have been successful are characterized by clearly defined and forceful management. While this can take any one of several forms, there must be an identified legal authority or 'board'. This may be the governing board of the institution as in the case with Stanford, Utah and Texas A&M, or it may take the form of a separate authority such as the Research Triangle in North Carolina and Arizona State University Research Park.

Execution of the programme must be carried on by a highly motivated full-time director and staff. There must be sufficient delegation of responsibility in order for the director to effectively execute a marketing programme, ensure adherence to project covenants, monitor day-to-day activities, and also negotiate with prospective tenants with assurance that he can 'close a deal' provided the conditions are within previously approved guidelines. Segmented responsibility, confused authority and operating ambiguity provide a sure formula for failure.

Marketing programme based on strengths and capabilities of the university

The days of placing a 'for sale' or 'to let' sign on a potentially attractive parcel of real estate near a university and expecting it to develop into a research park are long since past. In this era of intense competition for desirable science-oriented companies, there has to be a 'rifle-type' marketing approach to companies within selected industries which can logically be expected to benefit from the academic and research programmes of the university. The most successful parks have been able to match the university strengths to industry needs. These shared interests may take the form of a single researcher prominent in a particular field, or by an entire department which has strong academic and research capabilities compatible with industry objectives. The General Accounting Office study observed,

> The electrical engineering school at Stanford, the medical school at the University of North Carolina, and the bioengineering department at the University of Utah were all mentioned by industrial representatives as factors in their firms' decisions to relocate.[8]

This trend for high-tech companies to base location decisions in part on the recognized strengths of the university will continue.

Desire for quality environment

One of the reasons that industry has found the concept of the university-affiliated research park so appealing is the high quality standards for the overall appearance most have achieved. Entrances with attractive signs and professionally designed landscaping, careful attention to streets and screened parking, low-density building coverage with broad green areas combined to give the project a park-like atmosphere. Combined with the controlled building designs monitored by an architectural review board giving careful consideration to materials, colours, sign graphics and siting, the result can be an environment similar to the university campus which is attractive to scientific and technical personnel.

To continue to be successful, the park administration should first have a comprehensive set of protective covenants and be firm in requiring compliance to ensure that the project does not deteriorate after time. Exterior maintenance of buildings, upkeep of landscaping, and the installation of attractive sign graphics are the most critical elements in enhancing the quality of the park. There is increasing evidence that companies demand and are willing to pay for a park-like environment. Some developers in the private sector, where economic return is a vital consideration, are setting an outstanding example of building a beautiful environment into the project. Quality surroundings attract quality tenants.

Perseverance and staying power

One of the unique characteristics of a research park is the relatively long time period needed to become successful. Stanford has been in existence thirty-five years, the Research Triangle almost thirty years. Utah, which is considered almost a newcomer, started fifteen years ago and Forrestal at Princeton has been in operation ten years.

There have been examples of projects funded by state legislators which did not show enough progress to satisfy legislators in two years. Subsequent appropriations were not forthcoming and the projects failed. This prompted Governor Luther Hodges of North Carolina to advise, 'Be wary of taking funds from state legislators. They are like little boys who plant seeds and then dig them up every day to see why they are not growing.' Those who think that a project can be started and replicate what has been achieved at Stanford and North Carolina in a condensed time-frame are going to be sadly disappointed.

'The times, they are a changin'' in the development and administration of university-affiliated research parks. However, there are considerable satisfactions which can be derived if the challenges of change can be recognized and managed within the constants required for success.

References

1 US General Accounting Office 1983 The federal role in fostering university–industry cooperation. GAO/PAD 83–22, 25 May 1983, p 10.
2 Minshall C. W. 1983 *An overview of trends in science and technology parks*. Battelle, Columbus, Ohio. p 6.
3 Little A. D. Inc 1979 *The Saratoga (NY) Research and Development Center: development strategy*. August 1979.
4 Arizona State University Research Park. (Brochure). Tempe Arizona 1985. p 7.
5 Minshall C. W. 1983 op cit p 26.
6 Small town decides best way to lure high tech firms is to invest in them *Wall Street Journal* 7 August 1985 p 21.
7 Franco M. 1985 *Key success factors for university-affiliated research parks: a comparative analysis*. The University of Rochester NY p 289.
8 US General Accounting Office 1983 op cit p 18.

South Bank Technopark

Jeffe Jeffers
South Bank Technopark

South Bank Technopark is a nonprofit corporation set up to revive a run-down inner city location in central London by creating a high-technology zone. Established in 1982, the company represents business, education, local government and national agencies concerned with the development and support of new technology industries. The company, however, receives no funding from these sources but generates its income from fees earned by packaging developments or raising investment funds. It is, in effect, a private-sector company with public-sector goals.

There is now a well-documented drift of new technology industry in the UK to greenfield locations, particularly down the M4 motorway into the south and west of England. The reasons given are generally, cheap land and therefore lower building costs, lower local taxes, and abundance of semi-skilled and relatively low cost labour and the quality of life offered by these verdant pastures.

There is also a very expensive drive by the poorer development regions in the UK such as Scotland, Wales and the northeast of England to attract high-technology industry by local tax concessions, cheap buildings and wage subsidy, and of course their verdant pastures. In the meantime, the centres of the great cities are being allowed to die as industry is being wooed to these new locations. The cities are considered hostile to industry because their taxes are high, land and building cost are equally high and labour and management wage rates are premium.

So what can lovers of the great cities do about it? Our concept is not original, though some of the ingredients we bring to it are.

An area of London has been chosen (by us) to be London 'Science City'. The area has superb location and resources. It is only a few hundred yards from the House of Commons. The National Theatre is just down the road; Covent Garden, with its shopping and opera house, just over the river. There are over five hundred restaurants and cafes within a mile radius, and four hundred pubs. For the food of the soul the site is equidistant between St Pauls Cathedral and Westminster Abbey. The City of London's financial district forms one of the boundaries. It takes fifty minutes by subway to Heathrow and its extensive air network, and four major UK rail terminals are all within a mile.

That quality of life is compounded by the superb service infrastructure of suppliers available; the largest concentration of higher education in Europe, the headquarters buildings of most major national and international concerns, seventy venture capital funds, an intricate international banking system, two hundred trading houses and three hundred freight forwarders; in effect an inexhaustible resource of business infrastructure. It also has the largest concentration of management skills in the UK and of the highest calibre. London by itself represents 20 per cent of the UK market place.

Its drawbacks are equally striking. Land costs are high compared to greenfield sites and there are problems of site assembly. Local taxes are high, generally 300 per cent higher than development regions. There is a total lack of government grants and incentives. Finally, labour costs are high at both management and workfore level with a commensurately high cost of living.

It is difficult to break the cycle of decline, and yet in London the seeds of a high-tech zone already exist. For instance, there are 198 software houses in one small part of it. All are too small, undercapitalized; all are writing the same small business packages to generate revenue, but nevertheless it represents a pool of talent, a seedbed.

When I say this area has been chosen by us, I mean just that. We have no planning authority. The local borough councils are responsible for that and are politically changeable. To develop such a zone we must persuade and take people along with us. We are not seeking to attract large sums of public-sector investment, though they have an important role in our future plans. Our main concern is to demonstrate to the private sector the opportunities the London Science City offers for profit and for growth, whilst creating the jobs and local tax base inner London needs.

Our first goal therefore has been the creation of a demonstration project – South Bank Technopark. It has changed greatly during its gestation and building period in response to new ideas or insights, and to the flow of the market place. Technopark is a 75 000 square foot, three-storey development built at the southern end of Science City. It is built adjacent to South Bank Polytechnic, one of the UK's largest technology educational institutions and the Technopark is physically bridged into the Polytechnic.

Funded by the Prudential Assurance Company Limited (the largest insurance company in the UK, the largest investor in business, and the largest industrial landlord), the development, with interest rolled in, has cost £5 million. It is divisible into units from 200 square feet to 100 square feet and was intended to house new-start firms. The Technopark company provides the now traditional business development services and shared resources, conference room, book-keeping, shared telephone system at cost. We do not have a venture fund of our own, but 'play the field.' (A process we are currently evaluating). The building is now complete (1 September 1985) and is 84 per cent prelet. Prudential agreed to construct another wing of the building (25 000 square feet) starting on site in 1986. Prudential's financial return on the building is low, largely because they were nervous of the concept and therefore built an office block in case things went wrong. However, the project is important to them and to us for reasons other than pure financial return. Large pension or insurance funds in the UK have no experience of short letting. The norm is twenty-five-year leases to conventional tenants. At Technopark rental is by the month on a month's notice. No one is allowed to stay more than three years because, if you have not outgrown your space with us in that time, you have missed your technology window.

The pension funds have no experience of intensive onsite management, which will increasingly be the norm. They do not generally mix their real estate development function with their investment function. We are trying to demonstrate the connection between the two services and how they can mutually help the end profit.

We wish to demonstrate to venture capital how much easier it is for them to service investment which is geographically concentrated and how synergy can be utilized to bring growth to profit more quickly. In these respects the Prudential is no different to the rest of the UK investment houses. Indeed, its image is of being the most conservative. Their decision to support us is therefore of crucial importance in giving confidence to other potential investors in the depressing, lemming-like world of investment finance. Technopark is first of all an essay in changing traditional thinking and response patterns. For example, we are in the business of changing the way property investment is made, the way local government looks at the relationship between blue and white collar employment, the way higher education in the UK can get closer to industry and the final product away from pure research; making venture capital a responsive part of industrial growth rather than a short-term (five-year) profit stripper.

Of course, we are also subject to change. The letting of the Technopark is an example. We set out to create an innovation centre for new starts. The market place has shown us new roles and new needs and we have responded to them. We still have an innovation function but we also now have three other strategies: keeping technologically interesting companies in the area (because of lack of suitable real estate, London is continuously losing technology companies to other regions of the country just when they reach growth point); r&d from national and multinational companies attracted by the location, which gives us the opportunity to bat for the production phase; and technology windows. These we think are our most innovative features. We have three windows at the moment.

The London Medical Products Development Centre

The centre has two main functions: to prise electronic medical products from London's nineteen teaching hospitals and nine research institutes in the early research period and provide a commercial framework to prepare it for the market place; to assist, through product development and marketing expertise, the inventive skills of London's numerous small medical companies who are generally product-rather than market-led. Such an approach has tremendous potential in this fast-growing sector.

Telecom test & development

The denationalization of the UK telephone system has created considerable opportunities for new telecom/products. The approval system, however, is expensive and cumbersome and a serious drawback to small companies with new products to launch. We will therefore provide a test centre with a product development company attached. It will also provide a marketing and design service.

Both this and the medical products centre are intended to be fully commercial within five years, making their return from fees, royalties and licensing. Both also have the considerable advantage of being very effective tenant attractors. A business comes for the service, and stays for the space and support structures. They also give us a considerable insight into the state of the two arts.

Technology twinning
Most new technologies in smaller firms have a limited life of five to seven years before either the technology or larger competition catches up. Most US start-up technology firms rightly spend up to half their technology life developing their home market; generally they do not have, in their early days, the financial or personnel resources for extensive overseas operations. In effect they often waste half of their technology life before approaching a market which is the same size as the continental USA. When they do come, they find market resistance to what is often seen as US technological imperialism.

Dual development is the best answer for both sides of the Atlantic. It gives the US company market penetration at the earliest opportunity and gives the UK production and joint r&d. We are currently arranging two joint companies in the UK for European market coverage. In both cases, the UK partner will put up the finance, and the American the technology, the money buying 60 per cent of the equity. We have also twinned with one US Innovation Centre (New Mexico) and are in discussion with another two to offer their tenants this facility. UK venture capital is very interested in the concept and a future development may be each-way funding. We are hoping next year to create another window in biotechnology and food science.

The Technopark is a microcosm of our plans for creating the London Science City. Already its publicity effect has been considerable, though we have spent less than £3000 on advertising. Instead of expensive advertising campaigns, we do a lot of cold calling and telephone contact, and have built up a huge network of individuals in this way who talk about us and 'spread the word.'

However, the development of the Science City concept will involve us in more extensive publicity, trade magazine advertising, television, conference, organization, fairs, etc, and we are currently writing this strategy. We are also developing a small grants package to assist new starts, and will spend a considerable sum on improving the local environment in conjunction with local business and local government. We are budgeting to spend £3 million over the next three years. This money will come from local government sources and represents their importance as a lever in the process. However, this money's next purpose is to lever the private sector inside the plans objectives. It is a large task, still in its infancy, with a challenging future.

The new business incubator in America

Raymond Smilor
IC²

The new business incubator is attracting widespread attention as an innovative approach to economic development. By pulling together a variety of resources, it seeks to leverage entrepreneurial talent. New business incubators seek to maximize the potential of entrepreneurial talent within a community by providing the entrepreneur with services and support that complement his natural talents and enable him to expand his potential. The incubator can thus be a significant link between the entrepreneur, especially when he is technology-oriented, and the commercialization of his product or service.

Incubators can contribute to and benefit from a set of building blocks that make the technology-venturing process possible. These blocks include a healthy venture-capital industry, a solid financial base, adequate public and private infrastructures, a sound educational system and an extensive business network (see Figure 22).

Successful entrepreneurial development requires a synergy among talent, technology, capital and know-how. A new business incubator can be the integrating link that can increase the chances for success of new ventures for entrepreneurs. Incubators can provide a framework for fusing the critical elements of the entrepreneurial process for new ventures. They can also significantly telescope the learning curve, and thus give entrepreneurs more time to let their businesses grow, and more opportunities to learn from potentially fatal mistakes, as they broaden their own individual know-how.

Merely opening or establishing an incubator is not enough in today's environment. Businesses, even those which are being contemplated, must operate in a hypercompetitive environment. The business climate is fierce both domestically and internationally. The competition is between countries, states and communities, as well as between large and small firms and among industries. The environment in which yet-to-be-born and emerging firms must operate is particularly unforgiving. The ability to introduce new technologies or services to the market place poses several unique competitive problems. There is a gap between the firm and its potential markets. This gap results from issues such as: public acceptance, technological obsolescence, social concerns, channels of distribution, development of an aftermarket, overseas manufacturing, and the processing of moving to the next market.

To help companies meet the challenge of a hypercompetitive environment and to maximize the contributions of the small-business and technology-business growth sectors of American society, the promotion of new business growth has become an important facet of economic policy at the federal, state

Figure 22 Role of incubators in economic development

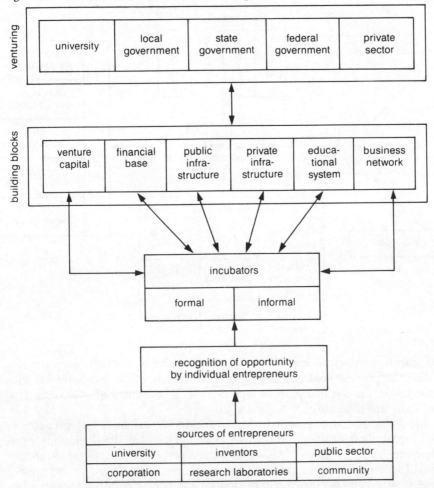

and local levels. Building indigenous companies has become an essential element in regional economic development.

Industrial relocation, along the central focus of regional economic development, tends to be a zero-sum game – one region or location benefits only at the expense of another. Indigenous company growth may be a more beneficial and necessary long-term economic development strategy for several reasons. First, it harnesses local entrepreneurial talent. Second, it builds companies which in turn create jobs and thus adds economic value to a region and community. Third, this strategy keeps home-grown talent – a scarce resource – within the community. Fourth, it encourages economic diversification and technological innovation by creating a climate that rewards productivity and innovation. In this context, new business incubators can be an important component in developing an indigenous company strategy in a region or community.

The incubator concept

Successful entrepreneurship takes a wide variety of talents. However, it is rare to find a potential entrepreneur who combines the technical expertise necess-

Figure 23

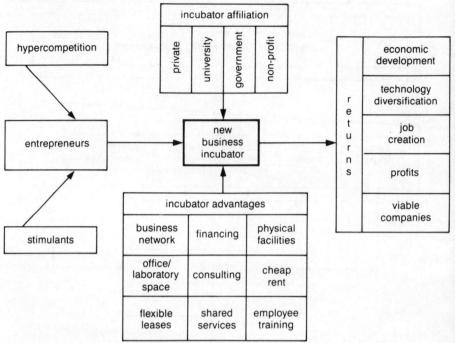

ary for technological innovation with the business acumen necessary for successful product commercialization. The concept of the incubator has thus emerged in the last five years to facilitate the development of entrepreneurial creativity and education (see Figure 23).

Incubator units are designed to assist technically oriented entrepreneurs in developing their business skills in an environment that simultaneously stimulates technical creativity. Although incubators vary in scope of assistance provided, there are some generic components to the incubator concept. After screening potential entrepreneurs, most incubators provide low-cost office and/or laboratory space, administrative services, access to library and computer facilities, skilled consultants, an inexpensive workforce in the form of graduate and undergraduate students, and special contacts with bankers, venture capitalists, technologists and government officials. In this environment, an aspiring entrepreneur is free to be technologically creative since his energies can be devoted to product development and not to the rigours of obtaining financing or managing an organization. All the while, the entrepreneur is associated with other entrepreneurs facing similar difficulties, thus providing an association which should, it is hoped, stimulate the entrepreneur's drive for success and help solve problems.

An incubator is not only an organization, but also a physical unit. Incubators start as a single building or group of buildings where the participating entrepreneurs can be housed and where, due to physical proximity, they will spontaneously interact. In the building, there may be space for a number of different entrepreneurs. The institution sponsoring the incubator will usually provide secretarial support, duplicating services, accounting services, technical editing help, computer equipment, conference space, health and other benefit packages, and access to university facilities and expertise for a nominal fee.

The advantages for a member of an incubator of being on or near a university campus are numerous: library facilities, exposure to state-of-the-art technical thinking and equipment, undergraduates that form a pool of cheap and technically skilled labour, a creative environment, and potential employment as a lecturer. Companies within the incubator profit from the technical resources of the university in a variety of ways. These companies benefit from the best available talent when they need it, without having to carry that high-priced talent on their payroll. And these companies receive the stimulus and catalytic effect associated with working alongside outstanding professionals from outside their organization.

Organizationally, incubators differ from one another due to their varying priorities. Priorities are different because of the funding that supports the incubator unit. Funding sources for these units include federal, state, and local governments, communities, universities, private individuals and foundations, and corporations. Incubators can be associated with any of these funding sources to varying degrees, and therefore, have similar goals but different priorities. The general goals of incubators are to develop firms, often technically based, and stimulate entrepreneurship. Incubators may seek to develop jobs, create investment opportunities for college endowments, expand a tax base for local government, enhance the image of college technical programmes, speed transfer of technological innovation from the academic and research worlds to industry, fill a perceived gap in venture capital financing by improving the quality of locally based entrepreneurial talents, and build a core of indigenous companies.

Science parks may accompany the incubator unit as another link between universities and industry. Located near universities, the objective of these parks is to attract both research and development and/or the manufacturing facilities of established technology-based companies. Science parks, also called technology or research parks, act as a lightning rod for technology-based companies and can be an area's lure for attracting companies and individuals from out of state. Science parks also give a university a method of further benefiting from the development of firms incubated in its facilities, since these firms are prime candidates for research park tenants.

National survey

A review of the selected results from a national survey on incubators provides insights on the structure, operation and diversity of this innovative approach to business development. Data on new business incubators in America was collected by means of a mail survey. The survey was conducted in July and August 1985. Traditional mail survey research techniques and procedures were employed when collecting the data, including follow-up telephone calls and questionnaires to initial non-respondents.

The original sample consisted of 117 incubators that had been identified from a variety of sources, including a data base developed at the IC^2 Institute, the US Small Business Administration, published reports and individuals. This sample included all the operating or planned incubators in the US at that time. Responses were received from 50 incubators. This represents an effective response rate of 43 per cent.

The number of incubators in the United States has grown rapidly in recent years; 88.9 per cent of the incubators responding to the survey have been opened since 1983, and one-third have been opened in 1985 alone.

These incubators are widely geographically dispersed in the United States and have emerged in every region of the country.

Objectives

Incubator managers/directors were asked to list their top three objectives in starting the incubator. By far and away, the number one objective was to create new jobs. Sixty-nine per cent responded that this was the first goal of the incubator. To make a profit and to promote economic development were the first objectives of 9.5 per cent of the respondents.

When the top three objectives are taken collectively, job creation still ranks first with 78.5 per cent response, economic development received a 69.3 per cent response, and entrepreneurship development had a 50.8 per cent response.

Participation and review

A wide variety of institutional types have been active in initiating new business incubators. As shown in Figure 24, 50 per cent of the owners or sponsors of new business incubators are from the private, for-profit sector, 25.5 per cent from local government, 10 per cent from universities, 6.8 per cent from state government, 5.8 per cent from private nonprofit entities and 1.9 per cent from federal government.

Incubator managers, boards of directors and special selection committees play key roles in recommending, reviewing and approving companies for inclusion in the incubator. Eighty-six and five-tenths per cent of incubator managers become actively involved in recommending tenant companies. For 33.3 per cent of the respondents, selection committees are active, and for 30.4 per cent the board of directors is active. For 50 per cent of the incubators, other groups or individuals recommend companies.

After recommendation, potential tenant companies are reviewed. In 80 per cent of the incubators, the manager is involved in the review process, while in 51.9 per cent the selection committee is involved, and in 28.6 per cent the board of directors is involved. Final approval is given by the board of directors in 62.1 per cent of the incubators that responded, by the managers in 59.3 per cent and by the selection committee in 42.3 per cent. In 42.9 per cent of the incubators, others are involved in the final approval process.

Relation to tenant companies

Incubators have established clear preferences for the types of companies that they would like in the incubator. When asked their first choice of tenants by industry type, 42.9 per cent of the respondents indicated light manufacturing while 40.5 per cent indicated high-technology. When the top three choices are taken collectively, 85.7 per cent indicated a preference for high-technology while 81.2 per cent favour light manufacturing. Incubator owners or sponsors and managers are making a link between their objectives of job creation, economic development and entrepreneurship development and the high-technology and light manufacturing industries.

Incubators have also established a set of criteria for tenant selection. Figure 25 shows what respondents indicated as the most important criteria for tenant company selection: 85 per cent look for a company to create new jobs; 60.5 per cent require that they pay their own operating costs; and 51.2 per cent require a written business plan. In addition, 37.5 per cent of the respondents favour

Figure 24 Incubator initiators by institutional type

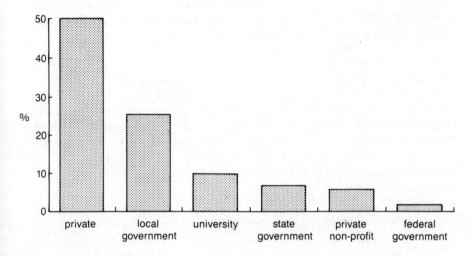

firms that appear to have a unique opportunity, 37.5 per cent require that the firm be a new, start-up enterprise, and 28.2 per cent look for fast-growth

Figure 25 The 6 most important criteria for tenant selection

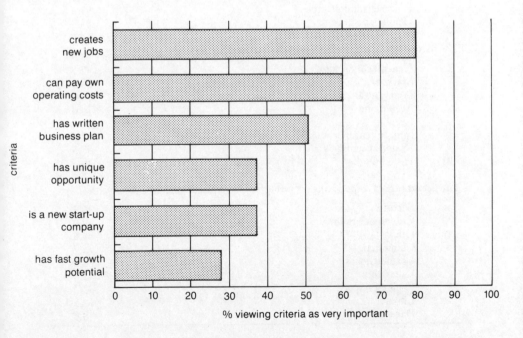

potential. The least important criteria were ranked in the following order: 92.1 per cent are not interested in expert references; 73.7 per cent do not seek equity in the companies; 69 per cent do not require companies to be in a specific industry; 63.1 per cent are not interested in a company having a proprietary product; and 58.9 per cent do not think it is important for a company to meet low-income goals.

Tenant companies

The survey developed data on tenant companies related to number of employees, months in incubator, annual sales, length of time tenant company was in incubator before graduation, and company location after graduation. Respondents to the survey reported the number of employees for 211 tenant companies: 42.2 per cent of the tenant companies had one or two employees; 79 per cent had ten employees or less; 12.7 per cent had eleven to thirty employees; and 6.4 per cent had thirty-one employees or more.

Table 17   Services provided by incubators

The percentage of respondents providing secretarial services:	
Word processing	90.0
Typing	80.1
Photocopying	85.7
Receptionist	77.5
Clerical	72.5
Filing	44.7
The percentage of respondents providing administrative services:	
Mailing	68.4
Accounting	61.1
Equipment rental	55.6
Billing	52.6
Contract administration	51.4
Health insurance	33.3
The percentage of respondents providing consulting services:	
General counselling	92.5
Marketing	85.0
Loan packaging	68.0
Accounting	73.0
Legal	66.7
Intro to venture capitalists	62.5
Financial contracts	57.5
Head hunting	39.5
The percentage of respondents providing various types of facilities:	
Security	90.0
Conference room	90.0
Other	84.6
Computers	75.7
Loading docks	60.0
Laboratory	42.4
Exhibition space	33.3
Library	12.5
Day care	8.6

Respondents reported on the number of months that 188 current tenants had been in the incubators: 13.8 per cent had been in the incubator one month or less; 27.2 per cent 2–6 months; 27.2 per cent 7–12 months; 19.7 per cent 13–18 months; 8.4 per cent 19–24 months; and 3.7 per cent 25 months or more. The relatively brief times in the incubator reflect the fact that the majority of incubators themselves are relatively new.

Respondents reported on annual sales for 42 current tenant companies: 9.5 per cent of the tenant companies have no sales to report; 28.7 per cent have $1000–$100 000 in annual sales; 16.8 per cent have $101 000–$200 000; 14.3 per cent have $201 000–$400 000; 9.6 per cent have $401 000–$999 000; and 21.4 per cent have $1 million or more in annual sales.

Table 18   Importance to clients of incubator services

The percentage of respondents rating specific secretarial services as *most* important:

Photocopy	54.0
Receptionist	53.1
Word processing	36.1
Typing	29.7
Clerical	23.3
Filing	8.0

The percentage of respondents rating specific administrative services as *most* important:

Mailing	39.6
Equipment rental	31.8
Accounting	24.0
Contract admin	20.0
Billing	12.0
Health insurance	10.0

The percentage of respondents rating specific consulting services as *most* important:

Accounting	60.0
Managerial	60.0
Business planning	59.4
Marketing	58.3
Access to grants and loans	57.6
Evaluating financial options	56.6
Intro to venture capitalist	48.6
Loan packaging	48.6
General counselling	46.9
Technical	46.7
Legal	41.3
Tax planning	32.1
Head hunting	12.5

The percentage of respondents rating specific facilities services as *most* important:

Other	57.1
Security	55.9
Computers	50.0
Loading dock	46.9
Conference room	45.7
Laboratory	33.4
Library	31.0
Exhibition space	13.0
Day care	5.6

Despite the relative newness of the incubator concept, some companies have already started to leave or graduate from the facility. Survey respondents reported on 30 companies that had graduated: 5 (16 per cent) have left in less than 6 months; 4 (13.3 per cent) in 7–11 months; 6 (20 per cent) in 12–17 months; 7 (23.3. per cent) in 18–23 months; 1 (3.3 per cent) in 24–35 months; 3 (10.5 per cent) in 36–59 months; and 4 (13 per cent) have left after 5 years or more in the incubator. Incubators seem to contribute to building indigenous companies. Of the graduate firms, 20 per cent stayed in the same neighbourhood as the incubator, 60 per cent remained in the same city and 20 per cent stayed in the same state.

Incubator services

Incubators provide a range of services for tenant companies. Services can be grouped into four categories; secretarial, administrative, consulting and facilities (see Table 17.) The survey also asked respondents to evaluate the relative importance to tenant companies of each of the services provided (see Table 18).

Summary

Incubators appear to be an effective and innovative approach to help entrepreneurs in their start-up phase with reduced overhead costs, expert assistance, and financial backing. Incubator facilities have been organized typically by using partitioned areas in existing building. New business can operate with a minimum of rented floor space and have access to shared services – secretarial, shipping and receiving, fabrication shops, storage, and special technical equipment.

Incubators have been established by a variety of organizations, including universities, private entrepreneurs, public/private partnerships, charitable foundations and by management organizations on a franchised basis. In most locales, there can be considerable value in the reduced overhead costs, access to specialized services and equipment that entrepreneurs could not otherwise afford, skilled and experienced business advice and assistance, and a supportive environment that arises from a number of co-located new businesses. Incubators can produce small business firms, dynamic growth firms and a more stable and balanced infrastructure for entrepreneurial activity. They can also serve to strengthen ties for furthur commercialization to research and industrial parks and the venture-capital industry.

For the entrepreneur, a new business incubator holds a variety of benefits. In addition to the operational benefits that come with being associated with incubator facilities, entrepreneurs gain access to education and training from critical business know-how. This is especially important in areas such as financing, marketing and tactical and strategic planning, as well as in business plan preparation. They may be able to tap important technical support in areas such as engineering, computer sciences, biotechnology, medicine, and other technology-related disciplines appropriate to their businesses. They may also gain access to important professional support, particularly in the areas of accounting and law. Finally, they gain access to a network of other entrepreneurs and business connections and may therefore reap both the tangible and intangible benefits that network affords.